U.S. and Them

The Re-Enchantment of a Cold War Childhood

U.S. and Them

The Re-Enchantment of a Cold War Childhood

Patricia Bjorklund

ALAMO BAY PRESS
SEADRIFT•AUSTIN

Copyright © 2016 Patricia Bjorklund

All rights reserved. No part of this book may be reproduced in any form without permission in writing from the publisher, except by a reviewer who may quote brief passages in a review.

Cover Photograph: *Cascone Family (1963)*, by Michel Nastasia
Book Design: ABP

For orders and information:

Alamo Bay Press
Pamela Booton, Director
Lowell Mick White, Editor / Diane Wilson, Activist

825 W 11th Ste 114
Austin, Texas 78701
pam@alamobaypress.com
www.alamobaypress.com
www.alamobaywritersworkshop.com

Names: Bjorklund, Patricia.
Title: U.S. and them : the re-enchantment of a Cold War childhood / by Patricia Bjorklund.
Other Titles: US and them
Description: Austin, Texas : Alamo Bay Press, [2016]
Identifiers: LCCN 2016944662 | ISBN 978-1-943306-02-2
Subjects: LCSH: Bjorklund, Patricia--Childhood and youth. | Cold War. | Children--United States--Social conditions--20th century. | Cold War in popular culture--United States. | United States--Social life and customs--1945-1970. | United States--History--1961-1969. | LCGFT: Autobiographies.
Classification: LCC E840.8.B56 A3 2016 | DDC 973.929092--dc23

For
Christopher, Richard, Victoria
and
Mom, Dad, John, Anthony, Joey, Chrissy

One of the hardest lessons of childhood is reckoning with the instability of the world. The earlier it comes the harder it is to take.
— John Lovett

Music, at its essence, is what gives us memories. And the longer a song has existed in our lives, the more memories we have of it.
— Stevie Wonder

Experience, which destroys innocence, also leads one back to it.
— James Baldwin

Contents

Introduction	1
A World Still Flat	5
Growing Up and Liking It	10
Good Catholic Motorists	14
Power to the People	18
Our Lady of Katz	24
Confessions of a Bouffant	32
A Countdown for Leaving	46
Champs and Chumps	64
U.S. and Them	81
A Taste of the Cold War	95
Almost Happy	103
Nine Lives in Purgatory	113
Wildcard	131
Fresh Summer Cuts	139
The Color of My Bus	150
Soul Train	164
Bamboozle	171
SYLP: A How-To	184
Good Car / Bad Car	194
On Good Authority	205
Just Like on Television	213
My Two Favorite Subjects	224
The Lion Sleeps	229
Sail On, Sailor	238
Keep On Truckin'	244
Afterword	254
Acknowledgments	257
About the Photographs	259
About Patricia Bjorklund	263

U.S. and Them

The Re-Enchantment of a Cold War Childhood

Introduction

I was perfectly happy growing up in the late 60s and early 70s, on the right side of God, family and country and measuring the time until Apocalypse by my Snoopy Timex. Life was tragic simply because no matter how bright the sun shines, it's going to set, one day for the last time. My heart understood. As for my head, I watched for signs of impending doom. As soon as I learned to read I checked the *Bridgeport Post* nightly to see if the sun was rising and setting on time or making any funny moves. I didn't blame my folks for the fact that we were riding in the caboose of civilization. My parents were brave; they were John Birchers, political activists with the American flag in one hand and my hand in the other. I stood on the edge of history and naturally I waited for some type of push.

Sometimes it hurts more when nothing happens. If only the Communist revolution happened the way it was supposed to, I would have written a book a long time ago. I wouldn't have had to wrestle with editors and publishers. Stress would have long been over. I'd have written and revised the bottom-line from deep in a bunker, in a safe but undisclosed location. If the cold war snapped into radioactive flames and God wanted to leave a few of us alive, I would have done the job I was born for: logging mankind's final chapters in a loose leaf binder. Tragedy? No! I was prepared to thrive on my enterprising spirit, delight in the mystery of rehydrated food, stir hope with a refreshing tonic of neon orange Tang. I might have emerged from the rubble of oblivion with proof that the conspiracy was more than a theory. It didn't matter to me if there was nobody left to tell.

Having the last word was better than being right.

Cascone Family, 1963....

A World Still Flat

I knew the world was close to its end the moment I took my first breath.

I knew it the way I was drawn to the smell of my mother's neck, the way I'd grown to turn toward the sound of my name—*Patricia*. I couldn't forget what I knew, even when I couldn't understand it.

On the day I was born, my mother didn't frump around the corridors of St. Vincent's in a linty gown and dingy slippers like the other groggy mothers. She slipped into her only expensive outfit: a classic wool skirt with matching jacket and pillbox hat. My father sat at the edge of the bed, still in paint clothes, but his T-shirt came fresh out of a pack of Fruit of the Loom. His hair was slicked back. His forehead was tan and shiny. He poked a plastic spoon at the starchy hospital spaghetti and the wilted green beans. "I'm paying for this so-called food," he told the nurse. "It's my business to find out just how bad it is."

My mother called out from behind the bathroom door, "It's a girl!" It was 5:55 pm, September 15, 1959. "Get ready. Here we come!"

My father balled his napkin, dropped it into a puddle of applesauce, and pushed the tray away so he could look me over and inspect me.

My mother strolled out of the bathroom cradling me in one arm and carrying her makeup kit on the other. "John, look! Isn't she lovely?"

"Not too far from it," my father said. "Is everything in working order?"

"She's perfect."

My father extended his giant hand, pointed a finger, touched my nose and from that moment on I loved the smell of paint and turpentine. "Her head's the size of a juice-orange but she's pink. Obviously, she's breathing."

"She's a miracle," my mother said.

My mother held me with pride. Her hair was perfect. Her coral lipstick was flawless. She had starry blue eyes and wore jiffy white gloves. She walked to the nurse's station in pink high heels and asked for the best bottle of formula they had. She held an Evenflo Nurser to my mouth. It had a deluxe silicone nipple and twin air valves to reduce gas. Each time I let go of the nipple, the nurser drew a stream of happy air bubbles.

My mother suffered with the knowledge that we were close to the Apocalypse, but after seeing me, she wanted to give happiness a try. My parents gazed at me, and I tried to focus my new eyes on them. The three of us drifted into the fog of happiness.

A hideous man appeared on the hospital TV. He gurgled and spit in a harsh foreign language; his guttural sounds snapped us out of our moment. My folks looked up at the same time and saw him—Khrushchev. My father cupped his hands over my ears, while his blood pressure began to soar. My mother lowered her head to cover my eyes, though her hopes drooped a bit.

Luckily, a commercial for Mr. Bubble came on. And a candy striper with marshmallow-colored slip-ons bounced into the room. She offered to take a few snapshots of our new family. I imagined a portrait, my parents and I beaming in sterilized linens. The hospital room was alive and buzzing. All systems were go! Tubes pumped. Control panels blinked and intercoms crackled as we posed on the edge of an adjustable bed with chrome safety rails. We basked in the glow of a surgical lamp and were surrounded by the hopeful advances of the modern world.

My father was a good man. He bemoaned the fact that we were forced to live in a world with communism. He yelled at the TV every day and cursed the public schools for producing the drug addicts and revolutionaries who rigged bombs and plotted assassinations.

As I grew, I remember my father explaining history to everyone he met, especially people who came to our house, for instance he loved to speak with Jehovah's Witnesses and to lecture kids who went door-to-door to Trick or Treat for UNICEF. He once had a conversation with the Fuller Brush man. The salesman stood on our porch wearing a hat, shirt and tie. They got to talking about the assassinations.

"JFK—too good looking for a coin or a greenback," my father said. "He became a monument before he was a real president. His brains were splattered on a sunny American street, in a princely American car, after his wife was given a bouquet of American roses. What does that tell you?"

"I'm not sure what you mean," the man said.

"I could get picked off right here as I stand talking to you. Come in, come in." My father gestured and they sat in the dining room. "Now, Martin Luther King—he's another one, a product of the mob, a man who believed in doling out hope by marching on streets—AKA, clogging the roads so we can't drive on them. What kind of patriotism is that?"

"Don't you think King and Kennedy are the two greatest men of our time?" the salesman asked.

"Neither one of them rose after three days," my father said.

My father handed the man a pamphlet. "In the big picture, they were just pawns. The assassinations are part of the Communists' intricate plan to infiltrate and then topple America."

The man shook his head in either sadness of disbelief but

he stayed and listened.

"Even our tap water is part of the conspiracy," my father said. "The fluoride they tell us will protect our teeth is designed to give us cancer and produce big profits for soulless government agencies."

"But why would our own government want to give us cancer?" the man asked. "Then how could we fight communism?"

"There are people in high places who want to destroy this country. The invasion from within paves the way. Constant threat and everyday violence intended to weaken, terrorize, destroy our will to resist."

"I'm like you," the salesman said. He stood up and opened his sample case. "I'm a practical man, feeding my family, doing the right thing. I'd like to introduce you to a quality line of household products that will enhance your life and save you money."

My father went into the kitchen, talking. "Our entire way of life is under siege." He game back with a glass of ice tea and handed it to the man. "Eventually, Americans will tire from witnessing elaborate funerals and the swearing-in of presidents we haven't exactly voted for. This country's giving up on justice and buying into the hippie shit—liberty for criminals, free lunch for minorities, and love beads for all."

"Well, I don't know," the man said. "Dr. King said love is the only force capable of transforming an enemy into a friend."

"People are forgetting who our enemies are! Nobody talks about Khrushchev anymore."

"That's because he's no longer in office," the salesman said.

"His *words* are in office," my father said." The Soviets haven't changed. Those son-of-a-b's are still hell-bent on spreading their atheist empire across the globe. The atmosphere is no longer safe since the Russians launched Sputnik and they keep shooting live commies into space.

Khrushchev pounded the podium at the United Nations, promised to destroy our way of life, threatened to bury us for godsakes--and nobody assassinated *him*!"

❇ ❇ ❇

Khrushchev's shoe served as the baton that ushered in my life.

My history began with my birth story and the story of my birth story was not just true, but sanctified and unquestionable, like the Pope. God emblazoned me with certain truths so that no matter what torture or brainwashing the atheists might put me through, I would always know who I was.

Before I started school, I had a sense of the world into which I was born. Like other kids, I remembered some things and forgot others. Some signs of the end preceded my birth and other historical moments occurred when I was just a baby. But in my mind, I'd seen everything. History was not just in my head, but it seeped into my pores and shaped every cell of my body.

There was a lot to be afraid of during my formative years, even, or maybe especially on television. Threats broadcasted from every channel. Soldiers died in Vietnam every night around dinnertime—and it was normal. I expected to see Vietnam the same way every day: an adult show I had to sit through until my father left the room. Police flaunted their guns. Black people clenched their fists. A white knight armed with a can of Ajax cleanser waged a never-ending war against dirt. NASA sent men out into space hoping to find peace or at least quiet on the surface of the moon. I was born knowing that no matter how many leaps mankind made, the world we actually lived in was still flat.

Growing Up and Liking it

The communist threat from without must not blind us to the communist threat from within. The latter is reaching into the very heart of America through its espionage agents and cunning, defiant, and lawless Communist Party, which is fanatically dedicated to the Marxist cause of world enslavement and destruction of the foundations of our republic.
 —J. Edgar Hoover, *Death of a Nation*

I didn't know it, but I'd grow to be an infiltrator. I learned more at home, crouched beneath the dining room table, than I did sitting upright at any desk at school. The table I hid under hadn't seen much dining and the room had become a repository of political literature that my parents said was hard to find and our neighbors said was hard to believe. I hardly read any of it. *The Naked Communist* featured the red silhouette of a man, unclothed and bald. *Death of a Nation* illustrated fists of an angry mob, and the cover of *None Dare Call it Conspiracy* pictured nine symbols that represented the path to the New World Order. I knew the score.

When I wanted to learn more I kept my mouth shut. I enjoyed the perspective of a small pet, hidden by the long end of a tablecloth. I heard the brisk sound of coffee, and I saw legs dressed for action: leotards and beige slippers with wedge heels. My mother sighed, rustled papers, lit a cigarette. She clicked the keys of her Smith Corona and tapped her foot in a way that said she was busy, not nervous.

When my father came home she yelled, "Don't traipse in here with those clodhoppers. I just vacuumed and JBS meets here tonight."

My father stood on the carpet fringe. His work boots were slapped with plaster, but it didn't look fresh. He leaned against the doorframe and began to unlace. He asked, "So, what have we decided to do about her so-called health class?"

"Here's what I've got so far: We are opposed to the airing of the filmstrip *Growing Up and Liking It*. As informed citizens, we object on the grounds that it usurps the God-given rights of parents."

"Don't dance around the truth, Jane. It's sex education."

My mother read aloud, "We respectfully inform you that we will not be sending our daughter to school that day."

"No, no." my father said. "Send her! Have *them* make accommodations."

"Let's keep her home," my mother said.

"Listen, these damn liberal bureaucrats are falling all over themselves to accommodate every cripple and retard they can find!"

"Watch your language."

"They're pulling freaks out of the woodwork. It's popular to have something wrong with you."

"John!"

"All these mandates—handicapped ramps, special education, it costs me—the taxpayer. So let somebody do something for *her* for a change—a *normal* kid."

"But how will she spend the time?"

"For what I pay, she can sit alone with a gilded Bible."

"Kids can be cruel."

"Let me tell you—life is crueler than any kid."

"Is curriculum spelled with one R or two? Pass me that dictionary?"

"Ah—either way, Jane, we're shoveling shit against the tide."

My mother uncrossed her legs and typed. My father sat down and rubbed his socked-feet that looked like gray potatoes. I pictured an unbroken chain of smoke from my mother's idle cigarette, its gray skin inching out over the lip of the ashtray and waiting to fall.

The fence Dad built, post to pickets, and me in my Assumption uniform....

Good Catholic Motorists

Before I stepped into Sister Leonard Mary's second-grade class, my mother turned to me and said, "You're going to start in room 2-B. Isn't that something? To be, or not to be. It's Shakespeare!"

But room 2-B was not to be the stage for tragic soliloquy. My parents had designs to home school me but they held off on it—and so I was blessed with an opportunity to get out into the world. Assumption was blessed with the chance to be a good school. The whole globe was blessed with time, time to correct itself before we fell off our axis and into Apocalypse. Room 2-B was a sanctuary of hope, a bright room of asbestos tile and concrete block walls painted industrial green. Huge pull-down maps depicted Earth as I knew it: slightly curved at the poles, but a world still flat enough to fall off of.

Sister Leonard Mary looked like someone who never feared an assassination attempt. She wore a long habit, high collar, yoke-bib, floor-length cloak over floor-length robe. So much holy garb. Was the cloak flame-retardant? Was the robe radiation-resistant like those heavy ex-ray vests at the dentist's office? Was the bib bullet proof?

I also viewed Sister in secular terms. She kicked up dust bunnies in her swift glide from the window to the door. The white boxiness of her habit made me think of Chinese takeout. The thick cord around her middle could have come off the deck of a battleship. I adored her accessories: cranberry-sized rosary beads—holstered to her waist—the soft clap they gave when she walked. I loved her black-rimmed, news-anchor spectacles and the shiny gold band on her finger that proclaimed to the world she was wed to the church.

Sister had the task of preparing thirty-three of us for the sacrament of first Holy Communion and she taught Communion prep like a hard science. She was serious on the subject of Original Sin, an indelible signifier of our fallen heritage. Original Sin, the notion that each of us was invisibly branded the moment we were born, occupied my mind even when I wasn't in school. I thought about Original Sin during a werewolf movie, how a man looked so normal right before he turned. Sin erupted like a canker sore with every full moon. Original Sin was inevitable sin.

"You'll be making your first confessions this week," Sister said right after we gave the pledge. "Suffice it to say you're not innocent children anymore."

She licked her thumb and counted out copies of what seemed to be a diagram of mechanical parts—everything under the hood of a car.

Daniel McCormick tugged at his plaid bowtie, turned around, and whispered, "What the H?"

William Dempsey cupped his mouth and muttered over his shoulder, "Beats me. Looks like a Ford."

Boys and girls passed worried glances around the room as they studied the mimeograph. Sister may have been overstepping her bounds—teaching auto-mechanics, a subject that belonged in the basement with wood-shop, the incinerator, and the Puerto Rican janitor known as Aqua Velva.

Flywheel, battery, carburetor, the parts were labeled like state capitals—landmarks situated on the outskirts of a rectangle named radiator.

"It's time for me to tell you a true story that's not for kids," Sister said. She nodded, and Jimmy Rhinegold knew to close the classroom door. Sister gave a quick stroke to the corners of her mouth.

"There lived a man and a woman, husband and wife. They loved each other in Jesus' name and they were blessed with child. Naturally, they gave our Lord thanks and praise when their son was born, and they promptly set a date to have the child baptized. Matter of fact, they were on their way to the church."

Sister glanced down and shook her head. "To this day, no one knows why that ongoing car crossed the yellow line at high speed—but it careened into the new parents' vehicle. Jesus, Mary, and Joseph! Mother and Father were thrown through the windshield and killed. Sister launched her hand into the air to show us the trajectory. "The baby was badly injured, but still alive. You see, the mother's body took most of the impact."

I loved Sister's true stories. They were full of pain and pain was the calling card of truth.

"Then Good Catholic motorists happened upon this catastrophe," she continued. "They found the child shaded by a flowering cluster of Bleeding Hearts. His white christening gown was spotless even after being thrown by the crash. The infant could barely draw a breath, but the tiny fingers on his baby hand were moving! The Good Catholic Motorists carried the baby back to the vehicle, where the whole front of the car was wrapped around a tree. The hood was peeled back in miraculous fashion. It was a gift from God because mutilation of the hood allowed the motorists access to the engine. They popped off the radiator cap, tore a strip of baby blanket and lowered it into the radiator to get it wet. They blessed the liquid in Jesus' name and baptized the child in the name of the Father, Son, and the Holy Ghost." Sister made the sign of the cross. "Drops of radiator fluid dripped over the forehead, anointing the child just before it died."

Sister sat down, pressed the back of her hand to her moist brow and exhaled as if she was tired from the ordeal. There was something urgent about her. Her gauzy habit bound her face into an oval. Her wrists were cuffed so tight her sleeves seemed to squeeze blood through the blue veins of her hands.

After a long stretch of silence, Sister snapped off her glasses and stood up. Her vinyl chair gasped. "This is a *happy* story, people! Let's get smiling!" She held up the diagram of the engine. "Through God's mercy, laymen baptized the child and saved his soul from Limbo! Now you can do this."

I imagined myself saving the werewolf, getting him to confess his curse of Original Sin before he went into his next lunar blackout. Of course, that was just a movie. Everyday there was real disaster on I-95, the strip my father called "the fast track to death in our little corner of hell on Earth". I'd witnessed unforgettable scenes—catastrophes that turned the throughway into an eight-lane parking lot, jackknifed tractor-trailers spilling fluids and toxic smells, windshields that looked like they'd been punched from the inside out with the force of a spaghetti and meatball comet, and guardrails mangled and strewn like severed appendages. I always wondered what it would've been like to get out of the car and walk among the victims. My father said the city of Bridgeport was damned, but a damned city is full of desperate people.

I wanted to save lots of people, and to be bona fide, maybe wear a signifying armband, I asked Sister, "Do we get an official patch? Where can we find canteens of Holy Water?"

"This isn't the Girl Scouts, Miss Cascone." She puffed up in the cheeks, picked up her eyeglasses, stared over the rim with a look that doubled her chin. "Mr. McCormick— crack open some windows."

I felt foolish and ashamed long before dismissal when Sister coiled the scarf around my neck in the cloakroom and said, "You'd better stick to studying long division, Lady Jane."

"What?" my mother said later, as she sliced carrots into thin half-moons that floated in a galaxy of chicken soup. "What exactly did you do wrong?"

"Nothing," I said—but like any kid in Catholic school, I was never absolutely sure.

Power to the People

Cities had reputations. That's what town lines were for: to keep reputations where they belonged. Bridgeport, Connecticut, was notorious for crime, public housing, and closed-down factories. But my father was a law-abiding, self-employed, single-family homeowner. We were neither rich nor poor. We lived in a city that had problems.

Fairfield was famous for picturesque streets lined with dogwoods and long winding driveways that hid mansions where movie stars lived. My folks convinced Our Lady of the Assumption Elementary in Fairfield to admit me, but they couldn't get the school to offer transportation.

"They're busing kids all over God's green earth," my father said, "but they can't talk one bus driver into one quick right turn. That's the kind of country we've become."

My father stayed angry about the bus situation but he drove me to school in his work van. It was boxy and red with weathered wooden ladders on top. We sometimes called the van a truck. It had a few dings and scratches from regular use, but it had commercial plates and all four hubcaps. My father had professionally stenciled signs on both sides, gold letters with 3-D effects, just like old Coca-Cola ads. The signs said: ***Grand Painting - John Cascone, Proprietor and General Contractor.*** Our phone number was creased by the sliding door.

The passenger seat felt like a ledge on a skyscraper, and the air stayed thick with paint thinner. Turns threw me toward the door or the stick shift, but mostly my father held me in place with one big hand. Buckets and droplights clanged so loudly we didn't have to talk to each other, and we didn't need to feel guilty for not speaking either. Upon arrival, my father came around to open my door and help me land on the curb like a lady. It wasn't unusual for a paint roller to tumble out with me. Sometimes my father tried to kiss me goodbye and sometimes I let him, but most times we hurried up. I think it made us both uncomfortable to take the van on church grounds and stop in front of the statue of Our Lady. Nobody on the playground ever said an ill word to me about my father or his noisy work truck.

Our car turned out to be an object of ridicule. Daniel McCormick coined it the *Shitty-Chitty Bang-Bang*. The kid was an idiot. Our Chevy wasn't souped-up like something from a Walt Disney musical, and it wasn't a jalopy either. Our ice blue Impala sported bumper stickers—one on the right and one on the left rear bumper—**I AM A SECRET MEMBER OF THE JOHN BIRCH SOCIETY**. I saw two heroes, a his-and-hers set, like matching towels. Those bumper stickers identified us as people with unpopular beliefs and secret intelligence. The politics of my situation required that I also view those stickers the way I imagined the kids from Assumption did—as red tags from a cheap store, proof of the inferior quality of our city.

The cars at school modeled the apathy you'd expect from a falling empire. I saw a happy face slapped on the bumper of a Cadillac. BMWs and Volvos touted peace signs. It was appalling. Daniel McCormick rolled down the window of his mom's Mercedes, punched his fist into the air and yelled, power to the people! My classmates were morons and their vehicles cost a fortune, but they stood for nothing. There wasn't a single luxury car with something to say about the state of affairs in the world. If my classmates' parents ever cared to say something noble with ink and adhesive, I would have known because bumper stickers *always* left a trace.

Sometimes my father needed to get on the road early. He didn't want to leave me loitering around the playground in the dark, so I had to learn how to take public transit.

One Saturday we did a dry run. We walked a few blocks to the corner of Hughes and Brooklawn Avenue and we waited. When the bus came, my father asked the driver to hold up a moment and my father proceeded to show me how to hold the railing, to pull myself on the bus without help, where to drop the coins, and how to brace myself if the driver started up before I found a seat. He said I should tell the driver to stop at the church but never to count on him to do so. He gave me landmarks to watch for, landmarks to pull for, and told me not to panic if I wound up at the mall.

We made it to Assumption, but we hadn't planned on what to do once we got there. The two of us exited the bus and stood before the empty parking lot. I looked for someplace to sit and my father told me to stand, and never to lean on a wall, gate, or fence because everything was someone's property. We stood under a huge maple tree, swung our empty arms, and we clapped and snapped our fingers to make galloping sounds while we waited for the return bus.

"Not bad so far, right?" he asked.

"It's fun," I said.

"Since we're standing in front of a church and within sight of your school, let's go over a little *Baltimore Catechism*, shall we?"

"Fine by me."

"Question—What is the Church?"

"Besides being a building, the Church is a congregation of people who profess faith in Christ."

"And what does the congregation do?"

"The congregation partakes of the sacraments."

"Continue," he said. "What about this congregation?"

"The congregation is governed by legal priests with one visible Head."

"That's *lawful pastors*," my father said. "Good. Who is the invisible Head of the Church?"

"Jesus Christ is the invisible Head."

My father patted me on the shoulder. "Are you ready?" he asked.

"To see the invisible Head?" I asked.

"No. To take the bus by yourself?"

"Now?"

"No," my father said. "Starting Monday, my little Peas Day."

"Yes, sir, I am ready."

And so it went. I was in second grade. I left my house with exact change and took my place on the corner with people who were not there on Saturday—the poor people.

We stood together but apart, spread out on the corner of Brooklawn and Hughes, a half-dozen of us. We all faced east to catch the bus heading west. I wore an emblem, OLA, which stood for Our Lady of the Assumption. The patch was shaped like a security badge of blue and gold embroidery and it was stitched to my Scotch-plaid jumper, right over my heart. The poor people at the bus stop had their own forms of identification. For instance, an auto mechanic with a smudged "Eddie," and a tan man in a "Groundskeeper" polo, folks with odd accessories like cleats and a pocket watch. I was raised not to stare, but the cleaning ladies had hairnets and horrible knuckles. I wondered if the poor people knew about the John Birch Society and communist conspiracy, if they believed in stockpiling food. Were they working to save up for a backyard bomb shelter? Probably not.

I was mostly happy to see the poor people at my corner. When they weren't there, it meant I was either early or late. When it rained, we were all stuck under our own umbrellas if we brought them. When I dropped a dime and it rolled into the sewer, the Groundskeeper gave me another one. We shared a pure and silent understanding. I don't remember thinking about the poor people as good or bad; I just hoped we didn't get bombed while I was on my way to school because I didn't want to take my last breath with a bunch of people who didn't know how to speak English. My father thought I rode a bus with full-blooded Americans, and I never told him otherwise.

Once we boarded, it was every man for himself. Getting a window seat was a priority since I didn't want to climb up on my knees and lean into a guy who smelled like motor oil as I reached for the cord. I tugged on the wire with precise timing, maintained an ear for a dull buzzer, an eye for a distracted driver. Getting to school before the bell required a sense of time as well as timing. I wore a watch with a thin white strap and an extra notch my father made just for me with a steak knife.

I made it my goal to get off a block before the church and adjacent playground so the kids didn't see the color of my bus. Everybody knew me as the Bridgeport public transit kid. Even so, I refused to herald my arrival by popping out of a decrepit vehicle that featured an ad for women's cigarettes and the slogan *You've come a long way, baby.*

My bus was incredibly ugly, a big green canister from the 1950s, with round headlights and a rusty front bumper. There were uneven blotches of paint—colors I associated with moss, frogs, and dollar-bills. Graffiti covered clouds of more graffiti and created a patchwork of camouflage that hid nothing while my bus crawled and hissed like a slow-moving target.

My bus smelled of meatballs and rubber tires. I'd already accepted that the stink of the so-called Park City had seeped into my pores. It wasn't just the beach of sandy-haired kids, the freckled faces and braces, the Kennedys, the McCormicks, and the Donnellys who called me an *eye-talian* and said they smelled something like garlic on me. On the front page of *Bridgeport Post*, Paul Newman called our city the "armpit of Connecticut." He wasn't the first person to call Bridgeport some kind of hole. My father often said our city smelled like dirty socks but that was not the worst of it. He never got past the day we woke to find both my little brothers' tricycles *and* our dog's house had been stolen. We stared at the bald spot in our yard with a pile of poop where the doghouse used to be, and then turned to the vacant place on the porch where the boys' trikes were last seen. The dog paced and my brothers wilted with disbelief.

"What do we do?" I asked.

He took the lock off my bike and cinched the rickety gate of our picket fence shut. "I could understand it if they stole your Schwinn," he said.

I was never sure what my father meant—about the nature of crime in general or about our smelly city in particular, whether the crooks (always plural) had stolen items of too much value or too little.

Our Lady of Katz

I came into the house to ask my mother something, and I found her unhooking crystal teardrops from our living room lamps. Our lamps were adorned with gold cherubs and stood on marble bases, tall, proud replicas of something from the noble Roman Empire, lamps that proved we weren't the poor people in Bridgeport, Connecticut. My mother splashed ammonia into a basin and put the crystals inside to soak. The teardrops sparkled before she submerged them. I couldn't wait to see how blinding they could get.

"Get back outside," my mother said. "You shouldn't take your eyes off those boys, not even for a minute." I grabbed a Popsicle from the freezer, split it, and took half a lime outside, but a moment later I went back into the house, this time with the boys. She asked, "What now?"

"They want Popsicles, too," I said.

"Mommy, it's hot," Big-A said.

"Split another Popsicle and get back out to play."

"But it is too hot," I said. "Once they get sticky, the bees come after us."

"Okay. Down to the basement you go," she said. I opened the door for the boys and what was on my mind when I first walked into the kitchen came back to me: specifically, The Cat Lady, an odd woman in the neighborhood who'd been feeding cats for years, and a gold-striped cat I had been watching for a few days.

Connecticut was the land of four seasons, but our Cat Lady never changed for them. She wore the same lumpy wool coat, rhinestone brooch, and Russian-style fur hat. Her lipstick was treacherous. It seemed to spill out of the corners of her mouth. Every day she made the trek from parts unknown to Helwig's antique store. She carried crumpled shopping bags, overstuffed and apparently so heavy they caused her to waddle. We'd spot her tomato lips and her teeter from blocks away as she headed toward us on Wood Avenue. The lot in back of old Helwig's happened to be my hangout. Sometimes I brought my brothers, but it was no playground. The Cat Lady turned it into an infamous breeding ground for strays—activity we called *cat traffic*. My father called the lot *shit alley*. To the unsuspecting eye she was a harmless old lady, but I figured her for a communist spy. Feeding the cats was a distraction, a ruse. She infiltrated our neighborhood, trying to find out what the good side was doing. She never got a word out of me.

But one day it dawned on me I hadn't seen her. One day led to another. The Cat Lady didn't show and the cats meowed, paced back and forth, sniffed old tins and rusty can openers. They whined as if they knew it was the end of the world and they *cared*. I found it strange to go back and find the cats still loitering. A gold tabby with a pretty white bib stared at me as if I had food and an explanation.

I decided to share this information with my mother. She had forbidden me to go to Helwig's, but she knew I went anyway. I told her The Cat Lady was missing and now, without their leader, dozens of previously quiet cats had turned into a mob.

"They're rioting," I said. "If cats could raise fists they would."

"What?" my mother said.

"The cats have become a mob. Even the cutest one is jumpy, the one I named Golda."

"Her name is Irene," my mother said.

"No. It's Golda."

"I'm talking about the old woman," my mother said. "Her name was Irene Katz."

"Who?"

"She died in her sleep…."

"What?"

"Under the Rooster River Bridge."

"Huh?"

"She was a gypsy," my mother said.

"No, Ma. Trust me, she was a spy!"

"Don't be silly," my mother said.

Big-A interrupted us. "Mommy, I'm thirsty!"

My mother emptied the last of the Kool-Aid in a plastic cup and she let the empty pitcher gurgle down into the sudsy water. "Ok, now back down to the basement you go," she said. "And be a happy boy, will you?"

I looked at my mother. I asked, "How could she die outside?"

"The woman didn't have a home."

I'd never heard of anything like it—a person without a home. Cats could be stray—not people. I wanted to swear that there was no such thing. There were gypsies, though. So if she wasn't a spy, that meant that The Cat Lady—AKA: Irene—Alias: Mrs. Katz—had taken what my father called "the path of least resistance." He said people in this country were poor only because they chose to be. That meant Mrs. Katz sold her soul for booze and pills—and an insane amount of cat food and can openers.

My mother got all teary. She patted her eyes with the dishtowel.

"Ma, why are you crying?" I said. "Maybe you knew her name—but I was never introduced. I'm not happy she croaked, but now it's just a fact."

"I didn't raise you to talk that way," my mother said.

"Everything about her was suspicious. She never spoke. She looked Russian. She appeared and she disappeared. The

Cat Lady did everything spies do."

"That's no cause to be mean."

"I'm not mean. Truth is we never even knew her."

My mother washed and rinsed the Kool-Aid pitcher with its etched grin, and set it smiling upside-down in the drain board. She reached for my hands but I put them behind me and looked away. Then she grabbed my forearms and squeezed them with her wet hands. She shook me a little until I looked up.

"She wasn't a Cat Lady," my mother said. "Her name was Irene Katz."

"Okay," I said. "Can I go now?"

"Look at me," my mother commanded. "I want you to see what sadness looks like. Lower your head for a moment. Say a prayer!" She lowered her voice to a whisper. "Never be afraid to cry. Be afraid of people who don't."

I felt tension in my chest. I wanted to flex my muscles, pull away and run and keep on running. In the courtroom of my mind, I had the winning argument. I'd learned enough about the conspiracy against America. Once the Communists brought our country to its knees, everyone would know what sadness looked like. My mother's crippling sentiment wouldn't help. I'd be making Jell-O to keep spirits up. I would ration the water, stand over an open fire, and concoct a gray goulash to keep us alive. My mother would be crying us a river, weeping over a picture of what used to be.

When the moment had passed, I pulled my hands back and wiped her suds off on my dungarees. "I've decided Golda must be spared. I am her savior. That gold cat was destined to be mine."

"No," my mother said, and she began to dry her hands on the towel. "Let me rephrase that for you, *Patreesha*. I am *allowing* you to have her."

❀ ❀ ❀

Golda Meir. I'd heard the name ricochet around the

dining room at the GUUN meetings. I'd heard lots of odd-sounding words, places and people. Gaza Strip, Golda Meir. I assumed she was on our side. More than that, I loved the sound of Golda Meir—noble and pained.

But the first time I let Golda in the house, she ran off with a piece of chicken that my father had left marinating in a Pyrex of cooking wine, balsamic vinegar, and what seemed like an entire spice rack of oregano. He bounced out of the recliner and chased her through the house with a curtain rod.

"Here, Goldie," my father said as he jabbed the rod under the short side of the sectional sofa.

"Not Goldie!" I said. "Her name is *Golda*!"

"Com'ere, Golda, you little Jew," my father said.

"John," my mother said into the freezer, a baton of crescent rolls in her hand, "the walls have ears."

I didn't know my cat was Jewish. When she stole the chicken, all I saw was the effect of nature, the power that raw chicken had on a cat's brain. Whatever the Jews were doing, I figured it came natural to them.

I didn't know if Jewish was a religion or a country. At GUUN meetings I heard the Jews were rich and powerful, that they controlled the media. But I had seen pictures of what the Nazis had done to the Jews. Piles of bodies in black and white, horrors inside books at the school library, pictures I knew I wasn't supposed to see. The worst crimes known to man were the sins of Adam and Eve. The second worst crimes were the Nazis torturing and killing the Jews. I'd heard that the Jews had no home, that they'd forever be chasing their land. But that meant Jewish people couldn't have controlled everything. We had a plant called a wandering Jew and it didn't go anywhere. It didn't make sense.

Whatever I couldn't understand about the world I put into a folder marked 'For Later,' and I filed it off into a quiet corner of my brain. Eventually, all would be revealed. But early on in my childhood I understood that my parents, and the GUUNs, and other members of the John Birch Society simply didn't trust other people, especially people from other countries, people who tried to horn in on our bounty. And the bad guys didn't always have long hair and love beads, so Birchers couldn't relax.

Sometimes I couldn't relax with what I heard, all the loose ends. If the Jews controlled everything, I wondered why they had to fight for a home. We bought Alaska from the Russians. If the Jews had nearly all the wealth, why couldn't they just buy the small country in the sand? What other kinds of power could Jews have? Who was the original Golda Meir? Folder. Folder. Folder.

Even though she was ruled by instinct, I knew Golda was a good cat. I loved the hungry meow sound of her name. If Jews had power, then Golda did, too. Specifically, I believed she had nine lives. As a Roman Catholic, I wasn't supposed to believe in nine lives, but I did. There was the mystery of the virgin birth and the mystery of faith. I added the mystery of nine lives. Something can be real without being really clear.

I figured Golda had lived with the rich as often as she was left to the poor. She probably lived with an affluent Jewish family and wore a collar studded with emeralds that matched her eyes, so she died peacefully at least once. She must've lost one of her lives in a concentration camp, withered into a poor skeleton with gold fur and hollow eyes and then she was thrown into the Nazi's oven. She must've suffered a couple of mangy street lives. The empty lot behind Helwig's Antique Store was a cat ghetto of poop and broken glass. She must have dropped her share of litters there, suffered rabies, fleas, and heartworm. She must have woken up in the gutter as road kill at least once. I could see wear and tear on her. Golda's ear was torn like a ticket stub—proof of a movie already played—and paid for. God took pity on her and he kept giving her lives, chances to be happy. Golda didn't do anything wrong; she was traumatized for seeing her human mother die. Maybe Irene Katz came to our neighborhood to try and bring Golda and myself together before she passed. Maybe Irene Katz would come back with one of her own nine lives. Maybe Irene Katz was in Heaven. Maybe not.

Whatever crimes the real Golda Meir might or might not have committed as Prime Minister of Israel, I knew Golda "my-ear" was just a pitiful stray who'd seen more of life than we ever had. She looked ready to pounce, but I liked that. Tough does not mean uncivilized. If you looked at her face long enough, you'd see she was sad. She was tired of all the living and dying.

I had the feeling Golda was on her last life. But finally she wasn't guilty of having too much or too little. On the day she became mine, I wet my hand with tap water that I asked God to bless and I rubbed the fur between her ragged ears. She let me. Just a little baptism in case cats and people could live together in the hereafter, to remind each other of God's love of all species. I treated her to a can of Starkist—people-food. I ate some tuna first so she could see what I fed her was good enough for both of us. I forked out the rest and set it on an ivy-bordered saucer. She ate fast. She was toothy and a little dangerous, but she stopped eating and looked up at me as if she knew we were always meant to be.

Mom and us: Johnny-Boy, Big-A, and myself, about nine months before Joe-Bins was born....

Confessions of a Bouffant

What the caterpillar calls the end of the world, the master calls a butterfly.
　–Richard Bach

My mother kept our home clean and pretty, and if nuclear war claimed our Cape Cod at 327 Wade Street, I had no doubt she'd get our bomb shelter looking almost as cheery. Everything that *could* shine *should* shine was her motto, and my mother sparkled more than our spigots. While some women burned their bras, my mother made a strong case for the notion that housework should be done in Palazzo pants and turquoise accessories. Every room was a stage. Everything she touched was a prop and she was always on: bringing wood to life with furniture polish, kick-starting the vacuum with nude-at-the-toe pantyhose, fighting grime in a dark corner of linoleum. My mother was trying to show us how to face impending doom with class. I was paying attention. It started with indomitable hair! Lights, camera… spotlight on my mother's molasses-colored mane, go anywhere hair, a sophisticated flip with commanding curls, body and bounce, shine without oil, hair of today that won't be gone tomorrow, wash after wash, night after night, war after war.

My mother entered the dining room with her hair in a soft pageboy, Joe-Bins on her hip, and a ladle in her hand. "Patricia," she said. "Do something with that hair."

"I'm boycotting ponytails."

"Did you say boycott?" my father asked.

My mother smiled. "Get that hair off your face because I said so."

I slid an elastic band off my wrist and snapped my hair back into a ponytail.

"Who are you, Cesar Chavez?" my father asked. "How would you like to boycott TV?"

"No, sir," I said. "I just heard the word on the news."

My father's hair looked like it didn't want to be messed with: stiff with Brylcreem, wavy and dangerous as wet ink. He took his place at the head of the table and gripped the arms of the chair as if he were the captain of something and eager to set forth. "Well, let's eat if we're gonna eat," he said.

My mother served us with a genuine smile and enviable posture. But she held the ladle too high. She splashed broth at each place setting. Carrots and celery fell. Noodles hung and dripped off the side of my bowl. It disturbed me. I would have chosen less pageantry and less to clean up later.

"What a day," my mother said as she strapped Joe-Bins into his high chair. "Holy Mary. How can anyone send a kid to school with a raging skin infection?"

"An infection that's invaded our house!" my father said. "The war on germs—that's one more we'll never win. Ah, let's say grace." His fingers looked antiqued from painting houses all day. He pointed the butt of Italian bread at Johnny. "Look at this kid's face."

"It's impetigo," my mother confirmed.

Johnny's golden brown-hair was foolproof: too short to comb but long enough to leave a part on the side that he never had to make. His cheeks and chin were greased with ointment. The eldest of my kid brothers, Johnny-Boy had an easy life except for an occasional cut or scrape, or in this case, a lesion.

My mother passed me a terrycloth bib. "Please put this on Baby Joseph." My mother liked to say Baby Joseph had the hair of angels. But Joe-Bins, as I called him, made a name for himself by jimmying the fridge, eating half a stick of butter, and throwing up in the vegetable bin. The kid was down to his last ounce of innocence, a lock of hair that looked like a tail when it was wet. We set his highchair on my Twister mat. I struggled to tie his bib as he flailed like I was prepping him for execution.

"Whose sick kid was the carrier?" my father asked. "Lemme guess—Krasner's." He tore off a piece of Italian bread. "God forbid those people lose a penny for having someone sit at home with their sick child."

"John, they're just kids," my mother said. "Several of them have come down with it."

"Well it's a proven fact that kids don't need kindergarten or elementary school for that matter. It's unnatural for a child to be separated from his mother at an early age. That's why the boy's always crying when you go to pick him up."

My mother poured Hawaiian Punch into a sippy-cup for Joe-Bins. "I'm not sure about that," she said.

"The government is trying to standardize education, get all the kiddies ready for brainwashing. Read this month's *American Opinion!* There's an eye-opening article by Bob Welch." My father often spoke of Robert Welch, the founder of the John Birch Society, as if he knew "Bob" personally.

"I don't want to talk about this now," my mother said.

"Look at Anthony. He's got no worries, no infectious diseases. He's well-behaved and smart without any schooling."

"But he's only three," my mother said.

Big-A *was* well behaved, and so was his hair. He had the classic boy cut with honey-colored bangs angled across his forehead. We stacked a couple of phone books and propped him up in a regular chair. Kid was on the ball. We played with a magic kit and he figured out how to make it look like he pulled a penny out from behind my ear. He was not quite at the age of reason but ahead of his years.

"What's the problem, Jane? It's no secret to these kids or anybody else. We're living in the feel good generation. A crop of liberals like Dr. Spock are helping the communists ruin this country—duping parents into believing kids need kindergarten and even nursery school—so they'll be *happy* and *socially adjusted*."

"John...."

"—None of them need it."

"Certainly there are some benefits," my mother said.

"He's got enough toys—they all do. Propaganda. It begins with the lunchbox. Everybody's gotta have one or *feelings* will be hurt."

"Alright already," my mother said.

"Decent kids are being ridiculed for carrying a traditional brown bag ...."

"Patricia!" my mother said. "Get a napkin—stop that punch before it runs off Joseph's tray!"

I mopped up the juice with a stack of napkins and dropped the wad onto one of the mat's red circles.

"I thank God for the *Lost in Space* lunchbox Nonnie got for me," I said.

"You don't thank God for something like that!" my father said.

"It's the lunchbox of my life. I'll always love *Lost in Space*."

"Write that down, smarty pants. See if you believe yourself in six months."

"By the way, Dad, could you sign my permission slip?"

"Permission for what?"

"I want to take President Kennedy's Physical Fitness Challenge."

"Are you kidding? You don't need any challenge from a dead president," my father said.

"Yes I do! I know I can pass. I'll get a special pin."

"I don't want to hear about another government program. They've slapped us with seatbelts, mandatory sprinkler systems, and handicapped parking lanes. Let me tell you—Big Brother isn't going to regulate health or safety in this house."

"But, Dad, if half our class meets the challenge, we get to have a pizza party."

"I'll give you a challenge," my father said. "Give me twenty-five sit-ups—right now."

I didn't even ask what I'd get. I was stronger, faster, smarter and dying for any chance to prove it.

"Oh, John," my mother said. "Let the kid finish eating."

I dropped right there on the moss-colored area rug, knees slightly bent, hands behind my head. Johnny-Boy counted with me all the way to twenty and beyond. "Twenty-six, twenty-seven…"

"Patricia, come finish your dinner," my mother said.

"Soup's not going anywhere," my father said.

"It's getting cold," my mother said.

When I made it to thirty my brothers began to count. My father joined them.

My mother released Joe-Bins from the high chair, stacked dirty dishes, and carried them into the kitchen. I stopped at thirty-five, feeling good and dizzy. I stayed put and waited for my muscles to relax. Anthony came over and flopped down on top of me. Then Johnny climbed on top of Anthony. "Monkey Pile!" he said. Before I could shake them off, my father gave a Monkey Pile cheer of his own and proceeded to balance himself on top of the three of us.

We'd done it before and I always occupied the bottom of the pile. I liked being the designated underdog, fighting for my freedom, leaving tears and spots of drool on the cushion. As much as I liked Monkey Pile, I dreaded the game though I never gave my mixed feelings much thought.

But this time the pile up began on the floor instead of the sofa. My ribs and my face were pressed hard to the floor. I couldn't move or angle myself enough to breathe. I could neither slip beneath nor throw them off. I reached back, dug my nails into whomever or whatever I could grab. I threw all my strength into one final effort to lift myself off the ground with my arms. I shrank to the size of a period on a page.

I found myself sitting on the floor, panting—a stranger to

my own body, like a lip after Novocain. Shoulders, elbows and knees came alive and my head buzzed as if happy little bees made every move for me. I died and made it back! The tingling sensation had to be my soul returning to my body. The looseness of my limbs, the throbbing in my chest, the fuzziness in my mind, I paid attention to everything, sweet blank happiness. I'd never be the same.

But each breath pulled me further from the idea of heaven and pushed me closer to the facts on earth. Gravity had its way. Sore ribs, burning elbows, a stinging bottom lip. My limbs began to throb, not with miraculous bliss, but with the ache of a small life.

When my sense of calm totally evaporated, I felt washed ashore. Then I realized I'd wet my pants. My father stood over me. He grabbed an orange from a ceramic bowl of plastic fruit, palmed it the way a pitcher grips a ball he's about to fire into home plate. He gave the orange a squeeze that spit plastic air and he tossed the orange from one hand to the other—a hollow sound.

"You okay?" he asked, and he touched my chin.

I nodded yes.

"What happened there?" he asked. I couldn't tell if he was talking about peeing my pants or the fact that I had begged for my life and lost. Either way. I wished I could forget the ugly sounds I made. I found it impossible to look at him, but I wasn't able to get to my feet.

My father laughed. "How's it feel? How does it feel to almost meet your maker?"

Anger crept up through my veins, into my neck and a prickly heat spread across my face. I stared at my hands and watched them ball up into fists. My father tossed the fake orange at me. I think he expected me to catch it but before I could move my arms the plastic fruit struck my breastbone. I looked down on my lap where the orange had landed and there was the dark stain on my pants. Neither of us said a word. The longer the silence, the more it embarrassed us.

"You *bitch*!" I said. The words shattered the air. A surge

brought me to my feet and sent me running up the stairs.

I locked myself in the bathroom, a place of elevated cleanliness. I rested on the floor of Chiclet-size tiles. My mother blued our towels to an unearthly white, and she kept the grout pristine with denture fizz and a toothbrush. She often said a cruel tongue is the sign of a small person. I didn't want to be cruel or small. But I had suffocated in that Monkey Pile, and it became clear if I'd been drowning at Pleasure Beach, I'd do anything; I'd climb over my own kid brothers for air. The urge to live was a desperate and violent instinct. I knew what I was capable of. Worse than that, my father did too.

I went back to thinking about how I'd been given a gift and God's gifts never came easy. First I'd tell our priest what death felt like. But I couldn't think of what to say. The memory or feeling, whatever I knew, slipped further and further away. I needed a clear translation. I needed details, fast.

I rested my head on the floor and let the icy white tiles cool my cheek. I stared at the narrow copper pipes that rose up from the back of the toilet. And it came. Death is like a magician tearing a phone book right down the middle, and the phonebook is your heart. It's an incredible act of violence but after the tear, after your chest collapses and you lose the breath of life, you come undone. Pages of you scatter instead of bleed. And your last page flits like a butterfly, kisses flower after flower along the path to the savior. *That* was inspired truth! *That* was revelation! All my revelations came with a flicker of bliss followed by a bitter sense of being utterly alone. I had my speech. I just needed to write it down before it escaped me.

"Patricia, open the door." My mother called me Pa-*tree*-shuh, and I never told her how much I hated it. "There will be no more Monkey Pile—ever, ever again! Do you hear me? It's not a game. It's barbaric and it's over." She knocked on the door and twisted the knob urgently. "Now let me in."

"I can't come out yet," I said. "Can you bring me a pencil

and a piece of paper?"

"Don't play games with me."

"I'm not."

"I just had a talk with your father and those boys. Now I need to see my girl."

"Ma, can you please get me something to write on? I need a pair of clean pants and some panties too."

"Oh, good Lord! Hold on."

I heard her shuffle down the hall ranting about our house being a zoo and my father being a herd animal. Dresser drawers slammed. When she returned, I opened the door just enough to let her hand me my things, but she pushed her way in.

"Where's the stuff to write with? I said.

"Jesus, Mary and Joseph. Look at you—your face, your hair—you look like a little savage."

I looked at myself. I didn't see a savage. Worst case, I'd come down with impetigo.

She put her hands on my shoulders, and I looked at us together, portrait-style, mother and daughter, faces almost touching. Sharing a mirror with her was never good for me. This time my eyes looked a little swollen. I saw a puffy bottom lip, and my hair was a tangled mess around my copper-penny face. Not ugly. Not pretty. Not bad considering I had just spent one of my nine lives.

"You know what we're going to do?" my mother asked. "We're going to find your best features and *accentuate* them. We'll style your hair. Buy some barrettes. Tomorrow, you're going to walk into school like a young lady."

"That's stupid," I said.

"Stupid?" my mother said. "Come on. Is it going to kill you to smile? First of all—always believe that a smile make us prettier and takes ten years off a woman's age."

My mother had good reason to believe. She popped into our kitchen every morning as familiar and as welcome as the cinnamon on our toast. I was proud of her but I never had any desire to look like her. Besides it was impossible. My mother had a diamond-shaped face and mine was long. Her skin was pale and mine tanned. I didn't hold things like blue eyes and cheekbones against her. I wanted a perm so my hair could do its own thing. Poof! My hair wanted to shoot up like a dandelion or a mushroom cloud. I couldn't get her to let me have the hair I wanted, but I saw pity and where there is pity there's opportunity.

"Mom, I want to wear my hair in an Afro. First you get a tight perm, really tight, and then you tease the hair, mold it with glistening gel and shape it with an Afro pic that you can keep in your hair for decoration. That's how they wear it on *Soul Train*."

"Patricia. Number one—don't let your father hear you say that. More importantly, why would you want to do such a thing? Number two—you weren't born for the fickle masses. Get far from the madding crowd. Let it all go." She looked radiant. "You can be in this world but not of it!"

So, the only hairstyle I could have was hers. It wasn't from out of this world and it wasn't fair. Her makeover was no consolation, and I couldn't talk her out of it. But my mother's tangerine-colored lips were mesmerizing. She smelled like baby powder and Chanel no. 5. I wanted to believe she could change me into a person I didn't even know I wanted to be. I sat in front of the mirror and waited.

The vanity's Formica edge creased the back of my legs as she combed and spread Dippity-Do over my wild strips of hair. Pink sponge-curlers hugged my face. I wore a crown of jellyrolls. My mother opened the medicine cabinet and pulled out her tin of Bobby Pins, old Bobby Pins that had shed their soft amber tips. Each Bobby Pin clawed my scalp, but I winced from the sound, not the scratch. She rerolled a couple of curlers, moved my chin from left to right, knit her brow. I was a flyaway kite in the sky of my mother's blue eyes. She tried very hard to fix me, and I decided it wasn't going to work. I didn't need to wait until morning. I wasn't going to look at myself anymore anyway. Mirrors were for people like her, people who'd never done a sit-up in their lives, people who'd never faced death.

The next morning on the playground, Carol McDonald came my way. Carol wore her hair straight, shoulder-long, thick and yellow all the way to the sharp ends. She immediately came up with a jingle: *Patricia looks like Tammy Wynette and smells like Aqua Net*....I didn't recognize the tune but I fell for the rhyme and the attention.

Terri Healy said, "Man, where'd you get that do?"

"My mother did it," I said. Terri's hair was blond with stripes of dark and light woven into two stiff braids that didn't touch her shoulders.

Terri Healy suggested a test. "Let's insert this pencil and see if it holds or falls out of your hair." This experiment interested me in a science-fair kind of way. She plunged the pencil into one of the teased sections of my hair and it stuck, firm as a knife in the back. Terri poked her pencil in another spot and my hair held up yet again. Carol gave it a go. It was silly and fun and wild. It was a bittersweet success because when the Communists dropped into Connecticut, when they finally tumbled out of the sky in their red hammer and sickle parachutes, those girls would hardly be laughing. They'd be scrambling around with no plan, no place to hide. We kept fifteen thousand dollars worth of Bee Hive freeze-dried food stockpiled in a trailer in upstate New York. If there were any chance, we would live.

A sweet breeze of honeysuckle drifted into our airspace and I sneezed hard three times.

"God bless you!" Carol said. "God bless you! God bless you!"

"Thank you. Thank you. Thank you." I reached into my pocket for a Kleenex. "Know what? Once I sneezed 32 times in a row!"

Terri coughed up a sarcastic laugh. "Thirty two times? You shouldn't brag. You should get an inhaler before you blow out the rest of your brains." Terri's father was a neurologist, so she had to say things like that. I was certain her father was one of those men who believed we evolved from apes.

I tried the pencil test myself. I poked at my own hairdo in furious joy. "Look! I'm a pencil holder!" My hair held firm and I laughed myself woozy. I stepped back and landed on my own lunch box. When I bent down to see what happened, a pencil dropped from my hair and then another fell. I swatted and whacked at my hair the way I would fend off a swarm of angry yellow jackets.

"Hey!" Carol said. "Now it looks like you have an Afro!" I ran over to a parked car and looked in the side-view mirror.

"It sorta does!" I said.

I was almost the girl in the Afro! I moved to the music in my head. I let my shoulders roll back, swiveled my hips and took big, Keep on Truckin' steps until Terri Healy snapped, "What are you, retarded?"

"I'm Sicilian," I said.

"Is that why you're grinding like a perv?" Carol asked.

I picked up my lunchbox and left the pencils. It was over. They couldn't appreciate the art of sneezing or my *Soul Train* moves. There was no way for me to share the nasty truth with them. I headed back to class with everybody else. I thanked God for the laughs, for letting me play in Babylon a bit.

We got in our usual two lines, boys and girls, shortest to tallest and we followed Sister from the school, across the playground, and to the church for Confession. My acts of lying, swearing, and disobeying were forgiven every other week.

Sister gave the nod. I pulled the purple drape aside just enough to slip in and let the velvet door shut out the world behind me. A waffled screen glowed before me; a beam of solemn light shone on Father's hands. I had a plush kneeler, a grid to speak into, and someone on the other side to hear me.

I left the confessional, knelt at the altar railing, and instead of saying the penance father gave me for lying, swearing, and disobeying, I tallied my omissions.

1. I swore *at* my own father.

2. My hair: I knew I was guilty of a profound lack of charity in the face of my mother's kindness.
3. I had failed to explain my death and resurrection. Rebuking a miracle had to be a sin.

A row of potted lilies in pink foil had been placed at the base of the cross where Our Savior hung. I marveled at the details, the chiseled bones of Jesus's feet, his muscular calves, rippled stomach and pronounced rib cage. Jesus looked all-too-human, like a man who was once in very good physical condition. He was forced to suffer the humiliation of being exposed in public in a diaper-like garment. But the agony of nails and thorns! Oh, the pains we inflicted on our Lord with our sins. Jesus would have wanted me to tell Father Ryan what I knew about death, what I knew about ingratitude, what I knew about cruel words. I was a coward. My mother had said it often enough: Cowards die a thousand deaths.

At dismissal, the other kids whisked up their monogrammed duffle bags and streamed out. I lingered in the cloakroom with my jacket on, my hood pulled up, and my *Lost in Space* lunch box in hand. I could hardly bear the idea of taking my sins or my revelations back home.

I felt Sister materialize behind me like a ghost. I lacked the courage to face her.

"What's the matter, daughter," she said.

"Everything, Sister. Everything."

"Out with it then."

"I can't."

"You just confessed your sins. Your heart should be light."

"Yes, but..."

"But what?"

"I forgot to tell Father Ryan some things."

"You forgot? It's time to start remembering."

"I didn't actually forget, Sister. I just couldn't say them."

"You can say 'em right now. No need to turn around. Make believe you're still in the confessional. I can't see your face. Talk directly to Jesus."

"Bless me— *Fa*—Sister, for I have sinned..."

"Go on."

I lowered my hood. "I hate my hair. I wrecked what my mother did to make me pretty."

"And?"

"My father and my brothers piled on top of me."

"And?"

"I got smothered to death."

"And?"

"God brought me back to life."

"And?"

"I called my father a b-i-t-c-h."

"And?"

"That is all."

Sister turned me around. She knelt down and squinted. "You hate your hair? Clean up the foul language, missy. And next week, you explain all this to Father Ryan."

She rose, took my hand and pulled me toward her. "Don't worry, my child." She patted my eyes with a linty tissue. "It's not the end of the world!" Sister twirled me around and around triumphantly. She touched my frizz-flip-Afro as if it was the most perfect design she'd ever seen. "Your hair!" she said. "Now, somebody loves you a lot to do that."

I smelled honeysuckle as soon as I stepped outside. Buses groaned out of the parking lot. I took my navy sweatshirt off and tied it around my waist. It was hot enough for the beach. Maybe if my father came home early. I found a bouquet of hope in spreading a blanket and lying beside a transistor radio.

On second thought, I didn't need the beach. Every time we went I seemed to enjoy it less. I missed the minnows we already caught and killed, the crabs we'd torn out of their shells, the jellyfish we'd long since stabbed with the ends of our pinwheels. Sometimes I thought Terri and Carol were lucky for not knowing there were bombs earmarked for southern Connecticut, strategically aimed at Boeing Jet, Sikorsky Helicopter, and that nuclear submarine base in Groton. The communist attack on our munitions-rich state hadn't turned Pennsylvania into oceanfront property yet, but that day was coming. God wanted me to remember the world as it was; my memories were already packed.

    I found a good stick, a rod, and I beat my way into the brush, hammered the skunk grass, hacked a thread through the deepest green to get to the Rooster River, a raw world that smelled of onions. Up ahead, garbage bags littered the river's edge, the first sign of civilization. As I neared my house, I saw my brothers laughing, riding their trikes in circles in our front yard. I wondered when I should start to write down the names of all the people I ever knew. I would have started with Terri and Carol.

A Countdown for Leaving

I was nearing my tenth birthday the summer when American astronauts rocketed toward the first walk on the moon; I was in a hurry to catch up with them. I took my baby brother's car seat out of the back of our twilight blue '64 Chevy Impala and propped it up against the maple tree. I leaned the seat back far enough so that, when strapped in, I could handle the g-force that would pull like rubber bands through my body. I imagined myself as Penny on *Lost in Space*. Given the atmosphere in my house—my parents' contempt for left-wing radicalism and fear of imminent takeover by the communists—*Lost in Space* was the most realistic TV show I'd ever seen: Americans fleeing a world gone mad, sent out to colonize a new planet in the name of God, family, and country.

The problem with the world on my favorite TV show was dwindling natural resources due to overpopulation. The narrator defined the literal threat: ruthless competition among nations—nations that would resort to *anything*. From the very first episode, I was sold.

In real life, I'd heard the people in China were starving, Soviets lacked incentive to produce enough food. Our geography books showed God's love for America by the uneven distribution of earth's natural resources. America was not known as the home of the aardvark, or reliant on a singular crop such as mangos. It was neither a secret nor an accident that God set us apart from the rest of the world and he always had his reasons.

I extolled the virtues of *Lost in Space* to my father, hoping he'd watch and see the relevance; perhaps he'd see our future. He gave the show no more than five minutes.

"They should have shot Dr. Smith in the first episode," he scoffed and left the room.

My mother had no interest in space either. One day in the grocery store, I pointed out to her how, in honor of the Apollo 11 Lunar Mission, Tang was sprightly advertised as "yesterday's drink of tomorrow." She waved a baton of Minute Maid frozen orange juice and announced to everybody in Pantry Pride: "We won't be having any of that future stuff."

The wisdom of my favorite adventure show escaped my parents, but how in the devil could they fail to get excited about what Buzz Aldrin and Neil Armstrong were about to do? If we could have snuck some of our guys into NASA, they might be able to construct a secret lunar bunker. I'd choose survival on the moon over upstate New York any day. The fact that we planned to retreat to a trailer somewhere in the Berkshires might have depressed me if it weren't for *Lost in Space* and the fact that:

1. Every week, Penny Robinson's family had been surviving as castaways, living off the fruit of a hydroponic garden and the thrill of hostile alien encounters.
2. I failed to embrace the full meaning of annihilation.

My parents didn't want to hear about new worlds, latest gizmos or Johnny-come-lately countries. They harped on how much they wanted things to stay the same. I understood what they meant when it came to the Constitution, Holy Mass, and our survival plan, but beyond that I didn't get it. Stay the same as what? I never asked. I assumed the days worth repeating or getting back to were depicted in TV programs my father had watched and enjoyed in the 40s or 50s, shows where nothing much happened such as *Leave it to Beaver*. I didn't see how mindless civility could work for us. Let's say my mother wore a pearl necklace and dress full of crinoline to serve dinner every single night. My father would still pull into the driveway in a rattling paint truck, bound up the porch sweaty, tired, and ready to kick something like a jack-o-lantern that shouldn't have been so close to the door. Then he would barrel up the stairs and beat the Hades out of the Beaver.

But my mother didn't seem to hold the torch for any bygone era. She dressed like modern TV mothers with her oversized blouses and Capri pants. And she chaired MOTOREDE, the Movement to Restore Decency Committee. MOTOREDE set out to expose Betty Friedan, the radical who'd written *The Feminine Mystique*. Friedan was deep in the women's liberation movement; a riotous army of women who wanted to jump off the pedestal where God placed us and drown in the pool of equal rights. My mother stressed the point that equal rights meant women could be drafted; they might even have to pay alimony. The way my father put it, *The Feminine Mystique* encouraged women to take The Pill "so they could pull their pants down for everybody."

My father led a chapter of the John Birch Society (JBS). I sat in on a meeting where the men had discussed a book they approved of—Ralph Nader's *Unsafe at Any Speed*. The book wasn't pure propaganda and yet, somehow, it became a bestseller, "an overdue indictment of the auto industry's wealthy elite." My father loved overdue indictments. In this case, the brainwashed masses had stumbled upon a bit of truth about how car manufacturers cut corners for profiteers. Nader's book reflected change for the better! Maybe the apocalypse had been staved off for another month or maybe not—but for now the future of automobile safety was looking up.

My parents went door to door with petitions and clipboards, and they tried to get people to change their minds every day. I had no idea what I was supposed to stay the same as.

So everyday I blasted off for *Lost in Space,* always played the role of Penny, a pre-teen who didn't care what she looked like, Penny—an ordinary brunette in sensible pigtails and metallic space fatigues—I couldn't have looked any better than that.

I took my mother's old-style hair dryer, cut holes in the elasticized cap and wore it over my face; the spiraled tubing served as my oxygen umbilical. A transistor radio worked as a walkie-talkie. I had knobs from an old gas stove pressed into cardboard for a control panel. Christmas tree lights powered by extension cords ran into the garage and signaled when systems were go—gone—or under attack. I landed on planets as dusty as our backyard, dressed for action in a mod-silver raincoat, a crinkly vinyl with NASA printed over my breast pocket in Magic Marker.

I strode out of my cardboard module for a space walk. With my safety cord fastened around my waist, I gave the line a routine, precautionary tug before walking out into space. My brother Johnny rolled onto the scene on my old bike. I figured he wanted to play astronaut. I headed to the garage to get the dented colander he wore for a helmet and the safety mask he used as breathing apparatus. "Who are you gonna be," I asked my brother, "Major West or Will Robinson?"

"I don't want to play *Lost in Space*." He dropped his head down as low as the handlebars and opened his eyes wide. "I'm *Speed Racer*! Let's see how fast I can ride from here to the Flanagan's!"

It sounded good. I had my Timex on. Johnny rocketed from half a block down and I logged his speed. The finish line wasn't drawn precisely, so it was hard to determine if he was getting faster. We scavenged a coarse braid rope from the garage. Mr. Sheehan happened to back out of his driveway across the street. He rolled down the window.

"What are you kids up to?" Mr. Sheehan asked. We told

him about our racing idea.

"So, what's the rope for?"

"This is going to be the finish line," I said. "We need to tie it to a pole."

Mr. Sheehan got out of the car, left his door open and the rear end poking out into the street. He took one end of the rope and fastened it to the telephone pole in what he called "a military knot from back in the day."

"That is so cool!" I said as I tugged it. I grabbed the free end and snaked it back to our side of the street.

Mr. Sheehan saluted us from his station wagon and faded away. When I gave the word, my brother chugged down the street with red, white, and blue fringe streaming from his handlebars and baseball cards flapping in his spokes. I dropped the line just before he crossed it. He kicked out both feet in victory as he broke his own records, time after time. We laughed like there was no tomorrow.

"Okay," I said. "Here's something Evel Knievel might do. Instead of holding the line up and dropping it before you're about to finish, we'll do it vice-versa. I'll keep the line on the ground, and at the last second I'll raise it up over my head. You hunch down and cruise underneath. Think of it as a limbo stick!"

A fine idea, except that the end of the rope Mr. Sheehan tied to the pole was plenty high and my end was short. Johnny barreled straight down the middle of Pacific Street and the finish line burned his face at an angle. I had let go of the rope as soon as I saw he wouldn't be able to duck it, but the long line tore across my brother's face, swiped his neck, and draped over his shoulder. He hit the brakes and slid into a semi-controlled wipe out—just like Evel Knievel might do.

I ran over to help, to cast off the rope, to say I was sorry.

Johnny rubbed his cheek. Then he did it again, harder, as if he was trying to buff a scratch out of our mother's coffee table. I didn't know what to say to him as I saw a patch on his face like grated cheese, and then thick white ribbons of skin appeared. It gave me the chills to see how the skin coiled like pencil shavings. Before my eyes, a seared line emerged below his left cheekbone, across part of his bottom lip and down the side of his neck.

By the time I got him into the house and in front of our mother, that line blazed the spectrum of injury—it did everything from welt, to blister and bleed. By the time my father came home, the way the story was told, I had scarred my brother's face for life *and* nearly hung him.

My mother thought we should call a plastic surgeon. My father said a scar was a sign of character and since Johnny wanted to play football, he'd have plenty of signs. Mrs. Sheehan came over with some antiseptic cream that she said hospitals used on burn victims.

With gauze and ointment on his face, taking three baby aspirins every four hours, my brother seemed unfazed by it all, stretched out on the living room floor watching *Underdog*. My mother bought him coloring books and two new Matchbox cars. He pushed one across the bumpy carpet toward me.

"Sorry about your face," I said.

"It's okay," Johnny said. He lined the two cars up, side by side and then pushed one right up to the toe of my Keds.

"Does it hurt?" I asked him.

"Not really." He put the car in his palm and offered it to me, but I could not touch it. I walked away.

Even with my feet kicked up and doing Mad Libs on my bed, I found no relief in my brother's easy disposition.

When it was time for dinner, my mother called me out of my room. I didn't want to eat, but she insisted I sit across from Johnny at the table and look at what I'd done. The sweat of blisters, the deepening color—the line seemed to stretch his mouth into an exaggerated shape. He had a grimace like a sad clown.

That night while I was in bed, I heard my mother tell my father, "She needs a reprieve—a break from those boys before she kills one of them."

It had been an accident but at that moment, I took my

mother's words quite literally—that I could hurt, maim, or even kill—without intent. Of course the road to Hell was paved with good intentions and the very idea that anything could be merely an accident seemed impossible after I was forced to look at Johnny. It pained me—the foreverness of it all.

In the morning, my mother told me I'd be spending two weeks at my grandparents' house in Milford. It seemed too good to be true. Time with my Nonnie—who'd never raised her voice, who said yes more than no, who prayed the rosary. The biggest miracle of all was that she seemed to be the happiest person who ever lived.

I packed my entire bottom drawer full of pilly old bathing suits for the beach, and I brought my space raincoat to weather everything else.

❀ ❀ ❀

I stood on the neatly trimmed lawn with my Nonnie and waved over-and-out: to the Impala—a shiny blue bird, my father—his head craned for backing out, my mother—a pretty passenger even with Joe-Bins going ape in her lap, Big-A—barely visible in the back, and Johnny—hand pressed to the window to say goodbye.

My Nonnie was barely five-feet tall; when she put her arm on my shoulder, we must have looked like we were friends, friends who expected someone to take a snapshot of us. She kissed me on the forehead; we headed to the porch. We moseyed by the azaleas and through the green scent of Grandpa's basil. We strolled past the mirror-ball arm in arm; our reflection floated across the globe as one soft shape.

The house was full of smells. Her kitchen smelled like marinara and her basement was unforgettable for the toxic smell of mothballs that grandpa used to "varmint-proof the nether regions" of the house. "Today we're gonna make the ravioli, and you're going to be my partner instead of Grandpa," my Nonnie said. "Why don't you take off your coat and go wash your hands?"

I unbuttoned my raincoat and brought it to her hall closet. It smelled of crisp cedar. But my Nonnie's bathroom held the most powerful, lingering scent, the smell of Sweetheart Soap. I worked up a butter-like lather and as I rubbed under the spigot, I tried to avoid my image in the vanity. I wondered if there could be a world on the other side of a mirror. My side was cotton candy pink: mats, towels, tiles, toothbrush, the pelicans that splashed the shower curtain, and the crochet-doll that covered the spare roll of toilet paper—everything the color of sweetheart roses.

The sink was the altar of my Nonnie's kitchen. The window above it was adorned with stained glass images of our Lord and the Blessed Mother. In the pane above them, praying hands that seemed to applaud heaven were held to the window by a suction cup.

We rolled out enough wax paper to span the length of the dinette. She pulled her red vinyl stepstool out from a corner and used it to bring down a jade mixing bowl. I made a hill of ricotta and floated a pool of eggs, leaves of fresh parsley, and a sprinkle of salt and pepper on top, while my Nonnie flattened a blubber of dough with a red-handled rolling pin.

"Where's Grandpa?" I asked.

"He went to collect the rents," my Nonnie said.

"How come we don't go?"

"Those are sailors who need a room."

"What?"

"It's like the YMCA, Patti-cake. Where the boys go."

I didn't care much about boys but I liked my Sicilian Grandpa because he was naturally funny. He drank three glasses of warm water and ate an entire box of Sunsweet Prunes every day.

I used a fork and blended yolks into the ricotta. I made believe I was smearing bits of sun into snow. I scraped parsley from the sides of the bowl and churned the heavy mix until my arm hurt. "Does Grandpa do this part?"

"He does," my Nonnie said, and she leaned over the table

and flattened the dough. As she worked the rolling pin, her gold medallion of the Blessed Mother beat against her chest.

"Don't you think the world's gonna end?" I asked.

"Oh no. Not for a long, long time."

"But mom and dad do."

"I don't know, Patti-cake. I don't know. Maybe they're right."

"Don't you believe in communists?"

"Listen to what your parents tell you and say a rosary. That way you don't have to think about any of it."

"I already say the rosary."

"If you say the whole rosary every single day, the Blessed Mother worries for you."

My Nonnie knew things. She kept prayer books, pictures of the saints, and statues of the Blessed Mother in every room of the modest ranch she shared with Grandpa. They slept in the same room, but in separate beds, which signified uncommon devotion. My Nonnie and Grandpa were married and under the same roof and all, but they were not *together*. They were a *couple*, the way Mary and Joseph became partners to raise Jesus—it was a figurehead thing, a social duty, something I vaguely understood as "rendering unto Caesar."

We took turns pressing an upside-down jar to cut dough into circles. My Nonnie's dress was sleeveless, emerald green with happy metallic threads. Her arms were tanned, smooth and perfect. Her apron was tied at the neck and the waist, bleached so often I could only make out the pattern of lilacs from the gathers on the trim. A curl of her chestnut hair fell to her brow. She almost looked like a movie star—not like my mother but sort of like Sophia Loren—without the menacing breasts. My Nonnie used her forearm to slide the hair away, careful of her floured hands and her charm bracelet of birds and stars and half-moons.

"How much longer before we're done?" I had to know. I loved to be part of the creation of ravioli, and yet it made me sad, the part of me that measured happiness with a countdown for leaving it.

My Nonnie spooned a dollop of cheese on a circle of dough and folded it over into what we called clams. She set a couple in front of me so I could scallop the edges with a fork and seal the clams with nice even stitches. "Sing with me, Patty-cake," she said. "*And when we're dancing and you're dangerously near me, da-dum…I get ideas…da-dum…I get ideas….*" My Nonnie always sang the same song, and her ideas were always *idears*.

Nonnie spread jiffy-white sheets over the twin beds in the room where my father and uncle used to sleep. "Now we can bring the clams," my Nonnie said.

"Why do you put ravioli to bed?" I asked.

"The ravioli are resting; they need some air." She loaded a large tray and I shuttled ravioli from the kitchen to the bedroom. I faced them all the same way—an army of clam soldiers in perfect rows.

Grandpa came home with three black plums in a paper bag. "My, my, my," Grandpa said. "You girls work all morning!" His raspy voice and thick accent made it hard to understand him but fun to try.

"Why don't you go outside with your grandfather, Patti-cake," my Nonnie said. "I'll clean up."

Grandpa wasn't much taller than I was. He wore thick, black glasses, sherbet-colored clothes, and white shoes. He had moist skin and fleshy earlobes.

I thought he yanked his pants way up over his potbelly just to make me laugh. We ate our plums. He shlurped like a man and I licked the juice as it ran down my arm. I pinched leaves of basil the way he showed me, and I picked the reddest tomatoes. I followed him down the driveway to retrieve the barrels.

"Grandpa," I said, "why did you paint GC on your dented old garbage cans? Don't you know they're garbage cans?" He was an immigrant so I wondered what other messages he left for himself. AC for ashcan? FP on flowerpots? RS on the 50-gallon drum of road salt?

"My, my, my. What's this talk, Patty-girl?" It always

sounded like Grandpa was calling me petty.

"Never mind," I said.

My Grandfather took a seat in his parade chair and cracked open his newspaper. "I gotta do business," he said. Besides collecting the rents Grandpa checked his stocks in the newspaper everyday and read a column written by Griswold. I threw a pebble at the fencepost.

"Petty, are you happy here, with your Gran-*mather*?"

"Course, Grandpa. I love it here."

"Atsa what I wanna hear."

"The only thing I need is to see Apollo 11 touchdown!"

"My, my, my. What's this?"

"We're landing on the moon," I shouted. "Americans! I've been waiting my entire life for this."

"Oh! The man in the moon! Ross!" he yelled in the direction of the screened window. With his accent, Grandpa couldn't say Rose, and for years, I thought my Nonnie's first name was Ross. "Ross, get me the *TV Guide*. Let's check the time the man in the moon is on for Petty!"

"I'm talking about real men on the real moon."

"Yes, La luna!" he said, and he pinched my nose. He picked up his newspaper and folded it back to the front page. The story was right there. Apollo 11 hadn't landed yet but our astronauts were rocketing through space, hours away from the biggest event of all time. And I suddenly wondered where I should be. Who should I be with for the happiest moment of my life?

My Nonnie looked up at the plain-faced kitchen clock. "It's time to watch the stories, Patti-Cake." She grabbed my hand, pulled me into the living room. *Another World*, *The Guiding Light*, *Secret Storm*, and *Search for Tomorrow*. She zipped through the channels with Grandpa's remote. The remote was called the Zenith Space Command, a gold box with a mesh grid, a device that could access every channel from the farthest corners of the living room at the speed of light.

We settled on *Another World*. We sat together on the couch sipping Frescas. The woman on TV was sighing, gripping a doorknob. Then there was a close-up of her wedding band.

"Don't do it," my Nonnie said. "Don't ruin your family!"

The woman lingered outside the door and between worlds, agonizing. I was drawn to the stories for a glimpse into the adult world and because they reminded me there was about a thousand ways life could turn on you. The show flashed to a scene from the past. The woman from the doorway was laid up in a hospital bed, maybe sleeping, maybe in a coma, her hair was lacquered and she wore false eyelashes. The man of her past leaned over and whispered into her ear: "I'm the only man for you—the only one you'll ever love."

"He's full of malarkey!" My Nonnie yelled and got up off the couch. "You married the right man. This bum poisoned you!"

My Nonnie waved her fist in the air, a swiping punch someone makes when they miss. Music churned—a queasy organ sound, something between carnival and a funeral. I was dying for something to happen—kiss, confess, or shoot! A commercial popped on. It was a pleasant relief to see something that made sense—like a white knight poised to joust bathroom dirt in the name of Ajax Cleanser—and a woman who was certain her life was better because of it.

After the stories, my Nonnie opened the newspaper and read our horoscopes aloud. She told me I was Virgo: the Virgin. My horoscope said a secret admirer would send me a sign of affection. "You got a good one!" my Nonnie said. I didn't see how it could happen. A sign of affection? From who? Mr. Balentine, the deli-guy with the missing fingertip? He winked at me once. I never told my parents that.

Nonnie shared secrets with me. I figured I couldn't tell my parents about my Nonnie's horoscopes or the stories, either. I knew my mother would say things like 'pagan ritual' even though my Nonnie was Catholic. But I loved my Nonnie because she believed in so many things, like The

Amazing Kreskin. Kreskin could deal up a person's secrets from a deck of cards; he could bend a spoon with the power of his mind. I liked cards, twisted metal, and the idea that something good was going to happen to me.

We cleaned the house together, and she let me work the carpet sweeper. I rolled up the plastic runners and I waltzed over the rugs with mopping-motion over and over. I found it soothing, though I never understood how the carpet sweeper worked. My mother, a believer in Electrolux, said that my Nonnie's "contraption" was the equivalent of taking a hairbrush to one's lawn. "God love her," my mother said, "but the woman's been sweeping the same dirt around for 25 years."

After we spruced up the house, we took tablets of vitamin C and did calisthenics with Jack Lalanne. He wore ballet slippers and made them seem manly. Jack Lalanne breezed through deep-knee bends in a belted jump suit while two well-behaved collies looked on. When instructed, we used chair-backs for support as we lifted our legs to tighten up "the front, the side, and the back porch."

My Nonnie let me rummage around in the bedrooms. A crucifix stood on the wall between my Nonnie and Grandpa's beds. On the wall above my Nonnie's bed hung the most beautiful, pastel version of the Blessed Mother, the most holy and alive image of the Mother Mary I had ever seen. Mary's ocean eyes were not blue and not green, not of this earth.

Over grandpa's twin hung the coat of arms of the Knights of Columbus—a massive plaque which held two full-sized swords.

I peeked in on the raviolis. In the mirror between the two beds I saw myself, navy blue and white striped top, solid blue shorts. The room was dreamy. The shades were drawn and sunlight cast a warm amber glow. The air was heavy, a raw, unfinished scent. The top sheets glowed white as an altar, or pews packed with unborn cherubs.

I stood in front of the mirror, took a ravioli off the bed and slid it underneath my stretchy shirt and held it there. I did the same for the other side and there I was, a girl with breasts. On the wall behind me, I could see the framed print of Botticelli's Venus, her naked body, hovering above a chevron. She covered one breast. I cupped my breasts. The dough softened against my warm skin—it curved and molded to my ribs and became my flesh, real to the touch, breasts perfectly shaped for hands. Below my breasts, there was suddenly a slope—a waist. I turned sideways, took small steps, practiced walking like a full-grown lady. I took the ravioli out of my shirt, and placed them back on the sheet believing I knew exactly what I was in for. Being a woman was sort of fun but heavy on the chest.

❈ ❈ ❈

Grandpa sat down to eat and he tucked the white linen napkin into the collar of his shirt. Nonnie unfolded her linen and spread it across her lap. I didn't like wiping my mouth on anything that felt like a curtain, so I kept a paper napkin balled in my hand. I shifted ravioli around in the big pasta bowl. I looked for the curved ravioli, my breasts.

My Nonnie asked me, "Did you get a bug bite?"

"Huh?" I said.

"Honey, you're scratching," Nonnie said.

So I was. The flour left me itchy. "I need to use the bathroom."

I rubbed my torso and my armpits trying to rid myself of the itch. I worried that my grandparents might be eating unclean ravioli. It was wrong and disgusting and with all the meat sauce there was no way of knowing. It was a stupid idea. I wished I hadn't put them back on the bed. I should have thrown my breasts out in the street where they belonged.

❈ ❈ ❈

My grandparents seemed to be up before the sun and fully dressed for their day—a day that ended every evening by 10 pm, when they said goodnight and retired to their Blessed Mother/Knights of Columbus beds. I never saw them in nightclothes but there we were, the three of us, in the living room, in pajamas, sipping hot Ovaltine at 10:30 at night, all because of the men on the moon.

My Nonnie's bathrobe gave no hint of her figure, but was utterly appealing: soft and bright as a baby chick, a zipper-front with a white tassel, quilted yoke. She pulled her feet up onto the vinyl-covered couch—spotless white ballerina slippers. My Nonnie looked relaxed and busy as she clicked her knitting needles—a new dawn of pink yarn was spread on her lap—the beginning of something, a scarf or a sleeve.

I wore pajamas and my NASA space raincoat.

Grandpa's pajamas were baby blue and spotted with palm trees and hula girls, under a green plaid robe, cinched beneath his belly.

"Don't give me no more hot chocolate at night—you hear me, Ross?" Grandpa put his Ovaltine on the TV tray near my Nonnie. He shook his head and shuffled into the kitchen with brown leather slippers and tall dark socks like tights. He filled a tall glass with tap water and spooned in crystals of Bromo Seltzer. "No more chocolate, you hear?"

My Nonnie smiled and nodded and kept on knitting. He brought his fizzing drink into the living room. Grandpa plopped into his chair, so funny, an egg-shaped man in mismatched bedclothes.

Grandpa looked at me and did a double take.

"Hey, Petty," he said. "You some kind of wise guy?"

"No."

"Whatta you got on over there? You wear your coat. You not comfortable in my house? You wanna go home?"

"This is a space suit, grandpa!"

"Ssssss, ahhh. Shhhhhh. Eeecha." Grandpa often spoke in unfinished words; it was as if he had sensitive teeth and he had sipped something too hot or too cold. "Tssss. It looks like we got a hole in the roof. It's stupid—a coat in the house!"

I gave him my arm. "Feel it," I said. "It's made of reflective materials similar to tin foil. Haven't you ever seen a space suit?"

"My, my, my. Okay. Come sit."

I sat on the rug next to grandpa.

"This is serious business, eh, Petty?" Grandpa said.

"This is gonna change the world, Grandpa. We won't have to live on earth anymore."

I stepped in and out the house, one minute gazing at stillness of the moonlit yard and the next sitting before the TV looking at the lunar module and white dust, knowing I'd never be the same person. I was a little scared as I waited to see what God might do once we touched his heavens.

The yard felt deeper. The field beyond the fence stretched out, a barren, seemingly endless horizon. The more or less than half moon was wedged in the sapphire sky above, like a nickel sitting in the slot of a gumball machine—waiting. I swore I could see the sweet speck of lunar module and I was sure I would see a shadow, a light, or a reflection of movement once our astronauts actually set foot.

Just before 11 pm, we watched it happen on TV: Neil Armstrong in full gear, taking that giant step, saying words about mankind. It sounded like a prayer, so wise and true, so unbelievable.

Walter Cronkite repeated the words: *One small step for man....* My grandfather kept his glasses on and leaned even closer to the Zenith. The astronauts' voices were interrupted by beeps and static. It was shocking that we could hear their voices at all.

"Do you see this, Ross?" he said. "Do you see this? Petty, there's your man on the moon!" He reached out to me and we shook hands. We turned to my Nonnie; we all shook hands.

I went out to my moon to see if it looked different. Clouds had crept over the face, reminding me of Johnny, the scar, a mark on both of us.

But then a happy idea came to me: Johnny-Boy was watching! We saw the same footprints at the same time, just from different TVs. What was he thinking? Where was he sitting? What space stuff was he wearing?

I had never been away from home, never had cause to call my brother, but I wanted to hear his voice. We couldn't shake hands but we could congratulate each other. What should my first words be since the Eagle had indeed landed? 368-6954. I went inside repeating our telephone number.

My father answered. "Well, well," he said. "How are you doing over there?"

"Fine."

"You watching TV?"

"Of course. I want to talk to Johnny."

"He's asleep."

"No he's not."

"Yes, he is."

"How can that be true?"

"He was tired," my father said. "You want to talk to your mother?"

"No."

❀ ❀ ❀

Grandpa had finished his antacid and his eyes were still glued to the TV.

My Nonnie put down her knitting and got up off the couch. She said, "George, it's almost midnight."

George. It hit me suddenly—his name—George Cascone—the GC on the trashcans was his initials. It was stupid, one of the dumbest mistakes I ever made. I hung my space-raincoat in the hall closet, turned down my bed cover, and put out the light.

Nonnie and Grandpa, their forver smiles....

Champs and Chumps

Experience, which destroys innocence, also leads one back to it.
—James Baldwin

Of course we had a dog. Herman was actually Johnny's dog because my brother fed him kibble and water. My mother found Herman shivering between the trashcans during a thunderstorm. His yelps made her cry. "John, look. Just look at him," she said to my father.

"I see, Jane," my father said. "It's a wet puppy. He looks mostly beagle." Herman looked raw to me, a breastbone with wings in my mother's arms. She said she didn't want animals in the house with children—it was unsanitary—but my mother was not heartless. Johnny and I made a bed in our cellar, a wicker basket and worn towels. For a few weeks Herman cried so much that we took pity and took turns going down to hold him in a baby blanket.

He got thick and furry. Herman spread out into lackadaisical patches of brown, black, and white. After he grew into his paws and stopped crying, he sat there at the foot of the stairs, like so many pairs of our shoes.

Herman lived outside but mostly in the cellar. It was spooky the way cellars are supposed to be: creaky door, plank steps, grotto-ish walls. The cement floor was gray and chalky with a dust we swept and vacuumed but could never get rid of. But Herman liked it. The way he splayed out on the cool floor made me think of a bearskin rug, broken and split. I shuttled laundry up and down the stairs and the dog didn't even flinch when I stepped over him. He clung to an old bone the way a kid clings to a teddy bear, but the bone was creepy, a shank with two smaller bones, or maybe it was a joint I saw poking out like a big crazy eye.

We had our own kind of fun. Sometimes I opened the cellar door and just to be friendly, I tossed a slice of salami down the stairs. Herman never got excited and he certainly never caught it. It was funny when a veil of bologna covered his eyes. Eventually, he'd shake his head and eat the meat off the floor. I bragged about our little gag and I called him meathead. It was our routine. If you had asked me, I would have told you he liked it. But nobody asked me what I was thinking, about dogs in general or about Herman in particular. Besides, it wasn't important. I had brothers to take care of.

My father remodeled part of our basement. He sheetrocked the laundry area and put in shelves. It looked swell except that he painted everything fire hydrant yellow. The caution-colored semi-gloss cast us all in a sickly light, and the cellar still had a dank smell of Cheer and Chuck Wagon. The Kenmore washer was a lifeguard chair. I made sure the boys weren't sticking a pencil in Herman's ear or trying to open a can of Drain-O. It was easier to babysit since my parents bought Big-A and Joe-Bins their own Big Wheels. They drove in dizzying circles.

Johnny barreled down the stairs with his tube socks flapping ahead of him. He stood in front of me with his hands on his hips. He said, "Hey, Patty! Wanna have a race?"

He looked the way he so often did—a thick kid in clothes that used to fit him: wide-striped crew-neck, Wranglers I called high-waters, and a fly that never seemed to zip all the way up.

We called it a race, but we didn't care who won. The point was to go wild: run over fallen mops and dodge family-sized towers of detergent. We manned the handlebars and scooted our little brothers' trikes. The boys weren't pedaling but their legs got tired from holding their feet up in the air. When enough was enough, I told them to go watch *Underdog!* They hobbled off their vehicles, climbed over Herman and up the stairs.

Johnny and I had the Big Wheels. I poured a capful of Downy fabric softener on the floor. We set the seats back and forced ourselves in. Johnny revved up his voice and gunned straight into the oil slick. He screeched for the sound of brakes. Herman lifted his head and then went back to ignoring us. Johnny wound up in a tailspin that rocked the shelf, knocked out a plunger, Drain-O, mothballs, and Miracle Gro. Loud, messy, the most fun I thought we could ever have.

It wasn't so funny when we stood up. Johnny's weight had cracked the plastic seat and bent the rod that connected the rear wheels. I used dirty towels to mop up the spill and Johnny put the stuff back on the shelves.

"This never happened," I said.

"What?"

"We never rode the Big Wheels."

"You mean make believe we didn't?" Johnny asked.

"Forget make believe. I mean what I said. *This never happened.* Got it?" My brother looked blank and nodded. I bent over to pick up the plunger and I spotted something—a brown spider. The creepy crawler disappeared inside the plunger's rubber lip.

"Kill it!" Johnny said.

I slammed the plunger down. We leaned forward expecting to find guts. But the spider ticked across the floor and up the wall. I grabbed the plunger, speared the wall and twisted until that goose was cooked.

"Look at that!" my brother yelled.

When the plunger kissed the wall it left a perfect circle of dirt. I thought of Bluto lip-smacking the hull of a battleship.

"A rubber stamp! Do it again."

I did. The wall belched as I pounded out another ring of grime. The mark was hilarious but the sound killed us. "Lemme try," Johnny said. I liked seeing the look of mischief on my brother. He slammed the plunger into the wall, and after the boom, he slid to the floor in a laughing fit. He took a gulp of air and his voice burst open like a pipe. His laugh was clumsy and sweet and unusual, a sound that courted catastrophe.

Teary-eyed and spent, we staggered up the stairs, split a Pop Tart, and plopped ourselves in front of the boob-tube, not friends, not enemies, elbow-to-elbow as if we didn't know how much we annoyed each other. All was forgotten until my father got home. When I heard swearing, I remembered what we'd done to the walls. I bolted out of the recliner and shut off the TV.

"Hey!" Johnny said. "Put that back on!"

"Dad's mad. Be quiet and stay put." I ran downstairs.

My father grabbed my hair, pushed my head to the wall and told me to take a good look. "What's this?" he asked. "And this? And this?"

I almost laughed. I could have said, I don't know and been telling the God's honest truth because he forced me so close to the damages I literally couldn't see them.

"Brand new walls," my father said. "I built! I painted! The audacity! This is your handiwork, isn't it? A sonofabitchin' hippie motif?"

"No. I was trying to kill a spider."

"Look at these walls! How many spiders were there?"

"I was stupid. I'm sorry."

"You're a destructive little shit and I'm on to you."

He was so furious about the walls he didn't notice the dip in the seat of the Big-Wheel.

Semi-gloss is forgiving. I scrubbed the walls clean and went to my room. I had to write I will not be stupid, 100 times, on notebook paper. I made the I's for each sentence by drawing a long line down the page then crossing it with horizontal dashes. It was quicker.

Johnny didn't have to answer for that round of mischief, but on many other occasions he did. Over and over I tried to explain the governing principles of the universe: never say *I don't know*. Never force Dad to chase you. If you fall—*get up* right away. If nothing else—*just don't cry*. Okay—if you *have* to cry, don't be so freakin' loud about it.

As we grew the difference between us grew, too.

My father said Johnny was a natural, made to play the *Real* American sport, football. "Real football, not that commie soccer crap," he said. "This kid's a powerhouse, built like a tree trunk. He's going places."

In other words, Johnny was born to play Pop Warner football. In other words, my brother's life revolved around games, scrimmages, and weight training. In other words, his practice uniform had to be laundered almost daily. In other words, he needed to be fed early so he didn't throw up when he hit the tackling sleds and dummies.

Even under a crisp blue sky and blinding sun, Connecticut football seasons were brutally cold. Still, I lived for the days at Pender's Field. My brother had perfect games with the Stratford Cardinals—times when he played the entire game on the offensive line, times when they needed him to play defense too, times when he made the local paper for sacks and even a fumble recovery. On the field, I called him Johnny-Boy!

Everybody said Johnny-Boy was born tough and his epic list of injuries proved it. He had a rope burn on one cheek because of me, and another time I hit him in the face with a golf club—two genuine accidents. Johnny fell off a swing and into a boulder; he had to have plastic surgery and get some false teeth. It wasn't long after he finished a long series of dental appointments when he fell, face first at an ice skating rink and knocked out his new fake teeth. He cast his fishing pole and caught himself more than once. None of his injuries fazed him. And those were all accidents from when he was really young, almost practice injuries. Since my brother had grown into football, getting hurt was part of the plan.

My uncle Joe was the equipment manager, so when I didn't have to watch the boys, I sauntered along sidelines for games and practices. No one offered me a spot so I could see. I nudged my way through every crowd and followed Johnny up and down the field. Even on the sideline he looked bold. I saw every icy-white breath he exhaled. I liked the way he stood with his helmet off, the way he kept it by his side, and his big hands bullied the face guard. If he was born to play football, I was born to see formations: a blitz, a shotgun, a screen. I followed X's and O's. Football excited and infuriated me. From the bleachers or the bench, I could spot a penalty before the ref could get the flag out of his pocket.

I caught a glimpse of myself in one of the coaches' 8-millimeter films: a long-faced girl, fists poking out of a green parka and into the air—a fool jumping and yelling, "That's you, Johnny-Boy!" It embarrassed me—the fact that my brother could watch the films and see that I was rooting for him like that—as if I was the kid sister.

But I knew he wasn't looking at me. He was watching himself—focusing on the play, preparing for each enemy. Like any sister, I didn't think about what brother meant. Johnny was just there. I had a sense of him. It was normal. I knew Johnny in a general way, the way I assumed he knew me. We didn't need to look at each other very closely—in person or on film. We knew enough.

It was my job to keep him on track, and he didn't make it easy. He was off in a fog, sitting on the swing feeding marshmallows to Herman or down in the cellar not answering me. When I'd had enough of him and his lackadaisical ways, I called him Seabiscuit. I knew nothing of Seabiscuit the champion. I was calling my brother a stupid animal, a horse that wore blinders and was bred to be manipulated. I was right about him in the way that all kids know where they stand in comparison to each other. We had roles according to what my father referred to as our *stations in life*. I was the oldest—a girl. Nothing novel about those details or what they meant in my Italian family. In my mind, stations in life were one and the same with Stations of the Cross—the pilgrimage of prayers to the suffering and death of Christ. The Stations of the Cross served to remind us that Jesus suffered the most. Our stations in life might seem hard to bear sometimes but they are necessary and doable. Nobody on earth is happy for long.

My humble station in life called for a little elbow grease and a lot of routine. My mother breaded the chops, but I cooked them. She teased, sprayed, and blotted at the vanity upstairs for her shift at Dunkin Donuts—her first real job. Big-A and Joe-Bins fit in the recliner together, happy kids watching cartoons. Johnny sprawled out on the living room floor—way too close to the Zenith—"for the umpteenth time," but my father wasn't home yet. I went back into the kitchen and tore iceberg lettuce. If I was my parents' right arm, as they often said, I was, by extension, Johnny-Boy's right hand, the hand that fed him. I set his placemat, portioned his food, and sat him down at just the right time. The pan soaked while I watched Johnny. He forgot to close his mouth when he chewed. He set his arms like parentheses around his plate and he kept a hand on his glass. I could not tell if my brother loved eating or if he just wanted to get it over with.

"I just saved his butt again," I complained to my mother.

"What are you talking about?" she said.

"He left his sweater outside—in the pricker-bushes. I picked off the thorns *and* hung it up before Dad saw. I didn't even get a thank you."

"Virtue is its own reward," my mother said.

"Question—Why does Patty wear a watch? Answer—so Johnny-boy knows what time it is!"

"You're mean-spirited."

"And he's a chump!"

"You should go to the mirror and see what your face looks like when you talk like that," my mother said.

"No thanks," I answered.

"I said get in there."

Standing in front of the mirror was easy for her, a woman who looked like Elizabeth Taylor. Being sent to the mirror—it couldn't have irked me more if I was Dracula. After reading sodium lauryl sulfate and the rest of the fine print on the back of a tube of toothpaste, I came back into the kitchen with an exaggerated smile and my mother handed me a stack of dinner plates.

"But," she continued as if I had never left, "I do think you have a point somewhere in there. Your brother deserves more chances to be responsible."

The next chance she got, my mother sent Johnny to Via Venito's to buy a couple of boxes of fresh ravioli. Mr. Venito sold them like postage stamps: twelve to a sheet, thirty six came stacked, separated by wax paper and placed in a box that could hold a small pizza or a large calzone.

"Anthony!" my mother said. "Don't hold a utensil in your fist like that." We'd barely finished saying grace and my mother's comment made it seem as though etiquette was what we were praying for. "Absence of manners shows a lack of breeding. People will judge you by such things." The American flag was standing behind her, and next to that stood a TV tray of Tax Reform Immediately membership cards. Joe-Bins sat in his highchair punching the cheese out of his ravioli while my mother demonstrated the civilized way to hold a fork. "And don't forget cultured people use a napkin."

My father scanned the table. "That's too much," he said to Johnny. "You." My father pointed at me. "Take four raviolis off his plate and put them on yours."

It happened often enough; still it was impossible to tell

when my father was going to order the redistribution of our food. He called us the backward Jack Spratt couple. My brother's clothes were hard to find, numbered sizes on racks that used to be labeled "stocky." But he wasn't fat, and I wasn't skinny. I set my plate against my brother's and raked the ravioli across with one move. Before either of us had a chance to start eating, we heard my father's fork hit his plate. "Son of a bitch," he said.

My mother put down her glass of iced tea. She asked, "What's the problem?"

"I'll tell you what the problem is. I think I lost a goddamn filling." He sucked on his teeth, pushed his plate away and spit into his napkin and studied it. After a moment he said, "That's not cornmeal or a grain of farina—that's a pebble I just ground into my jaw."

"What?" my mother said.

My father grabbed the bowl of pasta and poked around with the serving spoon. "There's dirt in here." He let the spoon fall into the bowl and he threw his napkin at Johnny. "You dropped them on the ground, didn't you?"

"They fell," my brother said.

"So you picked them up out of the sonofabitchin dirt and put them back in the box."

"John, it was an accident," my mother said.

My father rumbled into the kitchen and shoved things around in the fridge. He put salami and bread out on the counter. Johnny kept eating. He didn't look up from his plate.

"They should have taped that box," my mother called out.

My father slapped a couple of dry sandwiches together and went out the door. I sprinkled more Parmesan on my food.

My mother stood up, looked at the cheesy pulp in Joe-Bins' tray. She said, "Good God."

I went to the kitchen to grab a Handi Wipe and I passed the window where my father was in view. He leaned against his paint truck and chewed, sandwich in a half moon. No plate. No napkin. Johnny lingered at the table and I stayed around to make sure he wasn't caught with the four raviolis I gave back to him.

Vietnam was on. I sat next to Johnny on the couch and we watched our father watch the news: soldiers with mud on their faces, bloody bandages, dangling limbs, stretchers, smoke, screaming Vietnamese. Every night I knew we were lucky to be Americans in a safe place.

"Another day of the no-win war," my father said to no one in particular. "Our boys are getting killed because they're not allowed to fight. When Americans fight, they never lose. Here we are, the greatest military power in the world—hog tied by the U.N. Vietnam should look like Hiroshima already." He fanned through the *TV Guide* in disgust and then threw it between Johnny and me.

Johnny was sitting too close to me or vice-versa. I whacked him with the *TV Guide* and he elbowed me. I poked him. We stood up and yelled in each other's faces, "Move it! —No! You move it!" We shoved each other back and forth until we locked arms, fell onto the couch, and rolled to the floor.

My father told us we had five minutes to end it ourselves. He got out of his recliner and moved the coffee table out of the way so we had room to settle our squabble.

My brother had me pinned to the floor in no time. "Do you quit? Do you quit?" he asked through clenched teeth.

My mother came in from the kitchen, swatting at us with a dishtowel. "You stop—both of you. Stop it right now."

My brother held me down with my face to the floor. I wiggled an arm free and knuckled his forehead.

"John! Make them stop. This is insane."

"Let 'em work it out," my father said.

"Work it out?"

Johnny pinched my arm and then tucked it under me. I stopped resisting him.

Johnny squawked like a parrot—"Do you quit? Do you quit? Well, do ya?"

"Is she playing possum?" my father asked.

"They're not playing at all!" my mother said. "This is too rough! Johnny, come on. Get off your sister. I had the two of you so you could protect each other."

My brother held me down with his weight. When he raised his head a few inches, I threw my head back, a straight shot to his face, and he got off my back. As he rolled to his side, he cupped his chin.

"That's it," my father said. "Head back. Don't bleed on the carpet." That bloody nose made me the winner. I won a guarantee my father wasn't going to grab us by the hair and bash our coconuts together this time. Blood trickled through my brother's fingers and onto his t-shirt as he stood up.

"You savages!" my mother said.

"The kid gets bloody noses at the drop of a hat," my father said. "I was the same way."

"It's not right!" my mother said.

"A little bloody nose is nothing," my father said as he walked Johnny into the bathroom.

"You!" My mother pointed at me. "You know better."

I quietly checked my elbows and knees for rug burns. She ran up to her room. I knew one thing whether I wanted to or not: I never really beat Johnny. He was bigger, stronger. We both knew he could have hurt me. Sometimes he did. I was supremely good at the game, at letting him defeat himself. The textbook was in my head, the idea that we both wanted to be winners in the eyes of our father, and the law that said two objects can't occupy the same space at the same time. I understood. I wanted to win so badly I could not lose. Johnny wanted it so badly he could not win.

My uncle brought my brother home from a workout and told us Johnny was over the weight limit. Pop Warner Football's divisions were governed by weight. "You have to lose about 7 pounds by game day," my uncle said. "It's doable."

I did twenty-five sit-ups every time a Dannon Yogurt commercial came on. I was short and I heard people say that the taller you are the happier you'll be because you can carry more weight. I realized if I believed the tall-person theory I'd be miserable for the rest of my life. I'd always been the runt at school. Kids told me at the rate I wasn't growing, I'd be lucky to inch my way out of midget status. My mother loved to tell other mothers how she had me when she was sixteen, and my father was eighteen—and what a miracle it was to go back to the doctor's and find that she'd grown two inches taller after I was born. That was no miracle. It was bad luck. Two inches of height that should have been mine got confused and went to her. But that didn't mean I was unlucky. I'd just have to find my fortune closer to the ground.

Doing sit-ups felt right and I liked the way women looked eating yogurt on TV. I wanted to stir my fruit from the bottom, grace the spoon into my mouth without it touching my teeth, and think about how the yogurt was transforming my body from the inside. I'd emerge with a woman's figure, and like the gals in commercials, I'd produce a tape measure to prove it. I exercised but I never watched my weight. I watched Johnny's.

My brother handed me his gym bag and I emptied it of underwear, sweat socks and towels. My father went to the fridge, grabbed two cucumbers and skinned them. He rinsed a bundle of celery and piled the stalks beside the coins of cucumber. My brother didn't complain. He sat down at the table, crunched on celery and put medallions of cucumber into his mouth.

My mother sent me to Star Market with the usual: a list, a twenty, and permission to treat myself.

I handed my order to Mr. Balentine, the grocery store owner who ran Star Market with just the help of his son. He held the list under the cone of a desk-lamp. In spite of my mother's coaching, I stared at his hand. His ring finger was lopped off at the tip so it looked like he had twin pinkies.

Mr. Balentine shoved his hands into the pockets of his butcher's apron. "I've got a ham. Your mother will love it."

"My mother didn't ask for a ham."

Mr. Balentine slid a few invoices around on top of the deli case. "I didn't ask for this," he said. He produced a booklet, *A Businessman Looks at Communism.*

"I'm sure you didn't read it," I said.

"No, no," he said. "I read! Look."

He handed me the pamphlet and nodded.

I fanned through the pages and paused where I saw a passage underlined in red ink.

```
Labor Unions have long been a Communist
goal. The effort is frequently made to
have the worker do as little as pos-
sible for the money he receives. This
practice alone can destroy our country.
```

"You take the ham," Mr. Balentine said. "Pay me later. If she doesn't want it, bring it back." He wrapped it up in thick paper and wrote on the paper with a fat black pencil. "Here, hold it. Is it too heavy for you?"

"Of course not."

I carried the groceries across Wood Avenue. The bag wasn't too heavy but it weighed some. Mr. Balentine had written 12.2 lbs. on the wrapper.

I didn't want to think of the ham as the severed part of something, like a pig or a cow or a dog, but the idea came alive in my mind, weight and mass, something lopped off like Mr. Balentine's fingertip. I thought of my brother in pieces, cuts of meat: leg, loin, thigh, neck, rib, rump—raw pounds and ounces of him. I thought about telling Johnny— Hey, don't you realize you have to lose more than half of this ham?

Johnny was at the Y, in the sauna in a rubber suit. I wanted to see how it literally happened, what actually melted off my brother in the sauna and where did those pounds of him go?

My mother pulled the ham out of the bag, peeled back the paper, and held it like a large, precious stone. "Oh my," she said. "It's expensive."

"I told Mr. Balentine you didn't ask for it."

"No. It's divine," my mother said. "We'll take it. I think I'll start cooking this today."

We knew nothing of canned ham; ours were always fresh and decorated. My mother cut a grid of squares into the fat. She coated the ham with pink glaze, dressed it with whole cherries and yellow rings of pineapple. She tacked the fruit on the mountain of ham with colored toothpicks and dark pointy cloves. Finally she poured ginger ale over the whole thing, covered it with foil and slid the heavy pan deep into the oven. For days it would smell like Christmas.

When Johnny-Boy came back from the Y, my father told my mother, "He's got a little more reducing to do."

"I don't know how he's going to lose weight," my mother said. "He's a growing boy."

We kept an empty Choc-Full-O-Nuts coffee can under the sink as part of my brother's weight loss regimen. I handed it to Johnny. "Here. The smell of the ham will make you hungry. Your mouth will water. The more you spit, the more you'll need to." I don't remember where I first heard this spitting theory, but I repeated the instruction—even though I questioned the idea. I'd been ordering half-pounds of deli meats for years and the idea of even a quarter-pound of saliva seemed more than one person could produce. I never looked inside the can to actually see how much my brother could spit. Nobody wanted to see it.

Later I found Johnny in his room. He tore the foil, bit into a bar of Ex-Lax, licked his thick fingers as if it was real chocolate. He smiled as if he didn't know he would be doubled-up with cramps or trying to do his homework on the toilet. I don't remember whether it was the coach, or my father, or my Uncle Joe who first placed those little squares into his hand, but just like spitting into a coffee can, my brother had done it before. Nobody could ever get me to take Ex-Lax — not even for a million dollars and the chance to be the first woman on the moon.

On game day, my brother was the champ starting at weigh-in. The moment he got off the scale the coaches helped him suit up and gave him all the Hershey Bars and Gatorade he wanted. As soon as he hit the field, my father and mother, my brothers and I — we shouted, "Here we go, Johnny, here we go!"

Johnny won! We won! And when sleet fell from the sky we saw confetti.

We returned to our house in triumph. Johnny-Boy was allowed to eat everything we were having — two thick slices of ham with cherry and pineapple glaze, peas with pearl onions, buttered carrots, a big dollop of our mother's mashed potatoes and a hot dinner roll. Our places were set with real dishes, linen napkins, and formal utensils. I should have taken a picture.

Later after the meal, I sat on a kitchen stool, sipped my Coke, and watched my mother cube some of the ham for salad. She shaved the last bits for split-pea soup. Her hands glistened with grease and glaze. "Here," she said. "Let's give the dog a nice bone." I opened the cellar door and slid Herman his trophy. It tumbled half way down the stairs. Herman got up to fetch it. He loved it.

Later on into the boring week, my mother handed me a list of chores before she went to work. When I got around to the laundry, I put together a basket of whites: my brother's grass-stained uniform and a few towels thrown in to make a small load. I gripped the wicker, balanced it on my hip and closed the door behind me in one smooth motion. When I looked ahead of me to locate Herman, I found Johnny-boy sitting on the floor with the ham bone to his mouth. He saw me.

"What the hell are you doing?" I asked. He put the bone down and took his time when he slid it over to Herman. "Answer me."

He was supposed to say, if you don't tell on me, I won't tell on you—parlay his predicament with something I'd already done because that's how it worked. That was the game. Bargaining for survival is the secret every kid knows—without being told—like the scent of your mother's neck.

"Speak!" I yelled at him. He lowered his arms and rested his head on them. "You're disgusting. I can't stand to look at you." Herman lifted his head and turned toward me with droopy brown eyes. I dropped the basket on the landing and I ran. I shouted all the way to the garage, "He's eating rotten meat off the dog's bone. Come look!"

My father told me to take my little brothers outside and he closed the cellar door behind him. I knew he would talk and maybe slap something like sense into my brother. I pictured how Herman would slink off to hide behind the furnace. I knew my brother would cry savagely. I knew he'd run when he needed to stand. He'd be down when he needed to be on his feet. I knew it all.

When my mother came home from her shift, I was in bed. She argued with my father and then she ran up to Johnny's room. From behind my open door, I could see everything. My mother whispered to him and rubbed his back. She had him sit up in his bed. She gave him a cruller. When she left Johnny, my mother came and closed the door to my room without looking in on me. When silence overtook my room, I turned on the light and pulled the shoebox out from under my bed: a diary, a troll, some skeleton keys, and a few photos, one picture of Johnny and me together. Some damages can't be fixed. I studied our pose. If I could pinpoint happiness, I could trace the steps back to it. In the picture I thought would save us, we are standing on Main Street, on the curb with a sea of empty beach chairs behind us. It's early on the Fourth of July and we're there to save seats for the parade. I am twirling a tiny American flag, pointing my toe in my patent leather shoes. Johnny is sort of smiling but he looks stunned by the camera. We are standing together but not touching. The sun was directly behind my mother and when she snapped the photo her arms cast a winged-shadow over both of us.

U.S. and Them

My father worked in a white t-shirt, off-white overalls, and construction boots that were spattered with paint and crusted with Spackle. His fingers looked like wooden spindles, whitish as if they'd been stripped and then antiqued—and no matter how he scrubbed or what he wore, my father always smelled like turpentine—kind of clean and kind of poisonous. I never went out of my way to tell anyone that my father was a house painter, but I never denied him or what he did for a living. Maria said her father was an executive at General Electric. Terri's father worked at the New York Stock Exchange. Donna told me her dad was a corporate attorney, and I had heard enough. Corporate attorney, commodities trader, CEO: suit and tie occupations. With the luxury of sitting behind a desk, my classmates' fathers might as well be wearing slippers too. Whenever someone asked me who my father worked for, I was happy to announce that he worked for himself and more than that, I took pride in the fact that my father really worked for our bread and butter.

But I made it my mission to avoid talking about what my father did—what both my parents did—as patriots. I never said John Birch Society out loud. Saying "JBS" was the equivalent to asking everybody to line up for the final judgment. I didn't know what the Trilateral Commission was, but as Birchers, my parents spent a great deal of time trying to expose such socialist organizations. Just for having heard of forces such as the One World Order, I understood that ultimately each person chose to be on the side of good or evil. My classmates from Assumption—their parents were either in league with the conspiring elite or they were pawns.

My father headed the greater Bridgeport, Connecticut chapter of GUUN—Get U.S. out of the United Nations. Pronounced gun, not goon. Our dining room at 327 Wade Street was the base of operations. We had equipment: an eight-millimeter projector sat on a TV tray. A stand-up movie screen blocked the hutch and was flanked by six-foot American flags. We kept an army of folding chairs standing against the wall. We had a megaphone! On the night of a meeting, my mother piled Dunkin' Donuts on the table, perked the coffee, and waxed the bathroom floor.

I joined the GUUNs. I wasn't a natural member by birth. My entry into the world of patriotism actually came at an unlikely place and time: not in the dining room, not at a meeting or after a speech, but in the basement. I was watching my father cast plaster of Paris bricks for a wall in the kitchen he planned to reface. He poured a floury mixture into clear plastic molds, and after the bricks hardened, he pried bar after bar out of the plaster casts and stacked the bars like a Fort Knox of chalk. I didn't want to be run off the way my kid brothers were. I wanted to have a reason for being there. I wanted to count and handle the fragile plaster bouillons, so I asked questions.

"Dad," I asked. "Why do we keep so many American flags in our house?"

"It's considered an un-American activity to have organized meetings without the old stars and stripes present," he answered.

"Says who?" I asked.

"Says J. Edgar Hoover. Got a problem with that?"

"No."

"You know who J. Edgar is?"

"FBI guy."

"You're paying attention," my father said.

It bothered me—the notion that, for the price of the flag, Communists and Satan worshippers could legally congregate.

I thought back to a church carnival. I remember holding my ticket and standing in a long line for The Whip—me, my Dad, and our priest, Father Carlton. Father told my father and me about secret sects, ordinary-looking people who came to mass, walked right up to the altar to receive Communion—then spit the host out into their hands—evil conspirators. They took the Eucharist back to their clan where they desecrated it in Satanic rituals. If people who weren't even in the state of grace were allowed access to Jesus' body and blood, how safe could our country be?

"Dad, what about the people who use the flag as a decoy?" I asked.

My father looked annoyed. "Unfortunately, conspirators and even morons have rights. The question is—can evil co-exist with God's will?"

I thought my father was thinking like I was: the Constitution was probably way too liberal, and freewill was the worst idea God ever had.

Many nights after that, I could not sleep with such ideas—the dilemma of co-existence with evil or the rights of morons.

The next time the GUUNs met, my father said, "I have a seat for you if you want it."

My mother came into the room. "Don't you think she'd rather play Pokeeno with Carly?"

My father slapped me on the back. "You can't blame the kid for wanting to be the son-of-a-gun."

My mother put saran wrap on a tray of melon balls and headed over to the Sheehans for her MOTOREDE—Movement to Restore Decency—meeting. I stapled mimeographed GUUN agendas and handed out copies of *American Opinion*. My father let me sit next to him, sip from his coffee cup. My father had his own style, neat and ready for action. He wore a polo shirt, cardigan sweater, and pressed corduroys.

Mick Bovine sat across from me. Mick had the chiseled features of a Ken doll and he was spiffy—except for his dandruff. I knew Mick was a serious patriot, but he shouldn't have tried to look like a federal agent. It seemed to me he would have done better sporting a Hawaiian shirt and waving grill-tongs rather than wearing a navy trench coat and toting a briefcase slapped with the bumper sticker. It was a peace sign with the claim "Footprint of the American Chicken." A festive shirt and a tropical environment would have done him some good; whereas his fondness for navy blue always emphasized his scalp problem.

Farnum Bailey was a crisp, eagle-eyed man, a man I could imagine in the cockpit of an airplane. He was confident and he moved with speed and agility in very expensive suits. When retired generals came to the Klein Memorial Auditorium to talk about how American forces were hog-tied in Vietnam, Farnum was the man who introduced them.

Gregg Leary sat across from Mick. Gregg was in his 20s. He seemed average in height but most everything about him was miniature. He had stubby fingers, button ears, and other elfish features, like sunken eyes and wiry black eyebrows. His sand-colored desert boots were so small that they reminded me of my baby brother's Buster Browns. Gregg brought Skippy peanut butter with him to meetings and spooned it out of the jar, right there at the table.

"Let me get the plate Jane fixed for us," my father said. He walked into the kitchen.

Gregg slid the spoon out his mouth very slowly and he motioned toward me with the jar—as if to offer me some.

I waved him off. "Are you kidding?" I asked. "Why do you come over here with your peanut butter anyway?"

Gregg's eyes widened. "This is pure protein."

"So what if it is. We've got civilized food. My parents always put out a spread," I reminded him.

Gregg capped his Skippy, wrapped his spoon in one of

our luncheon napkins, and put it into his shirt pocket. "How old are you, Patty?" he asked. "I mean—are you old enough to be a member?"

"Why don't you ask my father, Gregg?"

The other men at the table laughed.

My father entered the room with a tray of cold cuts and Portuguese rolls. "Ask me what?"

I cleared a spot for our sandwich fixings.

"Our junior member here," Farnum said. "I'm glad she's on our side." Farnum grabbed the serving fork and speared several slices of Salami. "Did you know that Salami did not originate from Italy but from the Greek island of Salamis?"

"Now *that's* interesting," I said. "How did you find that out?"

"Books," Farnum said.

My father popped a small triangle of provolone into his mouth. "It's not so surprising about Salamis," he said. "Italy and Greece are the most advanced ancient cultures."

As I understood the GUUN mission, we were calling for the United States to sever all ties to the United Nations, an international body that was founded by Communists and other socialist members, nations, and individuals whose common goal was a Godless one-world government. I was more inclined to read about the island of Salamis than to read the GUUN literature—but I didn't need to read much. The photos of the UN headquarters told the story: International flags surrounded the building. Other countries were staking claim—symbolically at the very least—on an institution planted firmly inside the greatest city in the US of A. Sure, Old Glory was one of those flags—but our very own banner seemed to stand as a legal loophole for conspiracy. The most powerful nation on the planet—why would we, why should we allow the rest of the world, especially the barely industrialized and less-than-free world, to scrutinize our manifest destiny?

My father liked a quote from Edmund Burke: *All it takes for evil to prevail is for good men to do nothing.*

"That's not just some little inspirational motto to keep under a paperweight," he said. "It's a warning—a wake-up call, maybe our last!"

I understood that I had to know more than my fair share about the sad state of affairs in the world. American citizens had fallen for the propaganda and become puppets. The puppets were:

1. People stupid enough to claim a pet rock
2. Women who took the pill
3. Folks who failed to realize that the so-called peace symbols they flaunted were actually the calling cards of Satan
4. The growing number of citizens who voiced more skepticism about the will of God than the existence of Sasquatch

For the rest of us, the literate, un-brainwashed, God-fearing Americans, it was triple-duty. This was why the John Birch Society carried the moniker: For God, Family, and Country—an authoritative equation as solid as the Holy Trinity. The Birch Society's forecast for America's future was bleak. Most people didn't want to know the unhappy truths, but I knew I was born to face them.

Jim Sheehan, our neighbor and my best friend's dad, was the co-chair of GUUN. I liked him. He was a bit older than my father. He made more money; the family lived in a stucco house, the kids had gyroscopes, and they always brought us back maple syrup from Montreal. It seemed to me the most painful personal cross Mr. Sheehan had to bear was his strong resemblance to one of his arch enemies: Richard M. Nixon. He had Nixon's hairline, nose, jowls, even his physique. Like Nixon, Mr. Sheehan was a shirt and tie guy. Mr. Sheehan had gone to MIT. I didn't know what that stood for, but I understood that he was one of the few people who had not been corrupted by an institution of higher education. He had fought in the Korean War, and now he was a civil engineer employed by Hubble. Mr. Sheehan stayed tight-lipped when I asked him about the Sputniks eavesdropping on us from space, but I got him to tell me about trench foot, and he gave me the real facts about army rations, specifically, a meal they called Shit on a Shingle. Though my father wore coveralls and Mr. Sheehan wore old suits to work they still seemed more alike than different. They were men who took the state of affairs in the world personally.

Mr. Sheehan was also a man who actually liked to hear my stories. For instance, I told him about a day I spent on Pleasure Beach, grassy dunes on the quiet side of a rickety wooden bridge—the time I discovered a mass of heavy, rubber-like hosing in a polluted section of the sound. I stood at the shore and kept reeling it in—whatever it was. I glanced back at my mother who was far away but gesturing like a flare trying to wave me off. I ignored her. I pulled up about twenty feet of what police later said they believed to be human intestine. My mother was distressed, and even in denial over the whole episode: the entrails, the crowd, the body bag. She was mortified by the fact that I had to give my name as the person who made the find. But when I told Mr. Sheehan about my adventure he slapped me on the back and laughed, and said, "You probably dredged up what was left of a gangster from Long Island."

I went out in the field with the GUUNs too. One Saturday I got dressed in my Sunday clothes and went canvassing with my father and Mr. Sheehan, going up and down the aisles of the mall parking lot and sticking GUUN leaflets beneath windshield wipers. One particular day we popped open a card table and stationed ourselves outside at the marble storefront wall between Parade of Shoes and Baskin-Robbins. I wore a white ruffled blouse and a yellow-check maxi-skirt. I was there for moral support, which I knew to mean that I represented *moral* youth, as opposed to the *counter culture*— i.e., impressionable youth who could be brainwashed into committing acts as horrible as stabbing a fork into Sharon Tate's pregnant belly, or having sex.

A leggy woman beamed out of her Mercedes: Jiffy-white gloves, canary A-line dress, perky dark hair—the Jackie-Kennedy-look you'd see all over Fairfield County, even in Bridgeport, Connecticut. The woman's hair was swept up on the top of her head and wound into a smooth, shiny bun. She paused, pursed her lips and looked away.

My father was unfazed. Mr. Sheehan pursued Mrs. Honey Bun in an attempt to hand her a pamphlet. It featured a cartoon image of a pistol with its barrel twisted into a knot—a stunt Bugs Bunny frequently performed on Elmer Fudd's hunting rifle.

"Miss," Mr. Sheehan said, "Imagine being held prisoner in a foreign land, an American citizen, pleading your innocence, seeking justice and a fair trial. Then—imagine finding yourself at the mercy of a tribunal, delegates from places like the USSR, Cambodia, or what they're now calling Tanzania."

"Uhm, maybe later," the woman said. She pressed her sunglasses deeper into her brow.

She strutted by my father. He said good afternoon. She paused. "I'm sure you're a conscientious citizen," my father said. The woman removed her white-framed Ray Bans. "I believe you're someone who cares enough to take some educational literature home with you."

The woman opened her beaded wicker purse, held it in front of my father and he dropped the pamphlet inside like a ballot. She said, "You gentlemen have a good day."

My father and Mr. Sheehan stood together and looked synchronized as they watched her walk on by.

Mr. Sheehan said, "Westport."

My father agreed.

Money or no, most people avoided our GUUN table as if we were selling tickets to the draft. It was hard to witness how the average citizen cared so little about our country's eminent demise.

As the woman's heels clicked off a short distance, I yelled, "We want out of the United Nations!"

"Hey, you!" my father said to me. "We're not the Black

Panthers here. What's with the fist?"

"I dunno. Nothing."

The sure things:

1. I liked being with my father, with the men, being mobilized.
2. I could never be turned into one of Charles Manson's minions.
3. Hollering at strangers agreed with me.

A man in a straw hat who looked like Bing Crosby headed our way at a tourist's pace. He asked, "What are you folks raffling off?"

"Sir," Mr. Sheehan said, "we're here today because the United Nations is threatening to take away the God-given rights on which our nation was founded—the right to self defense." Mr. Sheehan offered a friendly hand but the man raised his arms as if he were facing a hold-up.

"Young man, I've got arteriosclerosis," he said. "The hardening of the arteries," he said louder, and as if this was worse. "I'm just out for a little ice cream. My doc's not keen on the idea, but there you have it."

"Got it," Mr. Sheehan said.

The old man pointed a finger ahead toward the Baskin and Robbins. "It's a good day for a little pistachio," he said, "don't you think?"

"Sure, sure," Mr. Sheehan said, "Pistachio."

The man shuffled off in his huarache sandals and cardio socks.

After he was inside the ice cream parlor, Mr. Sheehan said, "Yeah, pal, make it a double—you and your doctor, cause we're all going to Hell in a hand basket."

I was beginning to notice that my father and Mr. Sheehan had their own distinct ways when it came to the enterprise of trying to save our country.

A sleeveless biker with club insignia came our way. My father called out to him, "The United Nations wants to take your gun!"

The guy wiped his face and bald head with a red bandana; he picked up the clipboard and nodded his head as he read the petition. He said, "Get us out of the United Nations... hmm."

"Can you imagine Americans giving up their rights for 'so-called' international law?" my father asked.

"It's all wrong," the biker said. "I'm with you on this, man, but I can't give you my John Hancock—nothing that can be traced."

"Who is it?" my father asked. "The IRS?"

"Nah. My ex-old lady."

My father leaned back and laughed. He stood in front of one of the concrete pillars with hands in his pockets—not a guy in drippy painter's pants, but a dark man in a smooth Banlon shirt and preppie khakis.

"This is my daughter, Patty."

I nodded as the biker introduced himself. I was no more eager to catch his name than he seemed in knowing mine, but I gave him free merchandise: American flag decals, Pray the Rosary Pins, and two copies of *None Dare Call It Treason*.

I watched the men ease into conversation, joke around like guys I didn't quite recognize. They understood each other, shared something I couldn't identify, even though I was looking right at it. It's not just that I failed to see any connections between conservatives and bikers, but I was mesmerized. I saw a boyish quality about them, the same jubilance I'd seen on the school playground. I started to see my father as a man of necessary urgency. He was shorter than the other two, but he was swift and muscular, olive skin, Brylcreemed hair, not just the father who quizzed me on the *Baltimore Catechism* and threatened to take away TV, but a dad who, despite my mother's protests, once woke me up in the middle of the night to watch a gargoyle movie with him. And now, here he was—my father—a man who only finished high school, a tough Jesuit prep school, just to win a car from his father—befriending one of the Huns.

I thought about an old black-and-white photo—the only picture I ever saw of my father before he married my mother. His hair was thick, wavy. He had a sly-clean look, like Elvis. His hands just rested in his hip pockets, his legs were spread and he was standing in front of his prized set of wheels—a '57 Studebaker that most certainly could have been a Harley.

One Saturday my mother shook us out of bed as if it was Christmas morning and she was the only one who knew it. We yawned as she corralled us into the living room. She opened the Venetian blinds to showcase a sky streaked with pink. "Look!" she said. "It's a gorgeous day—gonna be a hot one! Let's have some fun." She looked at my father. "I say we go out to the International House of Pancakes."

"For breakfast?" Johnny-Boy asked.

"For fun," my mother said. "Call it brunch if you like. You kids have never gone for brunch, have you?"

"You know we haven't," I said.

My mother looked at me. She said, "Just smile."

My father shrugged his shoulders. "Well, let's go if we're gonna go."

We quick-brushed our teeth, left the sand in our eyes and packed into the Caddy while the idea was still fresh. We rightfully came to a complete stop at the intersection of Wade Street and Wood Avenue—and from nowhere, our car was pelted with a monstrous plant—roots and all. A baseball-sized wad of dirt smacked us in the windshield.

"What the—" my father said.

My mother flinched and covered her face. "Mother of God!"

In the backseat, I was the first to hit the floor. I pulled Joe-Bins down with me, into the shallow rut of carpeting. It wasn't textbook—I mean I knew how to survive on the street or in the house, but I didn't recall ever hearing the protocol on what to do if you're in a motor vehicle when the atomic bomb hits. My father put the wipers on and the blades slapped the plant down on the driver's side and spread dirt in every direction. He rolled down the window and reached for the clot of soil with tentacles of green leaves.

"No! Don't touch it!" I said. "It's radioactive!"

"Don't be an idiot," my father said.

"Roll up the window before we're all contaminated by nuclear fallout!"

"I said, stop being ridiculous!"

"Well it's our life too!" I said.

My father turned to look at us. "Get off the floor for God's sake!" He turned off the wipers, tilted his head, and massaged the back of his neck.

"But who? Why?" my mother asked. "What just happened?"

"This is Bridgeport, Jane!" my father said. "The armpit of Connecticut, reminding us what an armpit is."

We pulled into the nearby Shell station and a happy bell rang. An elderly attendant hustled out from the garage. He grabbed the squeegee and raked the dirt off our windshield without asking how it got there. He asked, "Where are you folks headed?"

"We're just drivin'," my father answered.

"Ah! Since you folks are going to see a movie at the drive-in, I'll get those windows sparkling so you'll be able to see the picture just as clear as life." The man held up his hand. "Wait right here," and he walked toward the front office.

"Why did you say that?" my mother asked.

"Huh?"

"Why did you tell the man we're just driving?"

"I'm not on parole, here! Since when is it necessary that I file an accurate report of my comings and goings to *that* guy?"

"What are you afraid of?"

"I'm not afraid of anything, Jane. Where are you going with this?"

"I'm just saying, what's the problem? It's no secret. Why

didn't you tell him we're going to the International House of Pancakes? What's wrong with the simple truth?"

"Simple truth? The guy is deaf, Jane! If I told him we were headed to an execution he'd still be out there trying to detail the car."

Each of us, from our various windows, watched. The man said we were a fine family, and he gave my mother a handful of Bazookas "for the handsome bunch in back." We worked our wads of bubblegum and studied the man with the shell on his cap. He had arthritic-looking hands but happy wrinkles around his eyes, eyes as crisp and blue as aftershave. He pulled an oil-soaked roll of paper towels from one of the deep pockets on his uniform and from another pocket he produced a bottle of yellow fluid that looked like anything but Windex. We couldn't stop this Good Samaritan, all of us seeing how he delighted in this act of kindness. I only know I neither understood nor shared his apparent joy. The more he rubbed, the worse it got. By the time he was through with our windows, we would have had better visibility in a Pyrex that my mother had greased with Crisco.

We smiled and offered up a family-size bouquet of waving hands and cheery goodbyes. My father slowly rounded the block and pulled us back up our driveway. He said, "Everybody out."

My mother pulled out boxes of Life and Lucky Charms and let the cabinet door slam shut. She piled Rubbermaid cereal bowls and left a handful of teaspoons out on the table for us before she went upstairs.

My father gathered up the hose, the Palmolive, the Armor-All and the Minwax from the garage.

Herman came out of his doghouse, traveled the length of his chain, and spread out like a rag by the bucket to watch my father put a shine back on our car.

Golda grabbed a shady spot beneath the pricker bushes. She kept an eye on my father and the snakish movements of the garden hose as she licked herself clean.

Shoulder to shoulder, we sat at the island counter. We

looked out the window over our back yard. We crunched and slurped and we could see the threat of the unstable world right from where we were sitting.

A Taste of the Cold War

While my parents believed that the end of the world may have been near, they saw no reason why we kids ought to wait for it inside. My mother had colorful ways to get us out of her hair and into the great outdoors. One day she put me in charge of my brothers and gave me a pastel container of candy. "I want you to take these," she said, "and go outside with the boys and play nice." She shook the container that was shaped like a milk carton and handed it over to me as if it was the as-seen-on-TV product for playing nice. I approached the door and she grabbed my arm. "Wait a minute. Not so fast."

"Do you want me in or out?" I asked.

"Don't get wise with me," she said. She set the candy on the counter and grabbed the lotion off the top of the fridge. "I'm sorry, but you didn't get your peasant skin from me." She squeezed lotion into her palm and rubbed her hands together. "You can blame your father for this." She slathered my arms. "My people have history. We're from Rome, the heart of culture and civilization!"

"Rome-shmome," I said. "Rome crumbled and fell. Nero fiddled while it burned. I learned that from Bugs Bunny."

"Very funny," my mother said. "But you take after your father's people. If you don't want to wind up with pigskin you'd better watch out. You tend to get leathery."

"I don't care," I said.

"Well, you'd better start caring," my mother said. "Let me tell you about the contribution of Sicilians. Olive oil is great but it's not exactly a cultural advancement."

"Grandpa worked in construction," I said. "That's advanced."

"Your father can call it whatever he wants to," my mother said. "They're greenhorns! The fact is your grandfather carried stones from one place to another, and he didn't build any pyramids, either. They're peasants. The Cascones' greatest achievement is the mastery of the knife and fork. My people run circles around them and don't you forget it."

I wouldn't forget. I'd heard it all before. My father wasn't too fond of her family either. I stood in surrender so she could rub me down with thick white cream and reaffirm the superiority of her forebears. She squirted another dose into her palm, rubbed her hands and worked on my legs. Then she went for my face.

I lurched back. "I'll do that myself!" I insisted.

"Stop scowling," she said. "You know damn well why you need to cover your skin."

I didn't really know why I needed to cover up and for most of my childhood I was left to make strange sense of it. My father and I were the only ones in the family who never had full-blown sunburns. My brothers, all three of them, turned sissy-pink and blistered up like the south side of our garage. My mother had no problem with that, but I had to grease up with ointment and wear "loose and gauzy clothes"—on account of my peasant look—which seemed to genuinely pain her.

For years, I was uneasy about what I got from Sicilians. It was clear to me that my skin was a genetic flaw. The color for healthy people was either all white or all black and my permanent tan was indication of some disease I was uniquely predisposed to because of uncivilized Sicilians. I was the only one in our two sixth-grades who was asked to take the sickle cell anemia test. According to our school nurse, the prick in the arm procedure was reserved for those of African or Mediterranean decent. As an American by birth, I thought I was protected from foreign afflictions. The school's screening and my mother's purchase of skin creams for mountain climbers left me certain about the two biggest threats to my existence, the big Cs: communism and cancer. If caught by one of the Big-Cs, survival was hardly desirable.

I learned about painful diseases in the pediatrician's office. My mother lit up a Newport and became fully engaged in something she'd found in *Look*. I ditched the *Highlights* and grabbed a professional medical encyclopedia from a lonely corner shelf hidden by a vining plant. Polio, conjoined twins, malignant cells. Fascinating stuff. I was impressed by technology, too. The iron lung—an image of a head protruding from what appeared to be a room-sized muffler. The iron lung appeared to keep oxygen cycling and deteriorating organs pumping, though the person was forced to live the rest of their lives on their back, in a room safe from power outages. According to the pictures, people could visit someone who was confined to an iron lung. Visitors were tasked with turning pages of picture books and offering the afflicted person a sip of milkshake with a bendable straw.

Another page illustrated cancer statistics. One out of every four stick figures was Xd out with cancer. I came from a family of six and our number was up already. Cancer was Biblical, part of God's curse on mankind since the fall, the modern day version of leprosy. The only real difference between the two scourges: leprosy was created by God whereas cancer was engineered by communists. Our parents often went to funerals for people who died of cancer. Statistics were a reality; I sat my little brothers down and leveled with them about the Big C since my parents hadn't.

"The truth shall free you," I said. "Cancer attacks the body like invisible maggots, incessantly devouring of the beefy red muscle tissue and the yellow globules of fat. It eats away at the life-sustaining organs. This war happens inside the body where you can't see." I think they understood. I didn't tell them about the Communists and imminent invasion. Kids shouldn't live in fear of snipers.

I didn't worry too much about my cancer because the world itself seemed the bigger threat. Hiroshima, or that standoff between Kennedy and the Soviets for example—it would all get ugly in the end. Everybody's flesh would be burning or rotting eventually; they just didn't know it.

I put a drop of cream on my index finger and brushed it over my cheek the way I imagined Indians applied war paint. "Stop acting like a cat in water," my mother said. I rubbed a little more. Finally she handed the speckled Easter egg candy back to me as if it were something I wanted in the first place. She gave me one last greasy pat on the arm. "Off you go, but keep the boys in the yard."

The stale candy offerings did nothing to alleviate the staggering humidity. I drifted toward the swing set and motioned to my brothers.

"Step right up boys," I said. "Get your Dodo eggs here. Your mother searched to the ends of the attic to produce these."

Big-A just looked at me.

"Hey kid," I said. "Get happy. Be grateful you're not stuck playing with petrified gourds from last Halloween."

"I don't want any," Big-A said, and he proceeded to take little army men out of his pockets and stand them up in our bald, dusty yard.

I shook the box in Joe-Bins' direction. "Come on! You know you want some."

"No I don't," Bins said, and he gave me the Bronx cheer.

"Have it your way," I said. "There are kids in China who are starving for dodo eggs."

I put a piece of candy on the sidewalk and pulverized it with the heel of my Keds. I thought of hurling one at the back of the garage at close range but I sat on the swing watching my little brothers. They tossed little plastic paratroopers into the air. The red chutes would open—or they wouldn't. Either way, the weighted caps popped as the army-green men hit the ground. I imagined this was how the Communists would drop in on us. You could only hope their chutes wouldn't open. You could only hope they got caught up on telephone wires. You could only pray you spotted them before you felt a bayonet in your back.

My father pulled in the driveway, hopped out of his red work van with a half-gallon of Breyers Ice Cream in his hand—the triple-crown: chocolate, strawberry and vanilla—not even a bag. This meant he'd just stopped at Star Market, maybe to pay our account with Mr. Balentine since my mother needed more than twenty dollars' worth of groceries sometimes. Big-A and Joe-Bins flocked to my father tugging, pleading, reaching up trying to touch the ice cream. I walked up the back porch flapping my shirt to blot my sweat. My father chucked the Breyers into the freezer. He said, "That's for later."

The boys whined. My father kissed my mother on the cheek. He asked, "Where's Johnny?"

"He's at the Y with Uncle Joe," I answered.

My father looked at me. "Patty, take the boys back outside."

I pointed right at my brothers. "This is why you shouldn't get all excited over something like ice cream," I said. "You look desperate." I patted my forehead with my wrist. The lotion caused an unnatural sweat to bead up on my face the way Minwax reshaped raindrops on a car.

I sat on the top step, by the porch screen, and I could hear my parents talking.

"You know, Balentine pulled me aside today," my father said to my mother.

"How would I know?" she answered.

"He goes, 'Hey, you know your daughter—did you ever see how she mopes around the neighborhood with those kids? She looks like an 80-year-old widow. I wave, I give her candy—and you know, that kid, she doesn't even smile.'"

I got up off the porch. I didn't need to listen to the rest of that conversation. It was news to me that I wasn't smiling. I had the smirk under control. Now I had one more look on my face to master.

I sat on the slide, practice-smiling, when my father came out into the yard. He picked up the carton of candy eggs and shook it.

"Where did you get these?" he asked.

"They fell from the sky," I said.

"Just which section of sky did they fall from?"

"I don't know." I laughed. "Mrs. Gurney probably gave them to Mom—probably three years ago."

My father opened the spout, poured a couple of robin-blue eggs and rolled them in his palm. They clacked.

"Sound like dice."

"But they're not indestructible," I said. "Wanna see me smash one with my heel?"

"Sure."

I placed a blue egg down on one of the concrete strips of our driveway and gave my father a demonstration.

"You're right," my father said. "That thing cracked like the shell of a walnut!"

"I call them dodo eggs cause they try to pass this stuff off as candy but only a fool would even put one in their mouth."

My father sat on the swing next to me. "Say, you like to throw things," he said. "Why don't you stand over there, and I'll open my mouth and see if I can catch me one of your dodo eggs."

"What?" I asked.

"Let's try it," he said. "Toss one."

I reached for the candy but the Bins beat me to it. Before I ever had a shot, Joe-Bins thwacked the aluminum slide *and* clocked the doghouse as he ran. The kid wasted ammo. Our father was sitting on a swing with his mouth open.

"Hold on, boys," my father said. "Let's see what your sister can do."

My first toss blew by his ear and we both started to crack up. My father had a tough time keeping his mouth open after that.

I had better accuracy overhand, and my second shot would have been a ringer, but he laughed. The dodo egg hit him in his front teeth. I heard his pain. I tried not to laugh. My father stood up and put his hand to his mouth. The boys scattered and ran into the house. I got out of his way—but not before offering up the carton. I placed it down on the ground in front of my father and ran—the way terrified natives tried to placate King Kong with altars of fruit. But my father ignored me. He whirred past it all as he stomped up the porch and into the house.

A moment later my father came out with the container of ice cream and spoons—he had a smile on his face and no blood on his teeth.

"Nice shot, kiddo," he said. "I should have known better with you."

He held out his hand; I picked out a tall spoon.

We sat on a blue and white striped Sears Roebuck swing set, both of us, side-by-side and silent. We kicked puddles of dust with our feet and made smoke. I let a teaspoon of icy vanilla melt in my mouth, and when there was nothing but a fading bud of taste on the back of my tongue—that's when I tasted the ice cream the most.

Stylish Mom and Dad entertain at our home, circa 1970....

Almost Happy

"Saint Catherine, Saint Ann, Saint Jude! Where the Hell are they?" my father asked. He looked at my mother and paused. "Where have they gone? You think they all marched right up to Heaven?"

"Take it easy, John" my mother said. "I'm as mortified as you are."

"What did they do with the statues? It's sacrilege. I'm going to give these charlatans a piece of my mind," my father said.

"Don't," my mother said. "If you're that uncomfortable, find another parish."

Our car slowly rolled out of the parking lot of Our Lady of the Assumption. I watched our church and my school get smaller in the side-view mirror.

We didn't attend mass each and every Sunday—for perfectly legitimate reasons, sick kids or foul weather—but at least once a month we crammed into a pew together. In a matter of weeks somebody looted our church. All kinds of relics disappeared: statues of the saints, floor-standing candelabra, marble baptismal fonts, and incalculable feet of wrought iron altar railing—all missing. I knew the source of trouble: Vatican Council II had loosened restrictions and suddenly parishes engaged in their own brand of interior decorating. Our Lady of the Assumption was all caught up in the modern, streamlining trend.

My mother sighed. "It's just so tragic," she said. "Why would anyone want to turn an inspirational church so barren? Maybe the emptiness is supposed to make us yearn and reflect on the deeper, inner workings of our souls."

Johnny-Boy cleared his throat. He said, "Maybe they're just cleaning the statues."

"That's a fine idea, Johnny," my mother said.

"Yes. Very kind, too, kiddo," my father said. "But where have all the kneelers gone? You think they're cleaning the kneelers? That's what really gets me." He slapped the steering wheel. "How in God's name are you supposed to worship if you can't get on your knees?"

"You can still worship," my mother said.

"Maybe *you* can!" my father said. "They're throwing away saints, Jane! Which dumpster do we go to when we wanna pray to Saint Ann?"

"It's certainly minimalist but it's still a church," my mother said, "and we need to respect that."

"A church should look like a house of God!" my father said. "Not an empty loft. Pandering to the masses—I don't believe for one minute that's what God wants!"

My mother took off her lace veil, folded it, and put it in the glove compartment before she checked her hair in the visor mirror.

We pulled up to the corner shops on Wood Avenue—our usual Sunday stop. My mother sprung out of the Impala to get in line at the busy little storefront bakery. The air outside smelled like croissants. When she returned, my father reached across the seat to open her door and my mother angled into the car with a tower of boxes, which were bound together with red-striped bakery string. She balanced them on her lap, more than enough pastry for two families of six.

Of course, the Sheehans were that other family.

Jim and Olivia Sheehan came over from across the street with their kids. They were Birchers too. We huddled around the counter in our kitchen, grabbed napkins, and plunged our hands into cake boxes of donuts. My mother sliced a fresh log of apple strudel and poured orange juice into glasses with avocado-colored teardrops paint on them. The parents circled the pumpkin colored breakfast counter and sat on stools.

"Want an update on the other local parish?" Mr. Sheehan said. He cuffed up his shirtsleeves. "There's a carnival brewing in the parking lot outside the gates of St. Peter's, and inside, the crucifix of Jesus has been replaced by a bare wooden cross!"

"They're taking Jesus off the cross in his own church," my father said. "Those collared-punks with their mop-tops!"

"I wish I could say it's funny," Mr. Sheehan said. "These priests are literally turning their backs on God so they can *tune-in* to the congregation."

"That's right," Mrs. Sheehan said. "Father Bernard recited the entire mass, in English, and he faced the congregation. He even consecrated the hosts with eyes on the audience, not the altar or the cross."

"Maybe they have good intentions," my mother said. She centered four earthenware cups on their saucers. "But the real issue here is in the translation, right? How do we know if the words of the sacraments are accurate since the conversion of the mass from Latin to English?"

"The answer is no, Jane," my father said. "Sacred words can't be converted, and God doesn't need to explain himself to *us*!"

Mrs. Sheehan unplugged the Farberware percolator and served the coffee for my mother. She said, "I think Jane's got the key point here. We can't be sure the Eucharist is the Eucharist anymore."

My father tore open a packet of Sweet-n-Low, poured it into his cup, and twisted the paper until it resembled a toothpick. He said, "I wanted to show my disgust, get up and walk out in the middle of mass—but it was over before I had the chance. Thirty minutes at the most. Holy Communion has gone from a sacrament to something like a trip for fast food."

"Heaven help us," Mrs. Sheehan said.

I lingered in the kitchen, peeled layers of skin off my strudel.

My father grabbed the box of donuts that remained. My mother grabbed his arm. "Let me put some of those in a Tupperware for TRIM." TRIM—Tax Reform Immediately—another committee he co-chaired.

"Just a sec," my father said. He held the box in front of me and shook it a little. "What do you think?"

I eyeballed the marvelous selection: glazed, chocolate cake, chocolate frosted, donuts with shots, donuts with jelly, powdered sugar, Boston Crème, French twists, crullers. The world that produced such sweetness couldn't be totally bad, or maybe a variety of pleasure was proof that it was.

"Well, what do you think?" my father asked.

"I haven't finished my strudel yet."

"I said what do you think?"

"About what?"

"Stop playing dumb. What's the latest hijinks over there? Why don't you tell Jim about that pogo stick incident."

"Father Ryan hopped on some kid's pogo stick and he left divots in the newly-tarred parking lot."

"Is he overweight?" Mr. Sheehan asked.

"No. It's just that nobody noticed the rubber foot had come off."

"That's a real scream," my mother said.

"Well it's funny to me," my father said. "So much for trying to be cool. He's supposed to be a leader. What's the latest round of foolishness?"

"Nothing, really. I'd say we're singing more than we used to. It's sort of fun and inspiring. "

"Yeah—but you're not singing the time-honored hymns," my father said. "I'd better not catch you singing any of that Kumbaya-crap." He pushed his cup and saucer away. "Church isn't supposed to be entertaining. There's not enough flesh and blood—and too much guitar."

"It's such a shame you kids don't learn those gorgeous hymns," Mrs. Sheehan said.

"Ave Maria," my mother said. "Since I was a little girl at St. Raphael's—that hymn makes me cry. Latin is truly beautiful—the language of God."

My father rolled his shoulders, got up off his stool, and rested his foot on one of the pegs. "So, thanks for the choir update. Now what's going on in that school of yours?"

"I don't know what you mean," I said.

"You know exactly what I mean."

"Honestly, there's not much more I can say. Sister gave us *Good News for Modern Man.* It's not really ours—I mean we have to leave it at school. But it's a bible and it's good looking!" I looked at my mother. "The cover is pure white with 18 karat gold letters. It opens and closes with a zipper and a tassel!"

"There *is* no good news in the bible," my father said. "And saving your soul is the antithesis of fashion."

My mother adjusted the pearls around her neck, and I went back to picking raisins out of my strudel.

Mr. Sheehan slid his tie from his collar. "The new Vatican is particularly targeting the women."

"They're trying to keep God out of our family and our country," my father said. "The grannies are turning church basements into bingo halls, and they've got the teeny-boppers pitching banners for the peace movement."

My mother stood in front of the sink, looking off to something farther than any point in our kitchen. She said, "I'm not worried about peace or bingo."

"Well, you *ought* to be," my father interrupted. "The Bible says it is better to tie a millstone around a child's neck and toss him into the ocean, than to let him—or *her*"—he pointed at me—"lose his eternal soul."

"That's not what 'suffer the little children unto me' means," my mother said.

"The Bible means exactly what it says, Jane," my father said.

My parents went on bickering and I slipped out and up

to my room. I pulled the shoebox from underneath my bed, took out the Good News Bible and unzipped it. I opened it to a random page, looking for something good.

Proverbs, Chapter 2.

> 16 You will be able to resist any immoral woman who tries to seduce you with her smooth talk,
> 17 who is faithless to her own husband and forgets her sacred vows.
> 18 If you go to her house, you are traveling the road to death. To go there is to approach the world of the dead.
> 19 No one who visits her ever comes back. He never returns to the road to life.
> 20 So you must follow the example of good people and live a righteous life.
> 21 Righteous people - people of integrity - will live in this land of ours.

The Catholic Church *did* seem to be giving up the mysterious rituals that made her the one true church. The mass—which had remained the same for centuries—was unfaithful. It was changing.

I hadn't exactly resisted the changes. I wanted to know where Sister June Marie shopped for her sort of normal, but still nun-ish wardrobe, sturdy wools, reliable cottons and neutral cardigans. I loved her A-line skirts, and plain white blouses. Sister's look was humble, yet hopeful—clothes that were almost happy. But Sister's hem was way up since *Jesus Christ Superstar*. Her habit was half of what it used to be, and felt banners for peace and love draped concrete-block walls all over my school.

On the first Wednesday of each month, we marched from homeroom to church for mass. Father Ryan preached *Peanuts* sermons just for us! Comic-strip characters faced moral dilemmas, i.e., is it right for Snoopy to lie about his heritage, disguise himself as a full-bred instead of a mutt to have an edge in the Top Dog Competition? Charlie Brown caught Snoopy in a bald-faced lie—he understood. He forgave.

We no longer had to wear our plaid hats to that first Wednesday mass—those itchy wool envelopes that made me think of the Foreign Legion. The passé headwear stayed in our desks to hold pencils, sharpeners, and rubber erasers that could pass for chunks of cheese. I never told.

❄ ❄ ❄

The last time our class celebrated one of those Good News Masses, I squished in the front pew, in between Martha and Carol, when Father Ryan stepped down from the altar to shake our hands. "Peace be with you," he said. We took those words, peace be with you, and passed them out to each other like Communion wafers. Peace be with you. And also with you. Father shared a sliver of power and authority with us.

Father Ryan's hair was clean-cut but youthful enough to feather in the breeze of the tuba-sized church fan. His eyes beamed with the shimmer that precedes tears. If I lived long enough to have a boyfriend, I'd hope he had Father Ryan's face. I pictured him without a collar, imagined him singing a Bobby Sherman song—music like a spring of ice blue water— flowing out of grid of the pocket-transistor radio my father never knew I had. My father didn't know I'd been sneaking about the neighborhood singing,

> HEY! little wo-man, please make up your mind.
> You've GOT-to come into my
> world and leave your world behind.

The way of the cross didn't seem so sad. Each time we celebrated those Wednesday masses I was more certain of my numerous undeclared talents. I could have legitimized the bongos and the tambourine and helped Father Ryan bear the weight of virtue *and* fame. The Communists and Satan worshipers could brand me with my social security number or put me through weeks of Chinese water torture. Father Ryan was a man who could say words like *hey little woman* and really mean what he was saying.

I was thinking too much. Assumption had taken a toll. I wasn't as uncomfortable as I should have been. I'd seen way too much of Sister June Marie's ankles and shins. But my mind bounced back to happy. I was happy when Sister stopped trudging around in black oxfords and taken to springing around our classroom in airy-beige sling-backs with cork soles. Her shortened habit could pass for a hankie. Wisps of pale hair hung out. In the shine of her diamond-shaped face I recognized happiness, a forced fizzing in the gut, undeniable, almost irresistible—and dangerous for just those reasons.

If I rationed my occasions of joy, I would never get addicted to happiness, which was a fool's game in the valley of tears anyway. My experience with the seductive desire to be happy had to be my best defense.

A couple of Sundays later, we went to mass at Assumption again. I had no idea what my parents were thinking. I didn't expect to find the saints. But because we were there, I had to hope. I hoped Father Ryan would pound us with words that commanded happiness; I hoped he'd point out a grand design my parents couldn't conceive of. I wanted Father to say something about music being a gift from Heaven and sanctioned by the Pope. I wanted him to explain about all those statues—the bisque beauty and glazed blood that had disappeared. And what about my father's kneelers?

Father Ryan offered up a generic sermon about Lazarus. He made no attempt to explain the disappearances. He never told a joke or mentioned Snoopy, and maybe it was for the best. After mass we retreated to the Chevy in dirt-staring silence.

My mother shook her head and turned on the radio, a low click followed by faint sound. Stevie Wonder was singing…

My cherie amour, lovely as a summer's day…

I was no stranger to the words. My father hated the radio—he'd banned it from our car, but he didn't seem to hear. Stevie Wonder kept singing and the filling the car.

My cherie amour, distant as the Milky Way…

Along both sides of Stratfield Road, the estate homes flapped their awnings. The historic maple trees seemed to be waving—pushing our car along. *La-la-laa-laa-laa-laa.* We passed the Brooklawn Country Club, the duck pond near the 18th hole, the quaint strip of storefronts, the striped awning at El Dorado Pharmacy, and the barber shop spinning its ribbon like a million connected smiles. We cruised along with the radio on—like people on TV! I basked in the perfection of the universe. My brothers weren't fidgeting or taking up too much space. I adored the gorgeous waves of my mother's cotton candy hair; I loved the contrast between my father's tan neck and his jiffy-white collar. The air was sprinkled with Stevie Wonder's voice—lollypops of *la…la…la…* Music paved the way for our procession back to Bridgeport. The world was happy and filled with Sunday drivers. A thin, grassy knoll charmed the middle of the street. The motorcade was ours and nobody was going to get shot. I had the urge to blow kisses and toss bubblegum candy to people on the sidewalks, to the travelers, to the onlookers. *How I wish that you were mine.* The words and music became a pulse. Chocolate chips of time melted peacefully—as we passed away from Fairfield, Connecticut, a town of lonely circular drives. I waved goodbye to the Fairfield town line and hello to the city of Bridgeport, our city of cars that lined the streets and dotted the curbs and flowed down the roads like veins of a busy river. Each car with its own radio! I poked my head between my parents and looked at ours— our thankless Delco—the precise black lines between the numbers on the AM dial. It reminded me of a thermometer, and at that moment, no matter where our hash mark was set we registered the perfect human temperature. I praised the Lord for sometimes making life so clear to me: every car had a radio pressed into the heart of each dashboard like a soul. I thanked Him for the radio and for the revelation: at some point, whether we were listening or not, the same song pulsed through all of us.

Nine Lives in Purgatory

> Listen children, all is not lost, all is not lost, oh, no, no....
> —Chicago, "Saturday in the Park"

When I told my mother I wrote a play and my cat was one of the characters, she called it genius. When I told her I titled the play *Nine Lives in Purgatory*, she poured us a Coke and asked me if I was a happy girl.

"You know how happy I am," I said.

"I know you're an ace with sarcasm," she said.

"Mom, how would you feel if there was no Hell?"

"What kind of question is that? Leave hell alone. Tell me your play is appropriate for children. Tell me it's entertaining and upbeat."

"It is. It is."

"I wouldn't mind seeing your vision of space, even landing on a planet with ghoulish aliens. You're good at special effects."

"Mom, do you realize that when we land on someone else's planet, we're the aliens? I learned that from an episode of *The Twilight Zone*."

"Well, I'm thinking of lighter fare."

"The play is unique, the product of ideas that have tumbled around in my head for years," I said. She patted my hand. "It's mainly for you and Dad and the Sheehans. But it's no small production. We had to enlist some local Pagans."

"That kind of talk is unnecessary," my mother said.

"I apologize."

"Would you like to have more Birchers on hand?"

"We sure would!"

"Okay. The MOTOREDEs and the GUUNs—we'll have both meetings on the same night and your performance will top it all off."

"Thanks, mom. I'll need some carnations. I'd love to have long-stemmed, red ones."

"Flowers! Nice touch, kiddo."

"Oh—and Mom, can we not invite Mick Bovine?"

"What? How can we not invite him? He's on three committees."

"Please?"

"Why would you even ask such a thing?"

"He's creepy," I said. "I'm not comfortable around him."

"Why not?"

"I heard all the men talking after a GUUN meeting. I was in another room sort of listening…"

"You mean sneaking?"

"I mean sometimes I get hungry and I live here, and I heard Mick talk."

"Talk about what?"

"I heard Mick say he might blow up the Capitol!"

"What?"

"He said it's the only way to clean up Washington."

"Don't be ridiculous. That's not what he said."

"That's *exactly* what he said."

"What's wrong with you? Patricia! Don't you see? This is the kind of smear tactic the left wing uses on us all the time. You can't take words out of context or malign a person's character that way. The man's a patriot!"

"Can you can tell him to leave his briefcase home? It makes me nervous."

My mother pushed my Coke away. "Now you listen

here," she said. "We're going to clear this up once and for all. I don't just join organizations. I'm a leader, not a follower. Before I became a John Bircher, I wrote to J. Edgar Hoover—the director of the FBI. And I asked him about JBS. And you know what? He sent me back a typed letter—and he signed it. He said JBS is clean. He had nothing on them."

"So?"

"So let me put you straight. Mick never said anything close to what came out of your mouth. You made a big mistake. Period. You're not going to make it worse. Do we understand each other?" I nodded. "I'll get the flowers for your play. As far as I'm concerned, this part of our discussion never happened."

❀ ❀ ❀

Carly's basement was the best venue: tiled floor, paneled walls, and more space for chairs. Carly was like a sister to me, the only person I didn't have to fight with or explain everything to. We might have been best friends even if we weren't joined together by our parents' detailed survival plans.

Special effects were no small matter to either of us, so we raided our mothers' attics and linen closets. Glittery white felt and lace sheers made splendid clouds. Tin foil, cellophane, and reflective Christmas ornaments became the stuff of stars, moons, and comets. We worked like members of a happy chain gang; we took turns standing on a ladder, emptying shelves, passing item after item along: car batteries, flashlights, CB radios, gas masks, and boxes of rubber gloves. The toughest act of creation turned out to be making space. I sat on the top rung and took a breather.

"What if every star is a piece of God's spit?" I asked.

"Do you have to say it that way, Patty?" Carly asked.

"But maybe it *was* that way. I just had a vision of how God finished up with creation."

"Really?"

"I can picture God with a hunk of clay in one hand and

uprooting a tree with the other and he used the tree like an X-acto knife to add more groves to the Grand Canyon."

"I see what you mean, Patty. The earth's finishing touches came later, after God sort of thought he was finished."

"Yes. The further he stepped away from his creation, the better he could see it."

"Makes perfect sense," Carly said. "Not everything that was created was planned."

"Exactly! The Milky Way was probably a sneeze."

Carly always understood me better than I understood her.

It was easier to use the Sheehan's old Norge washer and dryer than to move them, so with assorted panels of old drapes and a picnic bench, we created a throne area, a type of loveseat for God and his Son. Tiers of pomp in royal jacquard spread out over the appliances and across the floor—a fairway of eminence. Anyone with eyes could see what we saw, such an inspired seating arrangement you couldn't decide whether to stand back in awe or try God's throne on for size.

❋ ❋ ❋

Mick Bovine was the first adult to venture down and he carried that darn attaché case, something I always had a vague fear of. He held it against his torso; navigated the short-lipped stairs like a man who expected to be pelted with a wet tea bag. The briefcase was distinguished by a bull's-eye set in the center, specifically a big red peace sign with the caption, **Footprint of the American Chicken**.

"Glad to see you, Mr. Bovine." I parked him in the front row. Like one of those mannequin ladies from a cheesy game show, I extended both hands and introduced him to the chair that was chosen just for him.

"So this is the stage," Mr. Bovine said as he sat down. "Can't remember the last time I saw a play."

"You're our double-agent at the University of Bridgeport," I said. "Don't they have a theater over there?"

"I never go to those things," Mr. Bovine said. He laid the attaché across his lap and set his Styrofoam cup of Sanka right on top of the peace symbol. "Hope it has a happy ending."

"I'm not one to brag, but you'll remember what you see here tonight."

I handed Mr. Bovine one of our homemade programs. "The edges crumbled in his hand. He asked, "What's this?"

"We cut sheets of brown paper bag and charred the borders for effect," I said.

"Wow. *Nine Lives in Purgatory*?" Mr. Bovine said. "Looks like quite an event you've cooked up."

"You've got the best seat in the house," I said.

Farnum Bailey, the lean, bright-eyed pilot, gripped the handrail. He was known for sharp pressed shirts and the rumor that his wife lived in an insane asylum.

And then came John Gimble; flannel, cardigan, creased dungarees, tidy and stern, I think he was retired military. Gimble once came to a TRIM meeting bearing gourds for my mother, a bag full of warts and moles. I never understood gourds, especially as a gift. Mr. Gimble traveled with a knotty wooden cane he didn't seem to need but he liked to say he wasn't afraid to use it.

Gregg Leary tiptoed down the stairs in his usual desert boots and snug chinos. He paced in front of the stage, leaned in and eyeballed everything. Gregg Leary had the nerve to touch the picture of the sacred heart of Jesus on the wall. I wanted to tell Gregg this wasn't a circus act where he might mull around looking for freaks, or evidence of slight-of-hand. This was a play. You look but don't touch, you sit in your seat and wait for the art to present itself. Eventually, he opened a folding chair and set it down in the darkest corner of the basement.

Cheryl and Rick Brown arrived as they always did, together, twin brother and sister, but we always thought they were married. They gave me their synchronized, windshield wiper wave, and they made their way down the aisle and took seats next to Gregg. Cheryl was a hunchback. Her affliction didn't scare me. I told myself there was a kitten balled up on her shoulder underneath the furry cashmere sweaters she wore.

Ted Lapous, the Greek guy, was a likable, retired history teacher. Many a night he sat in our dining room after JBS meetings and entertained us with his stories of ancient Greece, though he sometimes fell asleep in the middle of them. He wore old white dress shirts that he never tucked in, a stout man with cranky eyebrows and constant sweat. Mr. Lapous had brought a paper plate with food from upstairs. "Classic butter cookies," he said. "I hope it's okay."

"Oh, sure. We're allowed to eat down here."

"Everybody!" I called out to the crowd "—if I can just get your attention. Please feel free to help yourself to refreshments upstairs and bring them down with you. If you haven't helped yourself to a snack, you still have a few minutes to do so. Thank you."

Backstage in our makeshift dressing room, Carly squeezed into her Virgin Mary outfit, which consisted of a Peter Pan body suit, a baby blue blanket sash, and a pink sheet for a veil. The neckline, bordered with tight stitches, signified unyielding virtue. The veil emphasized innocence. The sash symbolized humility. Very Mary-ish. We weren't so young that the details of pious fashion were wasted on us.

Carly tended to the cast and last-minute details. We'd enlisted several kids from the neighborhood. The trio of Flanagan girls arrived on time and slipped into their long pale gowns. Timmy Flanagan showed up late. "I'm ready," he garbled with a mouthful of Red Hots, and as he jostled into his white Jesus-tunic, he dribbled pink spittle all over himself.

I turned to Carly. "Oh, no! Red stains! The little fool just ruined his costume." I looked around the basement. "We can use that grapevine wreath as a crown of thorns, and let the candy stains just stay there as blood."

"Oh—no we can't do that, Patty," Carly said. "Bloody Jesus is out of character. It'll change the whole tone of the play."

Carly was right. I'd written a masterpiece about modern forgiveness and overdue glory. Jesus's second coming would be white and triumphant, not thorned and bloody. I did a quick headcount, checked on Golda, and said, "Everybody freeze till I get back. I'm running over to my house for correction fluid."

I found my mother, Mrs. Sheehan, Rosa Scarpetti and Eleanor Gurney sitting at the dining room table sipping from their coffee cups.

"Here she is!" Mrs. Gurney said. "Woman of the hour! You're a babysitter and a playwright."

"I can't argue with that," I said.

"Your mother says you're her right arm, says it all the time. She depends on you," Mrs. Gurney said. "Salt of the earth, this one here, isn't she, girls?"

Mrs. Sheehan, Scarpetti, and Gimbal offered various words and gestures of agreement.

Mrs. Gurney continued. "Do you know that in his sermon on the mount, Jesus said we should be like the salt of the earth? And you know, salt was so valuable, the soldiers from ancient Rome were paid in salt!"

"Thanks, Mrs. Gurney," I said.

I led my mother into the kitchen. "Ma, can you round-up the MOTOREDE ladies so we can get started?"

She popped the top off the percolator. "I've got a couple more things to do here first," she said.

"But I won't be able to help Mrs. Gurney cross the street unless I do it right now," I said.

"I'll get someone else to help me," Mrs. Gurney called out. "The show must go on! But please, don't refer to me in the third person when I'm in earshot. Nothing wrong with my hearing!" She covered her mouth with her hankie and worked on clearing her throat, a sound like an engine struggling to turn over. We all waited until Mrs. Gurney was up and running at a rough idle.

"Patricia, I would like to say I'll be there with bells on," Mrs. Gurney said. "But the way I move, it'll only be one bell, and a cow bell at that!"

I laughed. "Mrs. Gurney, you are one of the funniest people I know!"

"Quit laughing," my mother said, and she squeezed my arm. "Go back to the Sheehan's and do what you have to. I promise we'll be there."

Of course they'd be there. The issue was when. I rummaged through the cigar box next to my mother's Smith Corona and grabbed the correction fluid.

※ ※ ※

"This white stuff stinks," Timmy complained. "I might have to vomit."

"Keep your voice down and don't be crude," I said. "Respect the part you are playing." I used a paper plate to fan the spots dry, and I heard my mother arrive with the MOTOREDEs.

"Oh, look at this," my mother said. "You talk about imagination."

"Mommy!" I ran up and hugged her. My mother looked stunning in black Palazzo pants and a plaid poncho with two large political buttons. One said **END THE ERA** and the other said **STOP NOW FOREVER**. "Mom, will you get everybody to take a seat?"

"Certainly. Now get into your costume. Do like the Mafia and break some legs." I went backstage and slipped a flannel gown over my clothes. As we went over instructions with the cast, Carly and I paused to listen to all the chatter. Mrs. Gurney asked for an ashtray and tried to clear more of the usual something in her throat. My mother would have ushered me into the bathroom and made me swallow medicine to bring the phlegm up. She hated what she called guttural sounds. I wondered how she could stand it with Mrs. Gurney.

"Where are we?" Mrs. Gurney rumbled. "Are those thrones? Is this Ferdinand and Isabella's court?"

"I think we're in Heaven," my mother said.

My father interrupted. "Look at the title Jane," he said. "Somebody's going to Hell."

"John," my mother said. "It says *Nine Lives in* Purgatory."

"The only difference between Purgatory and Hell is eternity." My father made this announcement as if he had first-hand knowledge that 30 minutes of the cleansing fires was as agonizing as 30 years.

"Wow," Mrs. Sheehan said. "What a transformation. I hardly recognize our basement."

"No kidding," Mr. Sheehan said. "What happened to my CB radios and batteries? Shouldn't move that stuff around."

"Maybe they're underneath one of those sheets," Mrs. Sheehan said. "Just let it go for now."

"We've certainly got an industrious bunch of monkeys here," Mr. Sheehan said. "And strong, too."

"Why is it so dark?" Mrs. Gurney asked.

"Good question," my father added.

"This is quite a program," Mrs. Sheehan said. "All their names are painted with scarlet nail polish on brown paper bags. Look, the seared border, the wrinkled parchment effect."

"Very creative," my mother said.

"Yes. The parchment—the parchment." Mrs. Gurney gacked like a talking bird. "That's why I'm guessing the play has something to do with Christopher Columbus. Maybe we're headed toward the new world?"

"What I'd like to know," my father said, "is how these kids got ahold of matches and where were they lighting them?"

Carly grabbed my arm. "Oh, my god."

I knew I should've got the show going already. There's a trick to working audiences. You have to get them hungry, but if you wait too long, it's like hand-feeding bears.

"Don't worry." I looked at Carly in her pale pastels, her sad Mary eyes, and heart-shaped face. "I bet the Blessed Mother's proud of you."

"But what if our folks don't like it?" she asked.

"We're not scared," I told her. But we both knew well enough that the parents are the first to turn on you.

It started with the end. The end of everything. Joe-Bins was the nuclear bomb. We covered him with a paint tarp and let him mushroom to his feet. We'd sprinkled the tarp with baby powder so when Joe-Bins flapped his arms he'd spread cosmic dust everywhere. We put out the remaining lights and banged on a metal pie plate tin to signify atomic apocalypse.

After a moment of silence, a stagehand plugged in the droplight we'd taped to the floor. The light beaming upward from an aluminum cone cast blinding light and unearthly shadows as God the Father came out and took his seat. He was flushed and visibly sweating in a rain poncho and a frizzed-out George Washington wig.

Jesus appeared and took his place at the right hand of God. Ramped up on candy, Jesus smiled and waved a little more than I wanted him to, but Jesus *was* a people person.

Our Blessed Mother was positioned in the corner. She had her own throne, a dainty resting place made from a five-gallon-bucket of Spackle that we cushioned with foam rubber and covered with gold lamé.

The three Flanagan sisters came on stage, angels outfitted in long bright nightshirts, no silly wing business. I named them the Pearls of Purgatory, and I was the main Pearl. All Pearls were armed. We carried concealed carnations—one long-stemmed flower tucked inside each of our long sleeves.

Matt Bueno served as prison warden. He hauled three criminals into God's court. Criminals were restrained: Nelson Rockefeller (bicycle lock and chain handcuffs), Billy Jean King (arms bound by extension cord), and Golda Meir (my cat was caged in an upturned laundry basket).

"Nelson Rockefeller!" the warden called out. "Traitor! Vehicle of the One World Order! Get on thy knees." The Pearls made a chant of his name: Rockefeller, Rockefeller, Rockefeller.

"Mercy, Lord!" Rockefeller yelled.

The Pearls chanted, "Ashes to ashes. Dust to dust. First man bleeds then he turns to rust!" Billie Jean King suffered the same fate, and when it was Golda Meir's turn to beg for mercy, I spoke for her.

Jesus extended his arms. "Father, may I help them? Can't we let suffering end with the destruction of earth by their own hands?"

God said, "You are my only begotten son in whom I am well-pleased. You will not suffer and die for them anymore. This time I am here to defend you. As they have sown, so shall they reap. Let them have Hades."

Jesus put his hands together and said, "Let us pray—pray to my mother to beseech my father to bring us all to the new world, not the new world order. Take us to a world of men and women, boys and girls, dogs and cats, music and fireworks, watermelon and strawberries, a world without Hades, a world without end, forever and ever, again and again, amen."

I gave the cue for one of the Pearls to press the start button on the dryer. The baby doll we'd planted inside rolled and kerplunked—the sound of the final cleansing cycle for the human race. The tumble and thud of the doll represented the deepest pain one could endure without actually being in Hell.

The Pearls circled the prisoners for cleansing. We pulled the red carnations out of our sleeves and whipped Rockefeller and King. We wouldn't hurt Golda Meir but we teased her in her laundry basket cage. We whipped the other sinners with all our might and they writhed as if they'd been branded by each flower. Golda loved it. We pelted her basket, and she stuck her paw through the slats and tried to snag the flower. We walked around in the circle and took our turns driving sin out of Rockefeller, King, and Meir with long stemmed carnations. We bruised the petals and broke the stems, and when the flowers could take no more, we let the dead lefties fall silent. The Pearls remained in a circle, joined hands and caaw'd. We sang the chant of angry birds—*Caaw! Caaw!* sounds—which grew into the full "Chorus of Caaw," a frenzied power. We stayed in the rapture of Caaw, with the dryer in the background, cycling plastic limbs. "Caaw! Caaw! Caaw!" I thought about Revelation—all the prophesied gnashing of teeth. When I looked out into the crowd and saw bewilderment on the faces of my parents, it seemed appropriate.

Jesus traveled to the corner to speak to his mother. He wiped genuine sweat from his brow. The spotlight turned toward Mother Mary for an operatic song we called the "Intercession Solo"—the scene where the sinners were supposed to plead to Mary, and Mary was supposed to speak to Jesus, and Jesus was supposed to write a new gospel wherein God the Father nukes Hell, and subdivides Purgatory into something like temporary, low-income housing. Everybody who wasn't zoned for paradise would be sent to a ghetto alongside Satan's retaining wall.

But Jesus kept fighting sweat and fiddling around with his bulky sleeves. He pinwheeled his arms until his fist hit the wall—and the picture of the Sacred Heart of Jesus fell to the floor and broke.

"Oy!" Mrs. Gurney shrieked.

A collective sigh from the audience caused us to let go of each other's hands and cut the Caaw.

Carly bent down as if she meant to pick up the picture of Jesus among all the shards.

"No, don't touch!" I yelled.

Mr. Bovine had his hand over his mouth. Mr. Sheehan pinched the bridge of his nose. My parents looked like they often did with their lips pressed into impatient lines—a "What's next?" expression I'd known my whole life.

"Something's burning!" Mr. Sheehan shouted. He stood,

pulled Timmy by the tunic, and tossed him into Mick Bovine's lap. Both our fathers ripped the throne apart. I scooped Golda up inside the basket. My mother carried Joe-Bins. Mrs. Sheehan corralled a bunch of cast members. The men threw open the door of the Kelvinator where the doll had begun to melt into the tumbler.

The basement fogged with smoke; people covered their mouths, kicked over coffee cups, clotted the stairs. I followed Farnum Bailey up the steps with a knot of adrenaline in my throat, an indigestible chunk of life, the taste of masterpiece but with the consistency of fiasco.

Sirens burned our ears. Firemen unhinged hoses, axes, and bulled their way to the front porch. My parents huddled with the Sheehans on the front lawn while the other guests were standing back beside their vehicles.

The Flanagans hurried to their station wagon, but paused a few times to look back at us. I heard Mr. Flanagan scold the girls. "Do I need to tell you not to whip each other in the face with flowers? What possessed you?"

Birchers hugged our mothers, patted our fathers on the back before heading off without much drama, except for Mrs. Gurney. The firemen wanted to put her in an ambulance due to her full-blown coughing jag. Farnum convinced them to let him drive her home.

I found Carly out on the lawn.

"What's wrong with you people?" I asked.

"What?" she asked.

"Damn your dryer! An accident waiting to happen—that thing was ready to blow and your parents are lucky I didn't get hurt."

Carly sat down in the grass and I did the same. We breathed the damp soil and looked out at the sapphire sky.

"Carly," I said, "I'm sorry they didn't get to hear you sing *Ave Maria*."

"It's not that." She tried not to cry. I tried not to see.

"What then?"

Carly shrugged. "I don't know what's wrong with me. I

guess I'm sad. I can't stop crying."

"Of course you can," I said. She buried her face in her veil and sobbed. "The first step to composure is to ask yourself if you have anything to cry about." I rubbed her back, small but complete circles. "Let me remind you that your house didn't catch fire. It was just a little smoke from your rotten dryer! Don't get emotional. Maybe I should cry because I'm going to get the blame."

Carly stood up and ran off—to be with her folks, I guessed. I didn't go after her. I was already calling up precedents to put the damage in perspective. What the heck? Burnt toast was a bigger catastrophe. And Mrs. Sheehan laundered her kids' sneakers all the time and none of the rubber treads ever melted. Why would a baby doll be different?

The Wood Avenue girls laughed their heads off and lit cigarettes behind the garage.

I said, "Hey! Show's over."

"No shit," Duplex Shelly yelled back.

I watched their blue wall of smoke cross the yard as I stood in my solitary cloud, listening to what sounded like metal taking a beating. In my mind I could see the firemen dousing the thrones, trampling our expensive drapes, gutting the dryer with axes and saws, stomping on my doll like a monster that needed to be killed.

When Carly came back, we reached out to hug each other at the same time.

"It's not my fault or yours, Patty. Even my mother says so."

"Doesn't matter whose fault it is," I said. "There are no do-overs in the world of Art or divine inspiration. I missed my moment forever."

"Don't say forever," Carly said.

"I told my mother about Mick Bovine—what he said about our Capitol. Do you know what she said? She said I didn't hear what I heard."

"She called you a liar?"

"Worse. She tried to change the facts, the data, the truth

that's in my brain."

"Well, I believe you, Patty."

"That's what I want to hear, because there's something rotten going on. Bovine goes to UB, sits in on all those brainwashing classes, says he's posing as a liberal, but how do we know which side he's really posing for?"

"You don't think he's one of us?"

"No. He's one of them. Worse. He's a traitor. You don't ever disrespect the Capitol of the United States. It's heresy!"

"Hey girls! Shh. Over here!"

"Who said that?" Carly asked.

We turned behind us to the see the outline of shrubs.

"It's only me."

"Gregg!" I kicked our end of a long line of bushes. "I know you're in there."

"You scared us!" Carly said.

"Show yourself. Stand up like a man."

"What's wrong with you?" Carly asked.

"I was just talking to your parents," Gregg said.

"That's a lie!" Carly said. "I was just talking with my parents and you were nowhere on the scene."

"Why haven't you gone home like everybody else?" I asked. "What are you doing in the bushes?"

"I just wanted to tell you girls not to be sad. You have nothing to be ashamed of." Gregg stood like a cardboard outline with distant streetlight behind him. His features were smudged. He kept one hand in his pocket and one on his head. "That was quite a pageant you put on."

"It's not a pageant!" I said. "Didn't you read the program? It's a musical tragedy—for children and parents alike. A classic, as we say."

"It was very mature," Gregg said.

"We're exhausted," Carly sighed. "In case you didn't notice, we had a little disaster here tonight."

"Did you get it?" I said. "Do you understand why God is going to rescind Hell?"

"You've grown up so fast," Gregg said. "You're young

women now. Maybe you menstruate. What size bras are you wearing?"

Gregg still had one hand on his head, but he spun his finger in small circles on his scalp as if he was winding a lock of hair, but he had no locks of hair. He had a zip. He cocked his thumb and made like he was holding a gun to his head and shooting, over and over.

Carly and I stood for a quiet moment and felt the chill in the air. Gregg bolted toward the next yard and into the darkness.

"Yeah, you'd better run, you freakin' pervert!" I yelled. I turned to Carly. "We can't share a bomb shelter with this guy."

"He's not one of us," Carly said. "Neither is Bovine. What the hell is happening? This is crazy."

"Psycho," I said.

"Why are we being punished by liars? Who are the good guys?"

"Right now, it's you and me, kid."

"He's a rotten SOB," Carly said, "a bad man, no—he's evil and he's fooled our parents. Bovine is just as bad."

"Do you wanna tell or should I? Or should we do it together?" I asked.

"We both have speak to our mothers," Carly said. "But please, not tonight."

"You're right."

My parents sent me home ahead of them as soon as the fire trucks left. Our backdoor was open. I ran Golda up to my room and came back downstairs. I opened the fridge and hung out there, moved side to side in front of the condiments and leftovers. My neck itched and I scratched it, realizing that I was still wearing my costume flannel with clothes underneath.

The pebble of ache in my chest wouldn't let me change into cooler PJs and close my door on the evening, even with Golda to snuggle up to. I wanted what was due me. I didn't want to be Mrs. Gurney's every-day-table-salt-of-the-earth—that person everybody needs but nobody wants to be. I wanted to blaze into trouble just to get to the other side. I wanted to be seen as an intelligent force, knee-deep in controversy, ready to take it. I was ready for a grand argument, two intellectuals, theologians or something like that. Hell was a slum. Entire continents and hundreds of generations from every civilization were crammed in already. Hell was so crowded it had to be measured in terms of people per square foot. No intelligent being could refer to Hell as a success. The whole system of governing souls was a failure. The premise of the play, the *idea* of getting rid of Hell was the best idea I ever had. I knew nothing would make my father angrier than the destruction of Hell and I felt singularly qualified to introduce him to the idea.

My brothers yawned and marched straight upstairs. My mother bolt-locked the kitchen door, and she turned to the sink and began to scour something she'd left to soak. My father stood beside her. He leaned against the counter.

I imagined I was impossible to utterly dismiss. I was ready for battle.

"Get to bed," my mother said.

"Now," my father added. He remained still—his tanned, folded arms, his permanent turpentine smell.

I sulked up the twenty-one stairs, stopped in the bathroom, rolled a wad of toilet paper and blew my nose. I wanted something so badly—punishment, sympathy, a review. I stared at the gray, sooty stuff on the tissue, a sign, I thought, of a really big moment.

❋ ❋ ❋

I told my mother about Gregg and I used the fewest possible words in attempt to minimize the fact that we'd been duped and worse. All we had was a small army of faithful citizens—how could God let there be enemies among us?

Gregg Leary never showed up at my house again. He didn't appear at Carly's house either. Gregg just disappeared.

Mick Bovine came to meetings sporadically, and by the time we noticed he'd stopped coming we couldn't tell how long it had been. Nobody told us what happened. I don't recall hearing our parents or any of the Birchers tell us not to mention this or that one's name and we dared not to ask.

I asked Carly, "Do you remember Gregg?" and she asked me the same question. We did this for a while; for months afterwards we asked each other for the truth because we knew we were the only ones who knew it. Eventually, we stopped questioning. But disappearing acts are hard to master and maybe impossible to control. After a while, I wasn't sure I could trust myself with remembering and forgetting. A vacuum can suck up more than dirt. The dryer, the play, Bovine's briefcase, we never spike of these things again. Except for the sadness, it's almost as if none of it ever happened.

Wildcard

We sat on the top step of Carly's back porch on a muggy Saturday, typical overcast sky but with a rare yellow light, the color cast off by the tail end of a storm we hadn't had, the color of a bruise one shade from healed.

"Now don't be fooled," I said. "Sometimes chaos is not chaos. Do you know what I mean by that? Want me to explain?"

"No," Carly said. "I get it."

"When things seem the most crazy, that's when a strategy will save you."

"I'm sure I'll figure it out as we go along," Carly said.

"Of course you'll figure it out, but I'm giving you an advantage, a heads-up on the rules."

"The rules of war?"

"Yes, Carly! War has rules. The Geneva Convention, for example, says you can't torture prisoners. Damn commies do it anyway!"

"I guess you're right."

"That's why you have me, so that you won't become a casualty."

Carly sat her Talking Crissy Doll in the grass and pulled the string from the doll's back—*Please dry my hair*.

"No playing with dolls today, little Miss Mouthy," I said.

"Okay. Two sides in utter opposition equal war. Commanders choose their squads. Don't take it personally if you get picked last."

"I won't."

"No one can attack home base. It's where you plot with your team."

"Can I stay at home base?" Carly asked.

"I suppose, but you can't win a war by staying home. I'm trying to teach you to be a soldier, not give you another place to knit. You need to put yourself in a position of danger sometimes."

"Sure."

"Both commanders synchronize their watches, and each side will have the same amount of time to find and store ammunition. If you hide the ammo, you keep your firepower secret. Capisce?"

"I ca-peesh."

"War is a free enterprise. If both sides agree, you can trade. Pinecones are the weapons of choice. Two or three small pinecones can buy one big one—it's a strategic thing."

Carly ticked the doll's cord again. *Hi! I'm Crissy.*

"Tell your friend to shut up," I said. "You can carry more of the smaller pinecones, which means you'll have more artillery. The bigger ones take up more space, but you can hurl them farther and that means you can fire from a safer distance."

"Sounds sticky," Carly said. "My mother won't put anything with pine sap into the wash."

"That's what my father's GOJO is for. Are you listening?"

"Of course. I'm asking questions, aren't I?"

"The only way to make a kill is to nail someone with a pinecone—and you can only hit someone when they're on their feet. Once you're hit—you're down, dead—you're a casualty and you have to stay down, right where you fall. Got it?"

"Got it."

"The last person standing wins for their entire army.

This is important. The last person could be you, especially since nobody will see you as a threat." I paused, rolled up my sleeves and pulled on my hood. "Well? Do you have questions?"

"No, I don't believe I do."

We headed to the lot. "Carly, see how our sidewalk is buckled from roots? See these gigantic breaks in the cement?"

"I see them."

"There's nothing in the rules that says you can't memorize the terrain," I said. "I've got these dangerous locations set to mind so I won't fall, so I can run and not have to look down."

But as soon as we got to Helwig's lot, I didn't recognize the terrain. I expected to know everybody, and I didn't. I saw Seth, Timmy, and the two Melechinskis. Irwin and T-Bone Melechinski were known for Levi cords and denim jackets. T-Bone's jacket was slapped with Rolling Stones' lips on the back. I had no contact with the Melechinskis but basic knowledge. They hung around Star Market to smoke. That was their MO. They puffed as if they were getting stoned off Marlboros, and they shouted random things when I passed with groceries. One day they screamed, *Bangladesh*! I didn't know about the bangle chant but Levi cords were okay.

"Patty," Seth said. "You know T-Bone and Irwin?"

"Yeah, well enough, I suppose."

The Melechinski brothers sauntered with their hands in their pockets. They nodded and said, "Hey!"

Then I faced a new guy.

"And this fellow here," Seth said, "is a buddy of mine from Unquoua Academy."

"Deuce," the guy said, and he introduced himself by saying "Deuce" again and flagging two fingers in the air. Pointy boots, doughy-gut, thick eyelids and a Beatles haircut, a strand of beads around his neck—this guy was the dictionary picture of dropout. My mind was blown by the idea that this card had ever been near a school except as a vandal, equipped to scale the fence in those boots. Deuce looked at Seth. He pointed at me. "What's she here for? To guard the ammo?"

"She doesn't play like a girl," Seth said, "and she stays on my team."

"Dude, I'm counting that as your first pick." Deuce said this as if he'd won something—or as if Seth had already lost.

"No shit, Sherlock. She's my first pick," Seth said.

"I draft the T-Bone for my first selection," Deuce said.

Seth picked Timmy, and then Erwin wound up with his brother.

"The deck is stacked!" Deuce said and he high-fived his team and kept two fingers in the air.

"What about Carly?" I asked.

"I'm an odd number!" Carly said. She sat on a long stone we called the tomb, and her doll stood like a sentry. "You guys are squared up without me." Carly pulled the doll's string—*Brush my hair please.*

We'd barely initiated the first wave of attack. I was just past the neutral zone; I'd taken cover behind a patch of thin pines and I didn't see the soup can; I stepped square on it, and fell flat. Before I knew what had happened, Deuce stood over me, fired a pinecone. I didn't cry. I had tears in my eye because I got hit near my temple. I yelled at him, sprung up, and spit in the dirt.

Seth's face flushed. "You piece of shit!" he said. He dropped the pinecones he'd been holding and emptied his pockets of artillery.

"I hit her before she was down," Deuce said.

"You're a liar, too." Seth charged at Deuce. They locked arms, grunted and squealed and croaked sounds, not words. They fell to the ground and rolled in the powdery dirt, becoming a cloud of fight—feet, hands, heads, tangled and too fast to follow—no strategy for either of them as far as I could tell. Deuce rose up. Seth chased and plowed Deuce into a tree and they hit the ground again, this time crackling and crunching atop scores of sappy pinecones.

When the scene slowed, Deuce pinned Seth, sat on his

chest. Seth grabbed a pinecone and shoved it into Deuce's face, crunched it and snapped it and rubbed the cone, shards of crystal sap against his nose. He cranked a fist and hit him in the head, the raw-meat-pounding sound of a punch in the face. I did not look away. Smudged khakis, untied shoe, heaving chest. Seth turned into a dirty black-and-white image, darkest where there looked like inchworms of blood crawling down his cheek, his forearm, his ear. He stood and cupped the knuckles of his hand.

Deuce got up, stepped backed. Seth stood still. They heaved in waves like the ocean. Seth's neck was thick and alive. He leaned forward as if he was ready to go at Deuce again.

T-Bone came over, grabbed Deuce, and Erwin stood by for support.

"Enough," T-Bone said. "Let it go." He dusted his buddy off with big swipes to the back. Deuce responded by pin-wheeling his arms as if he was still agitated. Deuce winged T-Bone in the ribs.

T-Bone retaliated, kicked Deuce in the shin.

"Listen, Ace," T-Bone said, "you haven't seen your face yet. You don't need another beating. Now back off."

Irwin Melechinski held Deuce's arm. "Me and my brother don't want to get involved, man."

When Deuce was left to stand free again, he pressed his nose with the fingers of both hands as if he just found it and snapped it back on. He pointed at me. "I see what kind of game you're playing. It's about that girl. Don't forget to kiss her, Sir Galahad! Cause I want to hear all about it."

"Whoa, you kiss her?" T-Bone asked.

"I do not," Seth said.

"I don't believe it," Deuce said.

Timmy grabbed Seth's arms. The Melechinskis held back the Deuce.

Right before our eyes Deuce's cheeks lumped, pinked, swelled, raised-up dirty cuts with bits of gray-white sap, an injury that needed to get worse before it could get better. Deuce deserved it all, every slug, every one of the dozens of scratches that the pinecone made on his face and nose and lips. I wanted to shove him and keep shoving him all the way out of our neighborhood and out of our lives.

Deuce grabbed the banana seat of his bike and he flipped the kickstand. I walked over as he saddled up. I looked at his face, couldn't say anything. He leaned in, rested his weight on his high handlebars and rolled away step by step.

Seth bent to tie one of the laces on his tan desert boots and victory blazed all over him. The collar of his shirt bore a beautiful tear.

"Did you get hurt?" I asked.

"Nothing you need to hear about," he said. "Well, that's the end of that." Seth stood up and scratched his fuzzy head. "What possessed you to trip and fall? You're never clumsy."

I couldn't think of an answer. I felt nauseated. I looked down at my wayward feet, my new, maybe too-new sneakers.

"I'm outta here," Seth said. He started with a hobble but then he jogged down our street.

"Did you hear that, Carly?" I asked. "Did you hear it all? I'm not a *typical* girl—and then—he blamed me for falling!"

"I heard," Carly said.

"What just happened here? I'm confused. What's going on?"

"Calm down, Patty."

"I don't know what to do," I said. "Should I be happy or sad? I don't know which words to believe."

"I believe the words for me are *never again*," Carly said. "This war of yours has been one grand fiasco! We're lucky the cops aren't bringing us home."

"What are you talking about, Carly? Nobody was going to call the cops. You're old enough to understand."

"I'm not the only one who's sick of your stupid war games!"

"It's called Combat!"

"Whatever you call it—this isn't Vietnam. Mrs. Flanagan has something to say about how you've got everybody fighting—and now a bunch of meatheads are involved, morons who are drawing real blood!"

I felt the bobber in my belly. I coiled crusts and ate clouds of bread to calm my stomach. I went to bed early just so I could whisper the words over and over: *she doesn't play like a girl and she stays on my team.*

The next day, Carly informed me that she wasn't going to Helwig's anymore. Her mother said it was too dangerous.

Sure, the lot was dangerous. Goat-wild grass, shattered bottles, mangy cats, and land mines of crap. But Seth and I had strategies. We raked the glass into heaps of atomic crystals. We outlined our parameters, painted symbols on rocks. We had a pit of stones to hide candy bars we called our rations. We never stepped in crap. Broken bottles never hurt us.

Before each maneuver, one of us agreed to slip into enemy territory, not looking to kill but to find their reserve stockpiles. When we got hit, we fell in a position that left a message to the living: a subtle arm stretched out pointing east, a dead leg with foot aimed at the left woods, body face-up means stash of cones beneath. Most of the time when we got killed we were exactly where we wanted to be.

Johnny and myself – holiday time at Nana and Grandpa Nastasia's home....

Fresh Summer Cuts

The pure and simple truth is rarely pure and never simple.
–Oscar Wilde

When my family happened to see Seth Stein's family, usually in our vehicles, we were all more than polite. We waved and they waved—two cars passing with a flurry of excited hands, a Catholic family and a Jewish family, happy to be neighbors who waved. Sometimes when dinnertime rolled around and my father asked me where I'd been and who I'd been with, I rattled off names: Sheehan, Flanagan, Tomasco, everybody's name except for Seth Stein. I had no proof, but I would have bet my P. F. Fliers that when Seth went home, he did the same thing. I knew what Seth knew—omission was the thinking man's lie. A lot of things were better left unsaid and all things better left unsaid came with secret instructions.

Similarly, our parents never told Carly and me we weren't allowed to talk to Shelly, but we never gave them the opportunity. Carly and I weren't exactly sure we wanted to be friends with Shelly in the first place.

Shelly lived on Pacific Street. My house sat on the corner of Wade and Pacific. We were allowed to walk up Wade Street to where it intersected with Park Avenue, which was a flurry of business: old Gothic and Victorian style houses turned into doctors' and lawyers' offices; gold-lettered shingles swayed out front as calling cards of local professionals. We didn't have the same clearance to stroll down Pacific Street, strewn with multiple family dwellings that erupted less than a block from our house. Pacific Street swelled with the problems of three-family houses too: dwellings without driveways paint-starved buildings, neglected lawns, broken homes. Renters came hand in hand with crime, public assistance and student radicals from the University of Bridgeport, people who brought junk in and never took it with them: warped shelves, gutted upholstery, stained mattresses. Our fathers didn't need to point out how this sprawl encroached upon our neighborhood of one-family sensibilities.

Carly and I figured we knew Shelly better than she knew herself. The girl had just moved into a three-family with a crooked front porch, a stone's throw from a traffic light. Shelly moved in to the first floor, no driveway, no father, no siblings, just her and her mother. My mom had made complaints to the police department about the Passoni's Bread truck—how it randomly appeared on that end of Pacific Street, a commercial vehicle parked in a residential zone, sometimes overnight.

Shelly didn't know that she lived out of bounds. She circled our block on her 10-speed until her gray sweats seemed to wilt into her solid frame. She cased my house so often it crossed my mind that she might have designs to rob us later. Carly and I sat on my front porch, slurped on fudge-pops, and acted oblivious when we heard Shelly's bike ticking around our corner for the fiftieth time. But we watched on the sly.

One day we were drawing flowers and vines with chalk, winding a regal design the length of our sidewalk on the Wade Street side. By the time I realized Joe-Bins had taken off, he'd flung his Pampers into the shrubs and had run halfway down Pacific Street, bare-butt. As he neared the bread truck, Shelly rolled out onto the sidewalk and blocked his path. She swung a leg over, slid off her bike and let it crunch into the hedges. She crouched in front of my kid brother.

Carly and I huffed onto the scene. "Thanks for catching Joe-Bins," I said.

Shelly stood up, pulled her bike from the thicket of shrubs, and got back on. "No biggie," Shelly said. "I was heading to my Karate class." She zigzagged her front wheel. "Why is he half naked? Is he trying to be a streaker?"

"Of course not," I said.

"He's just a baby," Carly said. "He probably has a wet diaper."

"There's no logical explanation for half the things my brother does," I said. I didn't want to share information Shelly wouldn't understand. As we spoke, four of Joe-Bins baby bottles and two pairs of Buster Browns were floating in the sewer in front of our house.

I inspected Joe-Bins. The kid had some berry stains on his mouth but that was all. Shelly told us her name and followed with a story, an episode she called her earliest memory. It was about a boy from kindergarten.

"This boy hit me in the ear with a lunchbox for no reason," Shelly said, and she pulled a few stray hairs back for us to see. "My first eight stitches."

I finally saw Shelly close up. I didn't see the scar and I didn't tell her how dumb her story seemed because I wasn't raised to be rude, and I never knew when Joe-Bins might bolt again.

When the doorbell rang, I snapped the top of my jeans, grabbed my Dr. Scholl's, and flew past my mother in her room watching TV, folding laundry. I shuffled down the stairs, gripped the banister globe at the bottom and I swung with the forces of nature. I was almost thirteen; every day I flew down those stairs like a satellite, with the idea that motion, weight, and centrifugal force propelled me into the front hallway, straight through the door and out into the world.

I opened the door to see Carly and Shelly. Shelly posed on the second step in her Eskimo boots—the color of a manila envelope—one foot wedged in the swirl of our wrought iron porch rail. The fringe dangled at her heel. Obviously the boots were new, and she wanted to show off—like the copy of *Seventeen* she held against her chest. The boots were sort of cool. Her vest was a bit much, a multi-colored patchwork of suede over a sheath of fake fur; her sweatpants belonged in a gym.

"Why did you come to our front door, Shelly?" I asked. "Epecially looking like a Woolly mammoth?" I stepped out on the porch. "Did you tell her to lay low?"

"I did," Carly said.

"Now you've heard it twice, Shelly," I said. "Come up the back, and never ring the bell."

Carly smoothed the back of her long denim skirt. "I told her we're not allowed to read *Seventeen* either. Instead of parading that smut around, why don't you roll it up—at least until we get out of the yard?"

"It's alright," I said. "My mother's busy and my father went to buy lumber. Besides, that magazine's just a good decoy for what I've got."

Nobody asked any questions. I clopped down the porch in my wooden shoes, one step in front my best friend Carly, and two steps ahead of Shelly who wanted to be. They followed me around to the back of the house where I made a stop in the garage. I reached behind a rectangular tin of turpentine, and a tackle box of rusted lures. "My radio," I announced to Shelly before she could ask. But actually the radio belonged to my father—who didn't even know he had a transistor radio anymore. I'd been tucking it under my coat or inside my blouse and listening to what the world was singing whenever the coast was clear. We headed down my driveway with its steep pitch, the chute that splashed my brothers out into the street when no one was watching. Lucky for us, there wasn't much traffic.

"Where are your little brothers?" Shelly asked.

"They're at the hardware store with my Dad. Let's hightail it out of here," I said. Helwig's antique store was as far as I was allowed to go, a single-block away from a dirt lot of freedom. Without Joe-Bins and Big-A bouncing around, the lot was just far enough away to have a cigarette or a séance.

Shelly kept the magazine folded and tucked under her arm. I noticed her T-shirt. I asked her, "What's Aqua Lung?"

"Man, that's Jethro Tull," Shelly said with an emphasis that told me everything and nothing.

"Well, Carly digs Elton John," I said, "and I can't live without Stevie Wonder, very superstitious, you know!"

I hadn't even turned it on when Shelly pulled my hand away and stole a quick look at my Regency shirt-pocket radio. She winced as if I was holding a dead bird.

"That's a box of static, a granny AM radio," Shelly said. "Jethro Tull is strictly FM, and in stereo."

"We don't need FM radio," I answered back.

No one would believe how many strings of perfect music I orchestrated with one crummy radio, four fuzzy stations on the dial—the magic I'd struck between my thumb and the coin-grooved edge. I wasn't just lucky. I was good—the type of thing you know but you just can't say. I never even told Carly how I literally prayed to hear my favorite songs; I had dropped hundreds of M&M's, one-by-one, into the sewer as offerings to God for the chance of rolling the knob and bumping one of my songs. I'd tossed unbitten Three Musketeers bars into Rooster River for Al Green—and I got lucky all the time! I was the queen of the airwaves between WABC New York, and WICC in Bridgeport, the luckiest person alive. I'd hit just the right spot to catch the Raspberries—Eric Carmen singing, "Please Go All the Way…" After that, I found The O'Jays singing "Back Stabbers"—a song that made me want to sashay and spin as if I was on stage in a sky blue tuxedo, and made me want to drum on the hoods of cars and point at strangers—*What they do? They smile in your face, all the time they want to take your place, the back stabbers….*

"I saw these suede clogs at 18-East," Carly said. "Patty, they're out of this world. Side-buckle and fur lined! I'm going to beg my mother."

"Those clogs sound classy," I said, "whereas Shelly's mukluks here are a bit questionable."

"Hey, that's not nice," Shelly said.

"Don't mess with me or my radio, Shelly."

"Fair enough."

"Let's change the subject," Carly said. "We can treat Shelly with a quick tour of our street."

"Okay," I said. "This yellow bear trap over here is the heart-attack-lady's house. Don't even stop for Halloween."

"Why not?" Shelly asked.

"Well, go 'head if you like it when somebody screams at you and bangs on the storm door with her wooden spoon."

"What's wrong with her?"

"Who cares? I just told you everything you need to know."

"This place here is where Seth lived," Carly said. She pointed to the green cape with the black shutters that used to be the Stein's.

"Who's Seth?" Shelly said.

"The boy Patty likes," Carly said.

"I never said that."

"Sounds juicy," Shelly said. She reached over to the shrub outside Seth's house and snapped off a branch. She bit on the broken tip of the twig and exposed wiry blonde shoots.

"There's nothing juicy about it." I noticed how rays of sun shot through the blank windows of his empty house—long, wide beacons with nothing to catch them.

"Oh, come on. Tell me!" Shelly said. She chewed some more on her twig until it looked like a tiny pitchfork. "What's the big secret?"

"The secret is that Seth and his three older brothers used to live here." I pointed. "We used to hang out at Helwig's—up there." I pointed. "Seth's brother, Scott, is in Vietnam. I can't point that one out for you, Shelly." She looked confused.

"Just say it, Patty," Carly said. "You liked him."

"We played Combat," I said.

"Combat?" Shelly repeated. A piece of twig was stuck to her lip like a thread. I imagined her pulling her ponytail around to her mouth, chewing on her split ends.

"*Combat*!" I said. "Like the TV show with Vic Morrow."

"Patty loves Vic Morrow too," Carly said.

"Now, *that's* true!" I said.

Shelly stopped walking. "Wait a minute. Back to Seth," she said. "Was he cute? Did you go out with him? Where is he?"

"No, I didn't go out with him." I ran a hand through my thick, choppy shag.

"Where is he?"

"New house. Two acres. Norwalk. They moved," I said. "It's called white flight, not that the term will mean anything to you." Shelly hacked at the shrub with her pronged stick and scattered leaves like confetti on the sidewalk.

"Seth was cute," Carly said. "His blue eyes and his buzz cut—a clean look, but he liked to wear plain white t-shirts. He needed more color."

"Since that plain t-shirt dude flew off to richville, maybe some new, really cute guys will move in," Shelly said. I turned away from the sun that glared through the window of Seth's old living room, and I plucked a cool dark leaf from the shrub in front of his house. I folded it at the natural seam and pressed until I felt it snap. It had been nearly a month since he'd moved.

Ahead of us stood the chicken wire that bordered Helwig's lot. The wire fence snagged litter like catch of the day, mostly foil and cellophane wrappers. We stepped over the trash and into the lot. Shelly sat cross-legged, leaning back against the gray-shingled building. The weathered screen door behind her featured a wooden panel and the faded 7-Up slogan—*You like it, it likes you.*

Carly sifted through the weeds with her foot, smoothed her skirt, and curtsied into a sitting position. She checked out the cover of *Seventeen* and fanned through it. "I'm looking for the Vidal Sassoon color pullout," Carly said. "'Fresh Summer Cuts.' Here it is. I could use a new hairstyle."

Shelly asked, "Why don't we turn to 'Famous First Kisses?'" She scooted closer to Carly.

"Why don't we look at something real?" I asked. I dropped the transistor radio in the grass, and from the waist of my dungarees, I pulled out a brown business envelope, addressed to my father.

"Whoa!" Shelly said, and she pulled the envelope out of my hand.

I took it back.

"Go easy," I said. "I've got to return this just the way I found it."

"Oh my God!" Carly said.

"They're really doing it," Shelly said. She grabbed the pamphlet.

"There's just no way you'd find that trash in my house!" Carly said. She held her ears and shook her head. "You wouldn't find fishnets or high heels anywhere on the premises, either."

"Face reality, Carly," I said. "Wedges *are* heels."

"Oh, man!" Shelly said. She pointed to a photo from the group titled 'First Tango in Paris'—a woman on top of a man, naked except for her garter belt and tiara.

"Who would let somebody film their honeymoon?" Carly said.

"Don't be ridiculous," Shelly answered. "These people aren't married."

"Take them away!" Carly said.

"Look!" Shelly said. "That wedding veil's bunched up between her legs—they're calling it 'The Milky Way!' This is truly gross."

"Ladies, this is life!" I said.

"Really, Patty!" Carly said. "You don't think this is just disgusting?"

"What's it matter what I think? At some point, this is

what it all comes down to."

"No!" Carly said.

"It's Biblical," I said. "It's the way of the flesh."

I stood up and looked down over their shoulders, at the pictures I'd already memorized—some confusing gymnastics, but mainly, I saw nakedness, the mingling of bodies as a force that two people chose to reckon with together—whereas most of life you bore on your own. Sex: a fact like death and taxes.

"This is more naked than the *Playboy*s I found in the closet at my father's house," Shelly said. "My mother's this type."

"The type to do this?" I asked. Shelly was hung up on the trio captioned 'Love Sandwich.'

"No—not with two men at the same time!" Shelly said. "I mean that she's been married and divorced twice."

"So, that guy who drives the bread truck—he's not your father?"

"Hell, no. That's Steve Mercurio. He ain't my father and it's lucky for him he stopped trying to act like he is," Shelly said. Her sweat pants were still tucked in to her mukluk boots, and she pulled at the matted fur that spilled over the top. "I'll do the sex, just like any other girl but it's gonna be with one guy, no divorces, no second marriages."

"At least you're realistic," I said.

"But someone's gonna pay for my effort," Shelly said. "That one lucky man will be making it up to me for the rest of my life—or he'll be a dead man." Shelly meant business, too. She had already beaten up the paperboy twice that summer for missing the porch.

"Okay, Patty," Carly said. "Forget sounding cool. You don't think about this stuff, do you?"

"Sure, I've thought about it."

"I knew it!" Carly said. "You're so screwed up! You know that?" She looked up mournfully at me like I had just died, or gone to Hell, or told her that we had to move.

"I didn't say tonight. I'm not saying I'd join this naked circus, but there are some facts here."

Carly picked up Seventeen again and fixed her eyes on a random page. "What were you digging under your parents' mattress for, anyway? Why do you always have to make life complicated?"

"You can ignore reality. You'll just wind up divorced."

"What do you mean, I'm gonna wind up divorced?" Carly asked.

"Come on," I said. "Who do you think looks at this stuff? Men—men who are married to women who hate having sex. Husbands get tired of all the faking."

"This ain't fake," Shelly said. "These women like it!"

"Nope," I said. They can't. They're getting paid, acting!"

To let someone know the secrets you carry around in your head—this was the hardest thing to do. I was always afraid if I looked into his Seth's eyes too long, he'd know everything about me. I was careful about the way I moved around Seth because I had a mind in my skin. I knew he did too. We had thrown water balloon grenades at his synagogue, and we blasted the stained glass of St. Peter's. We never talked about why. We'd crawled side by side through the tall weeds and tried to break windows with crab apples. That place where my arm just barely touched his was the most pure and dangerous place in the world. Unspeakable. Sex, that was God's way of rewarding you for being brave, for telling the truth. If you lied or faked, you'd be sad—like Adam and Eve. I just knew.

"What are you saying?" Carly asked.

"I'm saying I will never fake. I won't be doling out the good times like Strip-Poker Pam—but I won't be acting, either."

"Do you hear yourself?" Carly asked.

"Are you saying Strip-Poker-Pam acts with boys or loves them?" Carly asked.

"I'm saying you're being incredibly stupid." I picked up a pebble and threw it to scare off a nosey gray squirrel. I said, "Tell you what. You girls can stay here with your silly magazine." I grabbed my radio, tucked it into the breast pocket of my blouse, and then I leaned down and yanked the glossy away from Shelly. "I'll take this grown-up stuff off your hands. I can hardly bear to think what your phony lives are going to be like."

I slipped the envelope with the pictures back into the waist of my jeans, and while walking home I thumbed the cracked seam of the leaf in my sweaty hand and breathed in its sharp green smell.

The Color of My Bus

I turned on the lights and gasped—a grand piano. It was as if I opened my eyes and found myself arm's length from a walrus. And then my eyes were drawn upward, where framed pictures bordered the room. I read beautiful cursive names: Leontyne Price, Sarah Vaughan, Billie Holiday, Bessie Smith, Diana Washington, Marian Anderson—an army of proud, elegant women in black and white. I was never in choir, never played a musical instrument, but I'd taken class with Mrs. Reeves, upstairs, a mandatory half a year of Music Appreciation (followed by a mandatory second half of Home Economics), and so it felt better than passing a test to look up at the ceiling and recognize two faces: Sarah Vaughan and Billie Holiday.

A formal, statuesque woman with little patience for those who didn't appreciate her subject and an accomplished pianist, Mrs. Reeves was the only black teacher at Assumption. Always dressed in thread-perfect suits of every tropical color under the sun, signature pearls, and stunning brooches, Mrs. Reeves seemed to come from generations of rich people. She kept her hair in a glossy bun. She also wore dentures. I could tell by the s-sounds that trailed her sentences like loose slippers. Only rich people could afford perfect teeth. Mrs. Reeves gave me the feeling she was born for more than just teaching kids. One day during a rained-out recess, kids were sent to bounce around in the gym. Mrs. Reeves let me sit and listen to the same song over and over—"They Can't Take That Away From Me." I didn't know why I kept playing it, the hiccups of the record, bumps of the needle, a voice melting into the phonograph pulled at my sad strings.

It didn't seem strange or ironic, it didn't even dawn on me, that there would be a host of black female musicians looking down on me in a room where we were about to have a debate on whether or not Martin Luther King's birthday should be celebrated as a holiday.

The coolness in my chest I pictured as a nugget of dry ice, a hard yet vague element. I attributed my distress to the weirdness of the room: the glass wall—was it bullet proof? I thought about windows in cop shows, guilty men standing for mug shots and lineups. The other walls appeared to be soft tiles like pillows with millions of black holes. I did not attribute any of my tension to my position—that King's birthday should not become a national holiday. The room, the piano, the pictures all helped keep my mind off the real subject: My parents had suggested the debate to Mr. Norman via a note from home, a note that volunteered me for the side no one else wanted to take.

Thomas Kennedy became my opponent by proxy. Thomas refused to let anyone sign on to his team, and I didn't have that problem. I liked toying with the idea that Thomas and I would engage in a battle of the sexes, a chance to prove that boys in general had no clue as to what girls could do, and that Kennedy, in particular, was sadly mistaken to think he cornered the market on politics.

I had to give Kennedy his due in terms of connections. His three older brothers were local representatives and rumor had it that they were related to The Camelot Clan. Despite my father's views, all those people did was get elected and go to funerals. The Kennedy tree was a house of handsome tragedy. Maybe that was why they were so beautiful. When I cried my nose grew, eyes disappeared, and my mouth twisted into a kidney shape; I had the face of the Hunchback of Notre Dame. The Kennedys were beautiful, even in their anguish. Maybe it was a sign to the country that the world wouldn't see us as hideous or weak if we were forced to mourn in public.

Thomas could be a brutal opponent, though. He was the type who'd run over and punch a girl in the arm when the other boys were just yanking off our wool stocking caps to get us to chase them. Maybe he seemed so ruthless because he was trying to compensate for the epic rise and fall of his relatives. Maybe he didn't want to run for office. Maybe he didn't want to get shot. For as long as I'd known Thomas, I had the urge to offer him my deepest sympathies as often as I wanted to throw him into the pricker bushes.

The debate was scheduled to follow lunch, and I was eager to get both over with. We cleared off our desks and gave thanks. Our seating was ordered alphabetically, but we could get up and sit any place during the lunch period. As a Cascone, I sat at my desk in the first vertical row, the third seat—behind a Buskey and in front of a Donnelly.

While the rest of the alphabet shuffled around with their lunch boxes, I stayed put, as I often did. Maria Vasquez took a seat at the desk next to mine as she often did. When Maria first came to Assumption, she had to formally introduce herself, first in Spanish and then in English. In a garbled sentence or two, she told us her father worked at GE and her mother was a tennis pro from Chile. Her jet hair was striking. In a sea of blue eyes with freckled faces and braces, Maria stood out. Feathery lashes and dark features, she looked more like me than anyone else—and I resented her for it because she spoke with an accent, and I was an American.

It generally comforted me, my certainty that at least I was smarter than Maria Vasquez because English was her second language and she hadn't mastered it yet. But it didn't make sense how Maria ever got into Assumption in the first place. Were we taking and passing the same tests? An answer in Spanish couldn't have earned the same points as an answer in English. Still, I liked Maria for her dreamy eyes, and most of all, because she came and sat by me during lunch. I thought I valued our friendship; I thought it was deep—the way we didn't need to say that much.

I was taking on the debate for social survival—because I was on borrowed time. In my house in 1972, school was an option that my parents wanted to rescind due to radical times. In a class full of liberals, the debate might even jeopardize my quiet relationship with ESL-Maria Vasquez.

I took the Saran off my peanut butter and jelly and spun the dull Macintosh on my desk. I asked Maria, "What do you think of the proposed Martin Luther King holiday?"

She snapped the pop-top off a tiny single-serving can of Vienna sausages and poked at them with a real piece of silverware.

"I dunno," she said with an appealing accent and an open face, and I believed her. She probably didn't understand the question. She screwed the top off her thermos. I watched the steam rise. I smelled hot cocoa. The problem I had with Maria kicked me in the shin. Accent or not, she was like most students at Assumption, a rich kid with too many lunch options.

Questioning the nature of our lunchtime alliance, I balled the crusts I'd peeled from my sandwich and dropped them into my lunch bag. I wasn't sure what we had going for us. I wondered if Maria and I profoundly understood each other, or if we were content to "break bread" together precisely because we didn't.

We filed out of homeroom and followed Mr. Norman—history and science—the only male teacher at Assumption. Sister Beatrice got in line, "Just observing," she said. The second time I entered the music room I felt calm. It smelled of old wood and lemon oil. Students from both sixth grades filled the room, and I was deeply amused by the strange quality of sound. Every bit of noise was buffered. I heard the drag of chairs like there was cotton in my ears. I imagined no one on the outside of the glass wall could hear what went on.

Noises and words seemed to get sucked up almost before I could hear them.

Oversized index cards carried all the facts that my parents rehearsed with me, though I already knew them quite well. I stood to the right of the mammoth piano and recited the opening statement:

"While it's perfectly fine to have a Black-American holiday, we need to celebrate a good man."

Point number one: "MLK is a registered communist." I pulled the paper clip off my notes, produced a postcard-sized photo, black and white, Martin Luther King Jr. in a classroom full of lefties in training to be revolutionaries. "Marking his birthday constitutes a travesty to American patriotism." [Pass photo around.]

Point number two: "He was unfaithful to his wife. He was an adulterer." I had no documentation on that, but the accusation, the flaw in his character, no one seemed willing or able to deny.

Point number three: "MLK preached peace, referred to the Bible; however, riots, fires, and looting followed his so-called peaceful protests."

Bullet: Anarchy.

Bullet: Conspiracy.

Bullet: Would anyone like a copy of *Death of a Nation*?

Point number four: "Supporting themes": A stack of splintered ideas, hard to bring in to a paragraph beginning with States Rights, clotted with details I didn't quite follow. I had to read right off the card—the crutch of the ill prepared—and I resented it.

"Our Constitution is a republic, not a democracy. States rights were denied by radical Supreme Court decisions. EXAMPLE: Governor George Wallace...represented the people of Alabama, who, by their God-given free will," [make eye contact with teacher] "chose segregation, not integration."

I moved on to the closing remarks—which were really headings for other places where I wasn't going: Founding Fathers' intentions...leftist agenda...liberal court...Thurgood

Marshall. I read my final card verbatim and hoped that nobody asked me what the hell my closing argument actually was.

I sighed, looked up at Jesus on the crucifix and the army of black women saints, high on the wall above me. I checked my Snoopy Timex. A good five minutes had passed and the deed was done. I said, "Thank you," but wasn't sure why. In the back row, Sister Beatrice folded her arms, looked in Mr. Norman's direction and gave a tight-lipped nod.

I picked at my thumb and looked at the chalkboard behind me at a line of broken chalk and a contraption: a wooden gadget with a claw—each wire prong resembled a finger, tipped with a piece of chalk. The device seemed primitive. It reminded me of a hand, a hand with too many fingers of the same-size. I figured out the tool was designed to make straight lines for staffs and scales and notes—for people who were learning to read and write music, people who took lessons from Mrs. Reeves. I would have told you, if you had asked me, that I couldn't care less about scales and notes. But the idea that music was another language appealed to me. I had a desire to see the claw in action, to hear all its fingertips against the blackboard.

Silence choked the air. I wanted to sit down. The only available seat was the stool in front of that mammoth piano.

Thomas Kennedy began to speak. I saw him from the corner of my eye. I wasn't interested in what he had to say because I was just trying to take stock. I had done it. I thought I could rest my case, so long as I didn't relax too much because I tended to stand pigeon-toed. And whatever Kennedy was going to say, it didn't matter. I knew the seductive argument. I was tempted to be one of them, the happy, liberal idiots. How often I wished I didn't know about "The Conspiracy against God," the subplots against family and country. It was like seeing an alien. Who could I tell? The average kid just didn't want to know about the John Birch Society, about impending doom. I didn't know whether or not God would forgive their ignorance, forgive them, forgive their parents.

Like Kennedy, they had been duped; they had no clue about the One World Government, or the fact that when the bombs started dropping, southern Connecticut would be the first place wiped off the map.

I heard bits and pieces of Kennedy's speech. "Compassion...Jim Crow...slavery." Pretty predictable, but then he concluded with a question: "Why can't we treat all people as equals—as Jesus would?"

The class applauded and I played deaf. Lucky for me, my skin was dark enough to where, even while my ears felt blood red, I was sure that my feelings weren't showing in rashes of pink—like the blushing McCarthys, Phillip and Andrew— twins so pale Sister said they had built in lie detectors. There was some hooting; that wasn't in the rules. I looked down at my hands, bent the corners of my cards.

Mr. Norman stood up from his chair in the back row as if he was going to answer Thomas, but he didn't. He said, "It's time for us to give a hand to both debaters." After polite applause, hands went up.

We all knew we hadn't had a debate, just like we knew those hands weren't raised with questions for Thomas.

Terri Scully shook her tight white braids behind her. "Who are you to judge a man?" She paused and huffed and began again as if the question was burning inside her for years. "Who are you to judge a man when Jesus tells us, 'Judge not, lest you be judged'?"

I said nothing. Because what can you do when someone brings Jesus into the equation—by name? Like everybody else, I bowed my head at the mention of Our Lord. My mother had included at least one biblical reference, and I shuffled through my deck to find it. Problem with Affirmative Action: 'God helps those who help themselves.' I knew this was about welfare—definitely no ace. I felt the wool of my jumper scratching right through my cotton blouse.

Karen Buckley, a girl with memorable loafers (never a single scuff, adorned with pennies, so new and so polished that they actually looked pink) stood up and asked, "Would you have shot Dr. King?"

"Don't be stupid, Karen," I sniped without thinking. "Would you shoot the Pope?" Sister Beatrice held her head. Mr. Norman flagged his hands up in the air like a referee. I became aware that I was still standing and weary of it. I found a splotch of linoleum shaped like the USSR, and I thought about shrinking down and falling into the hostile square that I imagined as the Communist block.

I looked into my own hand, at the picture of Martin Luther King. He was sitting at a simple school-type desk. He had ponderous look on his face—like every bright student. He looked like a kid, not a revolutionary. I started to think about what I remembered about the day he got shot. It seemed another lifetime on the screen of the small RCA on top of the Zenith with the blown tube. I watched but didn't see much besides people scurrying. I stood before the class feeling that strange but familiar gravity, as if weights I'd forgotten I was holding, suddenly became heavy. I remembered hearing the newsman say, "Martin Luther King has been shot...The Reverend Dr. Martin Luther King Jr. is dead." I stood in front of my class in suspended animation. I remembered other things, too, like watching my folks—how they sat in their regular chairs, the way my father didn't get up to change the channel, the way my mother kept her clutching her oven mitts. They had no comments. They had no words at all. And I remembered my mother let me wear nail polish for the first time, that day, a light touch of pink, barely noticeable but a gorgeous detail. I walked around the yard with my arms out ahead of me and my fingers spread wide. I didn't know how long it took for nail polish to dry. I knew the world was much closer to ending *that* day.

"How would you like it," Terri Scully said, "if all you could look forward to in life was working as a maid, sitting in the back of buses, living in the ghetto with rats and roaches?"

I looked up at the black saints and the acoustic ceiling tiles, debating with myself whether to answer or not. *They* had the maids. *They* had Vienna sausages. *They* had real leather penny loafers. *They* had the yellow buses.

I wanted to remind them what public transit was, explain how I lived in Bridgeport, the city with the ghettos they spoke of. I thought of telling them the reason we didn't have bugs was because my mother rubber-gloved our house with a mixture of products that drained the color out of a bright blue bucket. I would have told them everything I knew — if I believed for one minute that all things were equal, if I thought anybody really wanted to know about the communist conspiracy and our imminent doom.

I believed Terri's question was one that nobody had any business putting to me. When it came down to it, we all believed that everything was God's will. And even our priests never seemed to have an answer for the riddle of inequality. Only God knew why everybody was getting shot, why he made some of us less equal than others, why my father was a house painter and Terry's was a neurosurgeon, why Karen Buckley got the lead role in every single play, why Maria Vasquez got A's in English. No one answered my questions. No one told me why, in all the generations of humanity, I had to be born into the apocalypse and be one of just a handful of people who knew it.

Mr. Norman draped his white-sleeved arm, like the winner's towel, over Thomas's shoulder, and a chorus of cheerleaders chanted the litany: "Thom-as, Thom-as."

I watched my teacher walk the undisputed champion around the piano and across the stage toward me. Thomas's flat-top and sideburns looked freshly trimmed. It was sort of like *The Dating Game* — consolation time — greeting the lucky bachelor who didn't pick you. I thought Mr. Norman was going to ask me to "love" Thomas, or Martin Luther King, or change the world as if it was all up to me, as if I was the one who was keeping us all out of paradise.

Mr. Norman stood between us, gave matching hugs. He left his hand on my shoulder a little too long. "Thomas," he said, "Patricia is not your opponent." Then I thought my teacher was about to ask Thomas to forgive me, to love me —

as if I was a person to be pitied!

"The fact is if Patricia hadn't been brave enough to raise the discussion, we'd fail to learn from each other," he said. "Democracy is a precious thing. We have to nurture it."

I didn't see myself as brave; indeed, my motives for taking on the "debate" certainly pointed otherwise. Courage. Bravery. Corny, stupid words. But I heard them. The axis of my world tilted just a little—but enough to melt a chunk of Antarctica.

I knew my teacher admired Martin Luther King. He believed we should not only celebrate King's birthday but celebrate his life. I was aware that Mr. Norman's views hadn't changed—except for how he saw me and I felt it—a moment of dignity that inspired me to show them more than my script, to reveal something truer about myself. An iceberg inside me was about to come loose. I had the peculiar sense of being almost free and almost lost.

"I know how it feels to be black," I said. I didn't know why I announced it. It came out of me, unstoppable, like forgetting to raise my hand in class or automatically raising an arm to blocking a punch.

"What?" Mr. Norman asked. His hand was pressed to his temple, a gesture that said everything was cool and he was listening, as much as it looked like he was trying to keep brains from falling out of his head.

"My cousin Manny's been calling me the N-word as long as I can remember," I said matter-of-factly. Voices tumbled from pockets of the room like loose change.

"Why didn't you tell your mother?" someone said. Other voices ricocheted, "Yeah, why?" Sister Beatrice's head was tilted slightly.

"My mother already knows," I said. "My cousin Manny does it all the time, whispers in my ear: 'You have a black butt.'"

I said it—I didn't spell it out. Kids laughed.

"Manny's no joke," I said. "He's pudgy, he's mean, and he likes to read. He has an appetite for little-known facts."

"Facts about you?" Kennedy asked.

"Facts about everything—like where to find a mailbox in the middle of Wichita, or he'd quiz you to make you look bad: What's the gross national product of Turkey?"

Kennedy laughed. "So, your cousin's Mr. Jeopardy!" he said. "Who cares? You're making a big deal out of nothing."

"Manny said he researched my relatives, said he knew all about the spoils of war and the conquest of women and the 'secret' history of my relatives in Sicily—descendants from Africa. At first I thought it was all lies, and then I started coming up with theories."

"What do you mean, 'theories'?" Kennedy asked.

"Well, first of all, consider the fact that my mother tries to keep me out of the sun—especially during the summer."

Mr. Norman had a serious but blank look. "I'm not sure I'm following you, Patricia."

"My mother's afraid I'll turn black. She puts lotion on me—skin cream made for airplane pilots, men who who fly above the clouds."

"It's probably just Coppertone," Karen said.

"No. It looks like toothpaste, smells like stuff for diaper rash, and doesn't blend in. I think it's even supposed to make your skin whiter."

My classmates looked at me with what seemed to be genuine concern. I decided not to tell them how my mother said I looked more like an immigrant than my paternal grandfather who was. I said nothing about my parents' ongoing joke that I was adopted from a black orphanage. Even if it wasn't true I wondered why the Patty jokes always centered around my having fallen from an African family tree.

"My mother says it all the time, 'When someone asks you what you are, just tell them you're Italian, and be proud of that.'" I asked my class, "Well, what else would I be? I mean, who tells a daffodil to be yellow?"

Karen swung her blond pigtails as she stood up and put her hands on her hips. She asked, "So, what's your point?"

I looked at Maria Vazquez in the back of the room, hoping she'd have something to say about dark skin or lotion or understanding me, but she didn't. She didn't look like a friend or an enemy. She looked totally confused.

I noticed Martha Cassady, hand half-raised. We were alphabetically close so we'd had opportunities to talk. Martha was not just the shyest girl in class; she was the whitest person I'd ever seen. She barely had eyelashes. Her skin wasn't translucent, which I would think exotic, but see-through like the cheap skirt that required a slip. Poor girl could have been an anatomy doll. We could see the whole map of her. I felt bad and I wondered what she had to share about her affliction of whiteness.

"It's not right," Martha said, "your mother, treating you like a second-class citizen."

I heard kids agree with her.

Somebody I couldn't see yelled out, "So, what are you?"

"What *am* I?" I repeated. "I'm the biggest secret in my family."

"What?" somebody chimed.

"They're ashamed of me." I looked at the Black women saints, rested my eyes on Lady Day. I said, "I'm not a regular white girl. I've got black blood, more than a few drops. I admit it. It's true. It's history. It's science. It's not as big a deal to me but my parents hate it."

"Hold on," Kennedy perked up after a long spell of silence. "You look pretty normal though, don't you? You sit wherever you want to on the bus. You drink out of every water fountain. What do you know about being black?"

I knew it—he'd been sitting back waiting, waiting to take his big shot at me. Martha had generated some sympathy. I was on the verge of some new status, maybe another cause that deserved consciousness-raising. Kennedy wasn't about to let me have anything like a free ride.

He pointed an angry finger. "Has anyone ever burned a cross on your lawn?"

"No," I said. "Of course we've never experienced a cross

burning in our yard."

I looked at Kennedy, and was just about to tell him what he could do with his finger, when Mr. Norman asked us, "Who is normal? What is normal, then? Is normal defined by what we feel? Is normal defined by what we see?" He walked to the front of the room and spread his arms, hands open, palms up. "Aren't we judging each other here? And aren't we judging each other even as we try not to?"

Not a single one of us answered. Sister Beatrice stared at the floor. I was judging that Thomas was a boy who always had to win, that as he cruised through life, he'd throw his own mother overboard as easily as a deck chair, if that's what it took to be a Mayor, or Senator, or whatever he was destined to become. I judged that I'd never fit in at Assumption for reasons spoken and unspoken. I judged that Mr. Norman was the wisest man in the world. I believed he saw me as a person much smarter than my grades, and of course, prettier than my looks. I believed that my teacher had a vision of me that matched the way I saw myself: the injustice collector, the person who nobly embraced inequality because that was the price of the ticket for salvation, the cross God wanted me to carry—just like he wanted Martin Luther King to carry it. It didn't look like things could change in this world—not for me and not for Martin Luther King, *saecula saeculorum*, amen.

I wasn't sure if being a Communist or an adulterer would force God to turn Martin Luther King away, but I hoped, from the sad middle of my heart, that he was in Heaven.

When I got home and up into my room, I took out my rosaries and stared at the crucifix, but I didn't pray on the tiny brown beads. I thought about Billie Holiday and the other black saints. I wondered what kind of church Martin Luther King was the Reverend of, and I wondered if we ever prayed to the same God. I thought about Martin Luther King trying to tell people about his dreams—how they just didn't listen—how lonely he must have been—knowing all he knew—having so few who understood. The world was almost over. If there wasn't a place for King in Heaven, how could there ever be room for me?

I never told my parents what actually happened at the debate. But the following day, Mr. Norman showed me the note he was sealing and sending home to my folks on official Our Lady of the Assumption stationery. It simply said, "You should be proud of her."

Soul Train

When Don Cornelius announced Al Green, I was front row, down on my stomach; the wool rug pressed itchy and hot into my elbows and through my blouse. I felt a sweaty rash dotting across my belly, but if I could hang in there, I could get the music from *Soul Train* on my tape recorder—a sly but brilliant maneuver because my father was right in the next room, converting the pantry into a bathroom. If he caught me, I'd face JUG—Justice Under God.

Right after the *Jackson-5ive* cartoon, I got up from the swivel rocker that squeaked like a pinwheel from the way my brothers threw themselves at the chair at the same time. I told the boys to wait for me in the yard. Instead of shutting off the set and following them outside, I slowly lowered the volume. Anyone who was in the house would have thought that TV was off. I crouched between the gold rocker and the hand-smudged wall where I'd secretly planted my tape recorder, where, the night before, my father watched the evening news unaware of what would unfold beneath his own chair. All I had to do was lift the skirt in back, pull out the microphone, attach the cord, stick the plug into the outlet and prop microphone at the base of the Zenith. The two mesh screens touched each other. I hid the length of wire with a couple of storybooks, an innocent arrangement. One of the claw legs of the radiator dug into the small of my waist and I felt the other leg grind against my hipbone. I thumbed the recorder's volume control to maximum, and I took about five seconds to depress the white play-button and the red record key at the same time so there was no audible click.

Al Green came on stage in a beige three-piece suit and open bowtie, just a man smiling into the microphone. He began without music, with idle musicians behind him, ready to follow. *Love and happiness*...Love was multi-syllabled moan, several seconds long, on and on and then—stop. Al Green grinned in the silence. What is love? Come on, say it. The band waited, I waited, the dancers howled as they waited for Al Green to tell us: *Something that can make ya do wrong, make ya do right*...Stop.

The dancers swooned, howled, called for him to come back to the song. He did. *Love*...He took the sound of the word love...and this time he pushed and pulled it across a stairway of notes. How long can he hold it? Does his Adam's apple move? The dancers howled, almost in a frenzy this time. Al Green smiled like the devil holding an empty microphone. And then his boot slapped the wooden stage: clap, clap, clap, clap, clap...*Love and happiness*...Al Green broke into song and sweat; the band breathed with guitar, drums, and organ—all rhythm—and a brass section from thin air. Sassy guitar licks and somber organ notes. He reached into the air, clutched notes from Heaven, and pulled them down to his heart. His song echoed from the place in him where God had strummed the chord of his soul. Salvation sunbeams and long-waisted women with chokers and halter-tops bounced and swayed in their hip-huggers with neon triangles flared out at their bellies. The Soul Train swelled and puffed, a blue sky background and marquis lights. I hated *American Bandstand*. My body slithered to the music, eyes fixed on the *Soul Train* dancers in their wild clothes, groovin' with eyes closed, without trying, body talk, and I understood, just like I always knew how to dance better than any of those kids, their bodies flinched to the music instead of melting right in. My arms quivered; my elbows burned. I rocked from side to side with Al Green, accepted the revelations as they came to me. I kept the recliner from squeaking, paused the button to edit out commercials. How did I come to have my whole family's share of Sicilian blood? My family thought I got too dark when we bathed under the same sun, but I was not ashamed. I realized my family was. Something in me was breaking free, and I wanted to free my family too. I wanted to tell them about how music sends waves that curl and crash in the center of my body. They would hate me for saying it. In my truest mind I worked out this beautiful plan where I'd tell the most truth I knew: how I realized I was more than a just a white person, even as I was less a black person. My heart beat somewhere in between, and I accepted the burden of this because I was inspired by God, and people never understand, but maybe my family wouldn't be afraid that there was anything wrong with them. If they knew I didn't fit, if they knew I moved and grooved and felt things more, if they knew I'd suffered more than they had, they'd realize I was closer to God. I was beloved, and the sex dance feeling was how God blessed me, and then maybe they could learn to love everybody including me. They'd realize how smart I was, and they'd celebrate Martin Luther King's birthday, and my friends wouldn't call me a pervert for the way I danced, and everyone would see how God had loved me all along, ever since that miracle in second grade when he made Father Ryan choose my name from the entire school as the one who'd crown the Blessed Mother on May Day—and then the second miracle happened when mother helped me make the crown of fresh flowers—but the flowers wilted and I cried but when I stood on the ladder to crown Our Lady—the flowers had turned brand new again. And I could tell everyone about my most amazing trip—when Jesus took me through the rings of the solar system because he knew I wanted to be the first woman in space and something broke in me when I realized I wasn't going to get into NASA. My parents would be proud when our priest asked me to come up to the pulpit and tell these stories like new scriptures, and I'd be a famous character from the Bible, and I'd heal people with my poems. My friends would be my disciples, and the boy I liked would leave his family's new house and move back into his old house next door to be by my side, and I wouldn't have to live in secret, or die a painful and agonizing death to get to heaven like the rest of the saints. All my fear and loneliness and shame boarded that visionary train and rode the rails until sadness turned into an epiphany of freedom, the one true joy that I was sure would last for eternity, or for the rest of my life, or until my father steamed out of the gutted pantry with a sliver in his hand.

My father marched out to the backyard with my tape recorder and a hammer. I watched him from my bedroom window. When it was done, I followed the lines on my wallpaper, Columbus's ships: the Nina, Pinta, and Santa Maria, a grid of longitude and latitude and a signpost that pointed to the "New World." I used to hate the nautical paper that was supposed to have been stripped, the walls that were supposed to have been painted so long ago that I didn't care about girlish colors anymore. The sailor motif had grown on me. I thought about all the hiding places ships would have for stowing stuff like a tape recorder or a diary. Behind my headboard there was a spot on the deck of the old Hispaniola where I stuck my old wads of gum.

My father stomped through the kitchen, up the stairs and bolted into my room.

"Here's what's left of your soul train," he said. He handed me a piece of my tape recorder—a chunk of plastic with slits where sound once came out. I studied it, the shape of a triangle and as a triangle it was not damaged. It was perfect, a very significant shape: The Holy Trinity, the food pyramid, the Bermuda Triangle, a flap of a white envelope, a paper football. He asked, "Do you have anything to say?"

I shook my head no. I marveled at the artifact. A triangle was a musical instrument, the chime for Heaven's doorbell. My father said something about time in my room and he left. I barely heard him. Without music and Carly, there was little I'd miss.

Being confined to my room was really the only way to keep my brothers out of it. The boys had flattened the tops and the bottoms to most of my board games so I got out the tape, figured while I was passing time I could fix the broken boxes of Risk and Life and Clue. When I heard my father barrel back up the stairs, I flung everything into the closet. I didn't want to get caught fixing anything. I didn't want to give him any reason to think I might be scheming to somehow bring my tape recorder back to life. I possessed a geometric piece of happiness and I wanted to keep it. He never knocked and he opened with his foot.

"Let me tell you something," my father said. "Someday you'll see who we are. We'll be in the history books, books you'll literally get to write. You can explain what happened to the last of the American heroes. The hardest battles are never the ones fought with guns."

I'd heard the hero/patriot speech before. My father was on a bender—the worst kind—the rant of a man who never drank booze. He spoke so close to my face I could hardly concentrate on more than his teeth. My tape recorder died for the cause and I figured I'd earned the right to be left to my solitude.

"Why can't you just stop talking?" I asked. "I'm sick of it. It's pointless to write the end of history if we were going to be the only ones left to read it. Maybe I should chronicle Joe-Bins' history of bedwetting? Maybe I can track the number of freeze-dried banana chips Johnny-Boy could eat in a day? How about if I follow mother around to see what she might use as an alternative to hairspray?"

"You're not funny," my father said. "But I can show you funny."

"You already busted my tape recorder and kicked my

door. What next?"

"I'm telling you to be very careful—or you'll find out." He left.

For a long time the promise or threat of hunkering down with emergency rations seemed like an adventure, something to look forward to. But I'd come to realize once we boarded that trailer it would be almost impossible to keep things to myself—even in my mind. I decided I did not want to record the history of a few survivors, crouch down in some tin can shelter with a flashlight and a loose leaf binder. *Hero* meant Vic Morrow on *Combat*—living on the front line—not scurrying around in the catacombs. If the world was going to end before I made it to high school, I did not want to survive in a communal trailer in upstate New York with an odd gang of patriots, $15,000 worth of freeze-dried food, and a half-ton of Triticale wheat packed in 50-pound sacks. I wanted to be part of the last human chain, humbly sheltered in the genuine fall-out cellar at Assumption like we'd practiced, my head ducked, hair splayed on the cool floor, hands holding the gritty heels of the kid in front of me, feeling the comfort of someone clinging to my ankle as they too, braced for oblivion.

And I wanted to play kick-ball, and cat's cradle. Those were things you couldn't do by yourself or holed-up with bouncing baby brothers. Boys—not my brothers, but real boys—were never least on my list. Even before Seth, I entertained the fantasy that Shawn Donnelly (lumberjack-plaid pea coat) would yank my hat off and run. I'd have to chase him the length of the playground, down to the faculty parking lot, to Mr. Norman's metallic blue Mustang Mach I. Shawn had freckles on top of freckles, splatters of color like Ovaltine across his nose, dotting off to his cheeks. We'd stand there awed by horsepower, mag wheels and a killer grill. I'd punch Shawn in the arm and snatch my hat back before he knew what hit him. You can't find *that* type of happiness while grinding Triticale for your daily bread.

As days went by, my parents acquired a TV tray of

literature from various religious academies and programs for alternative education, including the Reverend Lindstrom Home Study Course. I took solace in my room. I took stock: trolls, photos, and skeleton keys. And I had a diary—a refugee among poor math scores and a lip gloss too dangerous to keep— but I kept these things and the tape recorder triangle, in a shoe box under my bed—not hidden but not advertised. When we got word to head to the hills, I'd grab that box, a bag of clothes. I always believed I was the luckiest person who ever lived. In this case, my father spared me the task of sneaking out to the garbage can to sift for mementos. The significance of possession was lost to him. I thumbed the sharp plastic edges of the triangle and traced the smooth, unbroken side.

I knew hope was abstract. And also knew hope could be hammered into a hard fact—a tangible, triangle-shaped piece of happiness. Hope was something my father knew absolutely nothing about. I thought it was lucky for me.

Bamboozle

Bridgeport, Connecticut, was a place where an ice storm wasn't going to ruin anybody's day. The sky dumped six fluffy inches on top of snow that had already piled, thawed, and frozen again, just another day of angel cake over icing, but it was Saturday, so nobody even missed school. I bundled up and made my way across the street. All I needed to do to keep from falling was never lift my boots off the ground. I slid like a cross-country skier and let the snow plow up my leg in my shuffle to Carly's house for a long winter's day of Scrabble.

The back of the Sheehan's house was hidden, as nice houses in Bridgeport tended to be, behind manicured shrubs, mature trees, and a dark 8-foot fence with pointy fort-like pickets. Our backyards faced each other with a street between, so when I headed over to Carly's house, I came up her driveway. The garage was open, and I saw Mr. Sheehan with the hoods propped on both his Ford station wagon and his decrepit Ford Falcon. He whistled the "Colonel Bogey March" from *Bridge On the River Kwai* as he transplanted a battery from one vehicle to the other like a mad scientist with two patients and one brain.

"Hey, Kiddo!" Mr. Sheehan said as he looked up. "Like this snow?"

"It keeps my brothers off the street," I said.

He laughed like he so often did when I darted an answer back to him. "Careful on the walkway."

"Want me to shovel? I'll do it for free."

"I'm getting to it," he said. "Thanks for asking."

He saluted me as I stepped up to the screened porch. Two knocks and I let myself in the backdoor of their Mediterranean-style stucco house, and straight into their playroom.

The Sheehan's playroom was a distinctively functional place within a distinctive home: high ceilings, marble floors, arched doorways, and sconce light fixtures—sort of a medieval motif. The playroom struck me as a liberal concept, especially for John Birchers. The designated playroom suggested fun as an inherent right. I chose to think of the Sheehan's playroom as a cultural advancement, and not just for its absence of armored knights. At home we played in the bedroom, or in the cellar but every square inch of house belonged to my father and there was no 'room of play.'

The design of the Sheehan's playroom was also impressive: black-and-white checkerboard tile floor with built-in shelves for games and puzzles. The upper shelves were made of glass and served as a museum-style showcase for objects I considered obscure—a triangle, a miniature xylophone, a gyroscope, and a cowbell—festive marionettes from different countries dangled from pegs on the wall. The room featured a couch, beanbag chairs, tray tables, bins of toys, and classical music played from a grid in the ceiling. The Sheehan's playroom was as dreamy as a page from the FAO Schwartz catalogue I'd found in their mailbox—which had to have been the source of their furnishings. No way they found that stuff at Caldor's. I assumed this enlightened approach to children's entertainment was due to the fact that Mr. Sheehan had gone to college and Mrs. Sheehan was born in Canada.

"Hi, all!" I said.

The playroom fumed with nail polish remover, the lingering scent of Angela's Jovan Musk and Carly's favorite spray, Love's Baby Soft. Sarah sat in her feetsie pajamas with Little Kiddle Dolls in her lap. I hung my coat on one of the many coat pegs, left my boots on the mat. I tossed curlers and barrettes from the couch so I could sit and get right back to the Scrabble game where we left off.

"Smells like perfume and cabbage in here," I said.

Carly called out, "Mom, are we boiling cabbage?"

"No, dear," Mrs. Sheehan answered from the kitchen, behind a restaurant-style swinging door.

Angela came into the room wearing a lavender and lime-green plaid jumper, black tights, and purple shawl with balls of fuzz in the fringe. She squeezed into the couch next to me and pulled up a TV tray weighted by a mirror, cosmetic bags, brushes and creams. Angela rubbed circles of Ponds over her cheeks with a Kleenex and leaned over my shoulder.

"Angela," I said, "could you back off with the beauty cream?"

"*Bamboozler* is not a word," Angela said, pointing her greasy tissue at the board.

"The hell it ain't," I said, pulling out the dictionary. "Lookee here. '*Bamboozle:* to cheat, trick, confuse.'"

"You're making a noun out of a verb," Angela said.

"I let Carly make *Rockefeller* out of *rock*—for a crap-load of points too—not that it's any of your business."

"You're cheating," Angela said. Her white cream had melted, and her face glistened like a buttered turkey.

"Cheating? You never get in the game, but you like to play referee."

"You couldn't get me to play by your barnyard rules!" Angela said.

"And you should know all about barns, Angela, because you're a cow!"

"You're a little moron, Patty!" Angela said.

"A moron doesn't rack up points like this," I said. "He who bamboozles is a bamboozler."

"Your word is not in the dictionary," Angela said. She looked in the dictionary. "Bamboozled. Bamboozling. The only noun I see here is bamboozlement."

"It's implied," I said. "It stands to reason that where there's a verb, there's a noun with an iron fist!"

"Stop!" Carly said. "Be quiet, both of you."

"Tell Fatso to be quiet. I'm playing a game here."

"Shut up or I'm quitting!" Carly said.

I added up my points.

"You're just not smart enough to play by the rules, Patty," Angela said.

"Angela! You can't say that." Carly said.

"I can too say it. She called me a cow."

"You *are* a cow!" I said. "Why else would you people have a cowbell? This is Bridgeport, Connecticut. I'd expect to meet Bigfoot in church before I'd find a cowbell in a place where nothing's supposed to be moo-ing."

"You're stupid *and* rude," Angela said.

"Keep on talking like that and I'm going to take this dictionary and rap your skull with it," I said.

Mrs. Sheehan came in from the kitchen. "Hello, Patty. Would you like a sandwich?"

"Sure! Thanks, Mrs. Sheehan."

Mrs. Sheehan was in her nurse's uniform. Her hair was short, curly, and what they called salt and pepper. I liked looking at her. She was a tall, sturdy woman with a compassionate face, big boxy glasses, a white nurse's uniform, and a pin that said she was an LPN. The stethoscope, syringe, and antiseptic were the tools of Mrs. Sheehan's trade. She wasn't as particular as my mother about neatness, so there was something soaking in every sink and the smell of Clorox to keep you away from it. Mrs. Sheehan was pretty even without trying. She wore a plain wedding band and aspirin-sized pearl earrings. My favorite accessory was her nurse's watch: silver band, full set of numbers, and a second hand on its serious white face. I wondered if she ever said the words *time of death*....

"Ham and cheese?"

"Anything you're having," I said. "Thanks, Mrs. Sheehan."

She turned toward the kitchen door and paused. "What do I smell? What smells like skunk in here?"

Carly said, "Angela, are you trying depilatory cream again?"

"Obviously not," Angela said, "but there is a real stinker in the room!"

"Girls, girls!" Mrs. Sheehan said. "Is that necessary? Must you talk to each other that way?"

Must we? Mrs. Sheehan had a habit of asking questions. My parents cut right to the chase. They named the crime and the punishment: Knock it off or I'll break your legs; shut your mouth or I'll shut it for you. Mr. and Mrs. Sheehan left unfinished equations: How can we make it to church by noon? Is that not your Monopoly board on the stairs? How might you make it up to her? I envied Carly's multiple choice behavior options.

Mrs. Sheehan picked up a cereal bowl with a spoon and a few Rice Krispies floating in yellow milk.

Not even five minutes had gone by when Mrs. Sheehan blazed downstairs and charged by us. She opened the back door and called for her husband. She yelled, "Jim! Get in here."

"What?" Mr. Sheehan hollered back.

"Inside, quick!" she said. She waited at the door and let the cold air fill the room.

"What is it, Olivia?" Jim asked.

Mr. Sheehan stomped into the house and before he had a chance to unzip his bomber jacket or wipe his feet on the braided rug, Mrs. Sheehan grabbed his arm and pushed him ahead of her. "Upstairs," she said. We all stood up. "Girls, sit. Back to your game."

"Is the house on fire?" I asked.

"This is between us and Pete," Mrs. Sheehan said and she hurried to catch Mr. Sheehan.

The three of us left our posts and inched our way to the bottom of the stairs. We heard Mr. Sheehan say, "Spare me the drama and get to the point. Where did you get it?" We didn't hear the reply

"What does Pete got?" I whispered.

"They probably found his fireworks," Angela said. She hugged herself with her shawl and headed back toward the couch.

The event in Pete's room was hard to decipher beyond the high-pitched panic in Mrs. Sheehan's voice. Mr. Sheehan's words were blunt, economical. "When? Where? Who?"

When Mr. and Mrs. Sheehan came back downstairs, Pete wasn't with them—in fact, aside from their reactions, there was little evidence Pete was there at all. If Pete had ever been declared missing and if a cop asked me to give a description of the kid, I'd have said Pete resembled a tiger cub—a strange and beautiful creature with unnaturally green eyes and runny nose. On top of those eyes, the kid wore thick eyeglasses that made him look like an alien—a beautiful alien with allergies. With such a sketchy description, the detective would press for details and therein lay the truth: Pete blended in. You could say he was ignored. Maybe he went unnoticed because he was born into a cluster of pre-teen sisters, younger than everyone but little Sarah. Pete was the type of kid who wasn't on hand when we drew sides, the type of kid who was literally up a tree when parents came looking. I called him the camouflage kid.

Angela, Carly, and I sat together on the couch. Mr. and Mrs. Sheehan stood before us in fragile silence. Mrs. Sheehan bent over a TV tray and busted up solid walls of a jigsaw puzzle—a lighthouse that we'd nearly completed—she snapped off pieces and tossed them into the open box. Mr. Sheehan stood before us, khaki pants, flannel shirt, slope-nose, square jaw, still in his bomber jacket.

"He says he got it on the street," Mr. Sheehan said through his teeth.

"Got what?" Angela asked.

"Reefer."

"Marijuana," Mrs. Sheehan said.

"What street?" I said.

"That's what I'm asking," Mr. Sheehan said.

"I haven't got the slightest idea," I said.

"Where in this neighborhood do you go to find reefer?"

"We don't know," I said.

"We're trying to help Pete," Mrs. Sheehan said, and she stuffed her hands into her white pockets.

"You've got nothing more to tell me?" Mr. Sheehan asked.

"No. I don't know anything," I said. Mr. Sheehan stared at me. I didn't know what he wanted to hear, but whatever it was, he hadn't heard it yet.

"You're the eldest of all these kids," Mr. Sheehan said.

"I know how to get cigarettes," I said. "But I don't know anything about drugs. I know nothing about marijuana, and to tell you the truth, I hardly know Pete."

Mrs. Sheehan put a hand on my shoulder and looked at her husband. She said, "Jim, that's enough."

I watched Sarah, young enough to enjoy brushing the plumb-colored hair of her miniature doll. Carly, Angela, and I were shackled to each other by the fact that we were clueless in a different way. Pete the alien had been finding his way past Wood Avenue to parts unknown and in that way, he had bamboozled all of us. I wasn't sure if I admired or resented him for it.

Mr. Sheehan cased the room, slid books off the shelves, and shoved them back. He stopped and rubbed his temples. He stepped back from the shelves and stumbled on one of the kids' galoshes. He picked it up, opened the back door, and threw it outside. He swung the door open wide and proceeded to throw every single shoe and boot out into the yard, one at a time. When he emptied one basket, he grabbed the other: sneakers, slippers, sandals—everything four kids could wear on their feet in a city of four seasons— rapid fire off the porch and into the snow where they settled into the silent cloud, mostly invisible except for a tongue, toe, or heel.

My fur-lined pull-on boots stood alone.

Mr. Sheehan cuffed up his sleeves and pointed to the door. "Now you people get out there and pick up every one of your God-forsaken shoes," he said. He walked out of the room and headed upstairs.

Catherine's feet were in fleece pajamas; Carly and Angela wore socks. Mrs. Sheehan stood in marshmallow nurse shoes—I sprung up from my spot on the sofa.

"I can do this," I said. I punched my fists into the sleeves of my parka and kicked into my boots. "I'll scoop 'em up before he comes back." I took an empty basket and ran out to the yard. Mrs. Sheehan held Sarah in her arms, and they all followed me to the screened porch and watched me retrieve their shoes.

I spread newspaper on the floor beneath each basket and sat down on the couch with the minor puddles I'd dragged in. Carly and Angela were crying.

"That was sort of like an Easter egg hunt," I said.

"Patty, this is no joke," Carly said. "My parents were already talking about sending him to military school and that's a life sentence for Pete."

"You know, my mother's latest JBS recruit is a detective with the Bridgeport Police Department," I said. "We can't let this mess slip out."

Angela asked, "Why don't you just stop talking?"

I was haunted, not just for thinking about where Pete might be going, but for not knowing where he had been. Who was Pete? Who were these people with drugs?

Angela blew her nose a couple of times, and then she balled up her used tissue and stuffed it back into the box of Kleenex.

I never expected Mr. and Mrs. Sheehan to arrange for a man of the cloth to come and talk to Pete. For one thing, there were so few religious figures our parents trusted. Father Delmonico had passed away in the same house where we'd gone to hear him offer up Traditional Latin Mass in his basement. Father Carleton became our spiritual leader after that, and he offered up Mass in the basement of someone who lived in Sandy Hook, but rumor had it that Father Carlton went to PA to go to AA.

Whenever my parents whispered, I listened in. I thought I heard my mother say the Sheehans had been to a Greek Orthodox Church and that they met with a Presbyterian who agreed to be a Good Samaritan and make a home visit. I told Carly what I'd heard and she said her parents consulted with an Iranian, interviewed an Anglican, and settled on a Unitarian. Our parents decided it would be good to have both our families on hand to witness the event, what Carly expressed to me as "Pete's reckoning."

"Reckoning?" I repeated. "Is this guy from the south?"

"I don't know," Carly said. "But that's exactly what my mother called it."

"What if this Unitarian Reckoning involves speaking in tongues and playing with fire or dancing with snakes? Shouldn't somebody prepare us?"

"I don't know, Patty," Carly said, "but think of how Pete feels."

I hadn't.

I'd always assumed all branches of Christianity were lesser tiers of Catholicism, and they were somehow valid in God's eyes as long as they said the Mass in Latin. Other denominations were specializations, for special-needs groups. Greek Orthodox, for example, was obviously a church for Greek people who were naturally inspired by Pastors who looked like Telly Savalas. I'd never been in a Greek Church, but in my mind, the saints posed on marble slabs; the altar mimicked The Acropolis. Their hymns were hearty like *Fiddler on the Roof* and, of course, after their mass they drank coffee from cups that advertised a 24 hour diner. Greek Orthodox wasn't as perfect as the Roman Catholic Church. God didn't compromise, but He was more benevolent than my parents, so God believed in Affirmative Action.

Unitarian—rooted in the word unit. Had to be the military branch of religion, which made sense if Mr. and Mrs. Sheehan were thinking of sending Pete off to military school. Unitarian must have been the branch of Catholicism that produced Christian warriors cut from the cloth of Saint Gabriel, religious MP's and army chaplains—men who preached around real blood.

Carly and I sat facing each other, cross-legged, on bath-mat-sized throw rugs in her room. We churned out Spirograph designs. Carly cranked out exquisite flowery drawings while I specialized in ringed-blips that could serve as logos for nuclear power. We tried to anticipate the Unitarian's line of questioning. When we heard the doorbell, we bolted to our feet, but we came to our senses and slowed down. It seemed best not to charge into the living room too soon and give the Unitarian any ideas about sinking his teeth into us. I trusted the strength-in-numbers theory that protects all but one member of the herd from the hungry lion.

The Sheehan's living room, with its marble floors, stark stucco walls, and dark ceiling beams was designed for Inquisition-style drama, and the Unitarian positioned himself at the very heart of it. He stood in front of the terracotta fireplace, flanked by filigreed wall sconces. He stood with a claw-footed couch to his left and another to his right. He stood directly beneath an iron circle of chandelier.

A tall wiry man, slightly younger than our fathers, eyes as crisp as an airplane pilot's. He gazed into our parents' faces, looked into their eyes almost too long as he introduced himself. He dressed like a priest, but he wore a gray shirt instead of a black one, and the collar was different: the white space below his Adam's apple was not the square I was used to seeing, but more like a Band-Aid strip.

Pete's scruffy hair over a black turtleneck set him up to look like one of those morose sensations who produced the art our parents rebuked. If attire was part of Pete's plan of defense, I couldn't figure how it would work.

Carly and I sat together midway up the stairs. Mr. and Mrs. Sheehan flanked Pete on the couch. My mother and father sat on the other sofa.

"Well, as you know, I'm Pastor Faust, and I'm here to talk to Pete." He untied his shiny black shoes and parked them under the sofa. "I ask that all of you take off your shoes and feel with your feet. Allow yourself to feel. Feel you're on stable ground and know that each of us is grounded in the goodness of the universe."

Everyone looked stunned but complied. "I'm here to listen to Pete, but I'm here for all of you." He stuck his finger in his collar and stretched it a bit. "Reality is sometimes a difficult thing." He pulled the collar right out of his shirt and left it on the couch like an expired ticket. "But we have to deal with the world as it is. We've got to keep our minds clear in order to do the right thing." The Unitarian unbuttoned his cuffs, rolled up his sleeves, and Pete fell to the floor and onto his knees.

"Dear God, I am ready to accept Jesus Christ as my Lord and Savior!" Pete said, eyes closed, hands clasped. "I detest all my sins because I dread the loss of Heaven and the pains of Hell and because I never intended all this." Pete began to cry. "I ask God to grant me the courage to change the things I can change, and the wisdom not to change the things I shouldn't...."

"—What have you people done to Pete?" I called out. "He's praying like a Jehovah's Witness!"

The Unitarian put his hand up like a stop sign in my direction. He said, "Zip it, Skippy."

"All this I ask in Jesus' name," Pete said.

"Get up off your knees," the Unitarian said, and he waited for Pete to stand. "Jeezuus-shmeezus, son. You're fucked up."

Mr. and Mrs. Sheehan stared straight ahead, didn't shift in their seats, didn't cross or uncross anything. My parents looked at each other, and then at me. I covered my mouth. Carly covered her ears. Angela blew her nose. Pete looked up at the Unitarian.

"You've been getting stoned is what you've been doing, Pete. Quit with this Lord and Savior stuff. You need to stop dopin'."

My father stood up, ran his hands through his black hair,

and buzzed to the back of the room. He leaned back against the wall, arms folded, and ankles crossed—like the stocky, impatient men I'd seen on TV, guys who stood at the door of nightclubs, poised to throw people out into the street with a kick on the keister.

As the storm drifted from Pete's face, my eyes welled up. I became uneasy, vulnerable, and almost sorry for myself. And Pete seemed lighter, almost happy. He smiled like a child, not a sneaky son-of-a-Bircher. He put his glasses back on, a wide-eyed boy who was almost legally blind without them. Innocence filled up the room and found a small place to settle on me.

"It's okay, Pete," the Unitarian said. "Jesus was a good guy, but he wasn't perfect. My message to you is don't ever give up. We're here to live as part of this beautiful world. Now go and love thyself, body and soul. Don't tune-in to chemicals and tune-out on life."

My mother clasped her hands as though the reckoning was for her. She wore a billowing jewel-neck top—so remarkably white at the yoke where it gathered that it looked blue. She held her head up to heaven, eyes closed.

"We are here to fix the world," the Unitarian said. "Each of us in our own small way. This is joyful work!"

"But Minister Faust," my mother said, "There is so much evil. How do we embrace the world?"

"I'm not exactly sure, Mrs. Cascone, but I believe the knowledge is within you, within each of us."

My father cracked his knuckles. "Jim, Olivia," he said, "we're going to give you and your family time alone. Jane…"

As soon as my father said my mother's name, we all took our cue.

I went up to my room, sat on the radiator, and looked down at the happy white totems of snow reaching up to praise the blue heavens. But the other side of the road was strewn with was rubble, dirty nuggets, of peppered ice. In the middle, cars had forged ruts of ice that guided the tires that followed. It sounded as if the Unitarian had survived an Apocalypse already or he wasn't waiting on the same destruction we were. He proved to me that there was indeed a time and place for swear words. And he won Pete a little more time to figure out how to be happy. It was as tiny as a firefly but real, the idea that any of us needed a chance like that. I fogged up my window and drew tiny hearts and happy faces. I heard my parents in their room. My mother whispered. My father didn't.

"Jesus was a good guy? I hope Jim had sense enough not to give a dime to that goon," my father said. "The man revels in the fact that he's a thug himself, and a foul-mouthed one at that. What a fraud!"

I heard the door open and my mother head down the stairs.

My father said, "Looks like you want to tiptoe through the tulips with him, Jane. What are you on?"

SYLP: A How-to

My mother didn't finish high school, but she had me, and she read a lot, and this made her special, which is better than just smart. She read books: *The Naked Communist*, and *Death of a Nation*, and *None Dare Call it Conspiracy*, and many others. She was a Roman Catholic because it was the one true church, and she read everything the John Birch Society offered so she and my father could know the Truth with a capital T. She read the *Herald* and Bridgeport *Post-Telegram* to study the latest smear campaigns against JBS and to find out what the world was up to next.

She became chair of the Bridgeport chapter of MOTORE-DE, the Movement to Restore Decency. MOTOREDE was an ad hoc committee of the JBS, what they called a grass roots organization. A grass roots organization was one where the seeds of knowledge landed on good soil and took root. A hearty strain of patriotism grew right in our own back yard. My mother marched into PTA meetings and town halls wearing political buttons. One said **END THE ERA** and the other said **STOP NOW FOREVER**. Sometimes she wore several buttons at one time but always tastefully.

She recruited members, wrote letters to editors, called representatives, offered literature at the mall, attended public meetings, circulated petitions, spoke to pastors, principals, and politicians. Sometimes her causes led her door-to-door with Mrs. Sheehan, the co-chair of MOTOREDE. That's what it takes to try and save a country. That's what it takes to restore decency, an incredible amount of work from two women with a total of eight kids.

MOTOREDE seemed to fall under the domain of work that was better suited for women. For example, the MOTOREDEs made it their business to force the issue of sex education into the light of day when it snuck into our classrooms under the guise of Home Economics and Health. When teachers sent us home with a benign permission slip, which would've allowed us to see the filmstrip *Growing Up and Liking It*, my mother demanded a preview. She was a woman of action even as she stood dead set against the Women's Movement.

The filmstrip at school introduced the subject of menstruation. My mother found out the so-called educational clip was sponsored by the makers of Kotex—folks with clear interest in getting women to think about their mysterious nether regions—specifically so they could sell them the idea that having your period could be fun. The magazine ads introduced today's women, faces beaming with elation over products contoured so no one will ever know they were wearing them. No one needed to convince me it was all laughing gas. Females were being led to believe they could place their trust in a sanitary napkin—and that they could do pretty much anything they wanted on any day of the month. I would not be duped by Women's Lib propaganda. It was also in Kotex's best interest to encourage women to wear flimsy, vulnerable garments when they were flowing so they would have cause to buy and wear a 22-inch-long pad that promised revolutionary absorbency. I knew better. I could carry a 12 pound roast and a week's worth of canned goods home from Star Market easily, but it was all I could do to get one unwieldy purple box of 40 Supers across the street. The boxes didn't fit in a brown bag and they didn't fit in any bathroom. Disposal was a bigger problem than that. I once saw my grandmother sit my mother down and soberly suggest the toilet had backed up due to the *monthly papers*. I didn't have need of protection just yet but as far as I was concerned, a curse was a curse. A period was part of the biblical legacy of agony promised to Eve at the occasion of childbirth. A bouquet of daisies and a bottle of Midol would not appear on our kitchen table on the day of my period, and I couldn't have been happier. If the pain didn't cripple me, I'd give thanks and be humble about it. The last thing I'd want to do was insult God and my very nature by putting on a shameful performance of power and confidence.

I understood the purpose and the goal for each of the Birch Society's committees. I respected my mother's intelligence and conviction, but when it came to her committee work for Support Your Local Police—SYLP—her role seemed sketchy from the start.

The idea of supporting our local police—the ways and means eluded me. The Bridgeport Police were paid by our taxes. My father chaired the Tax Reform Immediately (TRIM) committee, and he certainly wouldn't go for more dole outs. In addition to our taxes, my parents were asked to pledge donations over the phone, and like most folks, they made modest contributions to support our police, because they appreciated the police, and with the hope that the thank you decal they received in the mail might ward off a speeding ticket or two.

But there were only a couple of ways to support the police as far as I could tell: one, decry anyone who jumped on the bandwagon of alleged police brutality, allegations that cropped up everywhere and which had to be false; and two, avoid disobedience, especially the civil kind. Supporting the police meant leaving law enforcement alone so that their efforts could be reserved for stuff like squelching protest marches and stamping out sit-ins.

Maybe I should have read the literature because I didn't get the tagline that went with SYLP either: *and keep them independent*. Police appeared to be nothing if not independent and absolutely free to do whatever they wanted. No way the masterminds of the communist conspiracy could infiltrate the police department. You couldn't become a cop until you'd been through brutal psychological testing, and so cops were impervious to brainwashing. Police were a brotherhood and they policed themselves. They'd beat the holster off anyone within their ranks who popped pills, or used too many descriptions like groovy, or snuck abstract art into their homes. I couldn't imagine any cop falling for anything like sensitivity training, even if forced to participate as part of a legal judgment against them for beating up a citizen-agitator or two. One look at the TV news on any given night and it was obvious the police had contempt for fads like consciousness-raising, and they had no interest in peace or love whatsoever.

The only support that could possibly be on the police department's wish list was more guns, faster cars, and wider bulletproof vests, enhancements that no Birch Society committee could help them attain anyway. What kind of support did the police need?

When I found out my mother and Mrs. Sheehan planned a trip to the Bridgeport Police Department, I wanted to know why I wasn't invited. I was more than just a good twelve-year old citizen. I was an informant, or I could have been. I already had to watch most of the kids in the neighborhood. I knew too much. If the police needed someone to keep an eye out for persons missing, suspicious or strange, I was their girl.

My mother and Mrs. Sheehan decorated themselves with rhinestone American flag pins and 18k gold plated birch leaf brooches. They dressed in classic navy and hound's tooth. They smelled like Chanel no. 5 and Taboo. I stood in the kitchen, in the crossfire of dual, but not competing, perfumes. They held clipboards that pinched wads of membership forms and SYLP bumper stickers. My mother said they were going downtown to the Bridgeport Police Station to inform the police that they were supporting them. I asked my mother if I could speak to her privately, and for whatever reason, she followed me upstairs.

"Ma, what are you doing?" I asked her. "Going downtown to inform the police that you're supporting them?"

"It's none of your business," she said.

"But just think about this for a minute." I pointed to her clipboard. "What are you going to do with those? Ask the cops to slap Support Your Local Police stickers on their cruisers?"

"This line of questioning is inappropriate, young lady."

"Okay. Then let me ask you this. Why can't I go?"

My mother ignored me, and I told myself I wasn't missing much. They weren't going off on a real assignment. Their trip was just basically morale booster, a form of light entertainment—like Bob Hope going to overseas to entertain bored troops on a safe military base.

When my father came home, he asked me where my mother was, and I told him she was paying a visit to the police department with Mrs. Sheehan.

"What are they doing that for?" he asked.

"Beats me," I said. "Can we come in now?"

"Why don't you keep your brothers outside while the weather's still nice?"

A little while later, Big-A chased Joe-Bins up the back steps. One of them hit the storm door hard enough to bring my father out of his den.

"Anthony's a liar," Joe-Bins said. "He promised to swap three of my cards for one of his cards. Now he won't do it. My baseball cards have perfect corners."

"Don't care about the corners," Big-A said. "I'm not trading any Bo-Sox." He held the card to his chest.

My father reached out his hand. "Give it here," he said. Big-A looked at my father as if he didn't understand. "Do you trust me?" My brother nodded. "Good. I'll hold the card in question. Whoa! *Carl Yastrzemski*! One of the greats! Pennant, triple-crown—you can't trade a guy like this!"

"But he said he would," Joe-Bins whined. "He promised. I've been waiting and waiting. Here! Look at my cards too."

"Okay, boys," my father said. "Hmm. This is a case where

three-for-one isn't always what it seems. You see, Joe-Bins, Big-A is wise to keep his card."

"But…" Joe-Bins said.

"But nothing, son," my father said. "These team cards aren't worth anything."

"But Big-A said he would trade!"

"Look, let's slow down and really consider your offer. It's hard to make out the individual faces on the roster cards and that's one reason why they lack value. Now, let's discuss the clubs you want to trade. The Expos? A team of foreigners! Milwaukee? City of alcohol! The Padres? A Spanish club! Whoa! Who's trying to pull a fast one here?"

Joe-Bins looked totally confused. "I just like the Red Sox," he said. "They're a good team with nice uniforms."

"Well," my father said, "your brother's no fool. Find another favorite uniform. And here's a tip—you want to get him talking-trade? Keep the cheap clubs and offer him some of your Yankees!"

My father gave the baseball cards back. The boys ran back outside to flip or fight over more baseball cards. I followed a good distance behind them, and just as I opened the storm door, my father gave me a long-arm-of-the-law tap on the shoulder. I stopped in my tracks but kept the door open a slice.

"There's no such thing as a free lunch," my father said.

I released the door and let it slam close to my face.

"Why are you telling me this?" I asked. "I earn more of my meals than they do."

"You were out there, a witness to their dispute. You *are* your brothers' keeper, you know."

"I'm not my brothers' keeper. I'm their babysitter."

"Watch it. You're about to run yourself into a ditch."

"I'm just a person," I said. "I don't have the power to stop them from their God-given free will."

"I find it hard to believe you didn't know what they were arguing about," he said.

"Even if I did, I can't break up a fight before it happens!

I'm not the police. I have no weapons to keep them honest."

"Instead of standing on the sidelines waiting for trouble, you could get involved. You could play with them. You might enjoy that more."

Maybe. Maybe not. I was sick over the implication that I had somehow perpetuated a fraud. I never aided and abetted a raw deal. I burned up with the feeling that I needed to announce to my father that I *was* one of good guys.

The SYLP Committee decided to support our local police by building a float and entering it in one of the local parades.

"You're creative! Hop on board! Get involved!" my mother said. I was no hippie, but I also wanted no part of a public display of love for the police. The Birchers had spent several weeks designing and crafting a 15-foot cardboard policeman's cap, painting it and setting it on the Sheehans' old Ford Falcon. The boys liked marching next to a colossal cap and visor, a prop that looked like it belonged on the set of *Land of the Giants*. And I'm sure it was good, clean fun when they stood next to Officer Friendly and threw Tootsie Pops into the streets. I quietly boycotted the entire activity, including the parade.

I came home from school one day shortly after and my mother met me at the door. Instead of changing into play clothes, she wanted me to slip on my checkered maxi-skirt and ruffled blouse—and make it snappy. She wore a pale blue A-line with matching belt and heels; her hair was teased, but not straying. My brothers stood behind her. The boys were dressed in matching shorts sets with suspenders. Johnny-Boy wore a button down shirt and suede Buster Browns.

"What's with the monkey suits?" I asked her.

"Watch your mouth," my mother said.

"Are we taking family portraits?"

"Just change your clothes, and when you come down, be wearing a smile too."

I mumbled up the stairs and got undressed. Before I could look in my closet I heard a police siren. It seemed to come from the back of our house. I threw on the t-shirt and jeans I found on the floor—and hurried down to see what was up. My brothers were already outside, swarming the cruiser; Joe-Bins sat in the cop car. He pressed a button or flipped some switch and set the blue lights into a hawkish panic—not the usual siren I was used to hearing when cops were in pursuit, but the dying howl of a grounded pterodactyl.

"Patricia," my mother said, "this is Detective Buchanan from the Bridgeport Police Department."

"Nice to meet you," he said. The man was tall, in full uniform, including his cap; he had huge hands and a Marine Corps ring—a bald man with a broken nose and a rugged, pink Irish face.

"Are you here to arrest Joe-Bins?" I asked.

The detective looked willfully confused. "Which boy is that?" he asked. He had a slippery grin I recognized from TV cop shows, on sly but familiar characters who said things like, *We can do this the hard way, or we can do this the easy way.*

"Joe-Bins is the runt. You might want to throw him into the cage in back," I said.

"Pa-tree-sha!" my mother scolded.

"Well, he's making us all deaf," I shouted over the siren.

"Joseph, come here," my mother said. She led him out of the patrol car by the hand.

"They're just having a little fun," Detective Buchanan said.

"Of course they are," my mother said. "I've always said when you're lost or in trouble, look for a cop. We don't want you children to be afraid of the law."

"I'm not afraid," I said.

"The police are not the bad guys," my mother announced. "The police are your friends."

The cop looked at me. "I guess that depends who your friends are, eh?" He chuckled. I tossed up an exaggerated grin and let it drop like a yo-yo.

My mother looked me up and down, and I realized my clothes were wrinkled.

"Well, nice meeting you," I said. I turned before he could

try and shake my hand. "Mother, do you mind if I go inside to do my homework?"

"Of course not, dear."

I jogged up the driveway, bounded up onto the porch.

"Patricia!" my mother called out. "Come back here—and take your brothers with you."

"You!" my father pointed. "Get in here."

I walked into his den—a small, windowed-in porch with louver doors and matching blinds. His knotty-pine desk was kid-sized but cluttered with serious business: invoice pads, stacks of bills, Naugahyde pencil holder full of miniature American flags, a crank-armed adding machine, and a veal-colored rotary phone. I looked toward the bookshelf and eyeballed the cover that always drew my attention, *The Naked Communist*—a black silhouette over glossy red—a bald man with no clothes.

"Front and center," he said. My father leaned back in his squeaky desk chair, hands clasped behind his head, with a foot propped on the lip of the open drawer. He asked, "What happened to the float?"

"Huh?"

"The parade float," he repeated. "It's ruined."

I tilted my head to think.

"Rocks, stones—someone's destroyed it."

"What do you mean, destroyed?"

"Cut the shit," he said.

"Vandals are running rampant through this neighborhood. Besides, the parade's over."

"That float was entered in more than one parade. What's the committee going to do? What's your mother supposed to tell the lieutenant? What happened out there on that lot?"

"Which question am I supposed to answer?"

"You're the ringleader. Out with it!"

"Dad, I'm telling you I didn't see anybody throw anything

at the float."

"You're a liar," my father said. "You look for reasons to throw things." He kicked the desk drawer closed and sat up in his chair. "A window gets smashed, a dryer catches fire, a kid needs stitches—every time hell opens up around here, you happen to be on the scene—wiping your hands like Pontius Pilate, coming up with more excuses—more loopholes than a friggin' tax attorney."

"I swear to God! I never saw a thing!"

"Spare me—and stop swearing to God! You like to play semantics, don't you?"

"No."

"Since you're not a liar," my father said, "you must be suffering from selective memory. How convenient for you. Well, keep this under your hat, smartass. The truth always indicts its source. And sure as I'm sitting here, it's just a matter of time before all this finds its way back to the guilty party, the source of all trouble around here—you!"

I retreated to our backyard play set. The rusty spine sagged low in the middle. I sat on the cracked swing but not with all of my weight. It still pinched the back of my thigh.

I did not see the rocks rip through the paper mache brim, puncture the visor, dent the tinfoil badge, and knock out the headlights on Mr. Sheehan's Falcon as it stood in full police regalia. I would have sworn to the police and to the president of the USA that I didn't see it happen—and I'd have been speaking the truth—because I pulled a red bandanna up over my eyes. With or without that blindfold, sometimes I only knew what I let myself see. Selective memory was a law of nature like gravity, a reflex, a force stronger than any kid. It was survival.

I had a conscience. I didn't see myself as a hero or a villain. I'd seen the innocent pay and the guilty walk away. But justice was a force that didn't explain itself —not to my parents, not to the cops, and certainly not to me. I just knew throwing rocks while blind felt good, and somebody had to do it.

Good Car / Bad Car

My father bought a Cadillac Coupe de Ville; I believe it was a '73, a surprise. We ran outside to welcome the new vehicle. The Caddy was stunning, but as I stepped off the porch, the yard became small and my family looked awkward.

My father circled the beautiful beast and snapped pictures. My mother admired the lines. Big-A and Joe-Bins stroked the tires. Johnny-Boy ran his hand across the chrome bumper; he kicked the front tire and stepped away as if he expected it to kick back. We all marveled and stroked the coffin onyx finish, just like in the movie *2001: A Space Odyssey*—the scene when the frenzied apes evolved to a point where they were compelled to paw at the mysterious black monolith.

My father wasn't the type of man who'd lose his head over a car. He put his arm around my mother's waist and strolled with her, acted like a man at a carnival who just won the top-shelf panda for his gal. He said, "Not only does it feel like riding on a pillow, there's more room for the peanut gallery."

"Luxurious and practical," my mother said. "John, it's absolutely stunning."

But my father's sparkling new Caddy shared a marquis with my mother's newly minted driver's license. Since we had become a family of two cars, suddenly the '64 Chevy became my mother's official symbol of freedom.

My father forbid us to use seatbelts due to the fact there were so many bridges in Connecticut, and there wasn't always time to unbuckle. But I found seatbelts can serve to steady the nerves.

Naturally, my mother drove as if she'd been waiting decades: check hair, lipstick, cigarettes, sunglasses, radio, start engine. She barreled the streets of Bridgeport, heavy on the gas, constant with the brakes, and reliant on last minute turns.

My mother loved to smoke, often with the windows up to protect her hair. The way she handled her cigarette reminded me of a veteran movie star who just had her nails done. She'd ask, *Be a darling and open my bag, would you? And see if you can find my wallet, and check the billfold—I should have a twenty. Then, sweetheart, I want you to dig into the side compartment where you should find my makeup purse—sweetie, the patent leather one, not the canvas, and be a dear and see if you can't find the bottle of Cover Girl...oh, darling, is it leaking? Don't get any on that envelope—we need to buy a stamp for it...Honey, watch what you're doing...Sweetheart, there's Kleenex in the front, not there. Look in the front-buttoned, outside zipper compartment. Now sweetie, see if you can read the name of the shade on the bottom of the bottle. Darling, you're a darling, you know that?* Digging through her purse was like shopping in a balled-up blanket from last weekend's picnic: puckered grapes, soggy teething biscuits, sweaty chewing gum, linty tissue, melted Life Savers. I always wound up with tobacco crumbs under my fingernails—and I was happier to sift through a mess than I was when she directed me to try and steer the car while she searched for something.

The Delco radio was the central nervous system of the car and everyone in it. Music made up for whiplash and nausea. But my mother was a button-pusher, a terminal case. When I played music on my transistor, I eased through stations on the dial and once I settled on a song, I stayed with it. Her finger was always on the ready. My mother gave a tune twenty seconds before she punched the music out of alignment, pushed us into a dimension of shrill madness and aimless static void. Dizzy and irritable, I had nothing melodious to hold on to as she sped in pursuit of something better. When she let a full tune play, I almost cried. She liked a song by Blood, Sweat and Tears. She only sang the chorus so I sang the rest for her:

> Hey, I'm a friendly stranger in a black Sedan
> won't you hop inside my car?
> I got pictures, got candy, I'm a lovable man
> and I can take ya to the nearest star.

My mother looked at me and I pointed to her. We sang the next lines together.

> I'm your vehicle, baby
> I'll take you anywhere you wanna go
> I'm your vehicle, woman
> but I'm not sure you know
> that I love ya (love ya)
> need ya (need ya)
> want ya, got to have you, child—

My mother sang the next line:

> Great God in Heaven you know I love you

She was part of my act or I was part of hers. We sang like a team.

She asked, "How the heck do you know the whole song?"

"I know things," I said. "I think everybody has one true song. I don't know mine yet but I'm telling you right now, yours is 'Vehicle.'"

"Why is it you don't have a song?" my mother said.

"I love too much music."

"You know what that means?" my mother said. "The

song's going to pick you."

❈ ❈ ❈

My mother got dressed to drive. She cycled through her wardrobe and when it was time for a milk run, a visit to the pediatrician, or a trip to the post office to buy stamps, she was ready with a fresh outfit. She still polished every crystal teardrop on the chandelier, but I couldn't remember the last time she had asked me to help her get the Venetian blinds into the tub for a bleaching.

My father said she was flying the coop too often. When he really meant it, he told my mother he didn't have the power to revoke her license, but he could eliminate her method of transport. "I can put the car in the *Bargain News* and sell it as easily as I can shove it off the Rooster River Bridge," he said.

"Patty, take your brothers outside," my father said. They argued long after we had to come in and go to bed.

The next day my mother rose early and had French toast and bacon waiting for us. By noon my parents put Johnny Mathis on the stereo downstairs and waltzed upstairs for a nap. We were outside having our own good time until they strolled out to the back porch together. My mother looked at my father the way a First Lady looks at a President—with a terrible, dreamy gaze—as if he's a monument already. I knew they intended to herd us into the car out of Romeo and Juliet style lunacy. Every time they had a fight, we had to do something as a family.

My mother sighed. "Let's all take a drive," she said.

"Just a leisurely cruise," my father added.

"We don't want to go for a ride," Johnny-Boy said. "My stomach hurts. We were just about to go in and start a game of Parcheesi."

"I'm with Johnny," I said. "I've already got the board set up."

Our father kissed our mother on the neck. "Everybody in the car," he said.

The very idea of driving around aimlessly was a recipe

for trouble, and from where I had been sitting for thirteen years, somebody besides me should have known better. We had a long history of family-drive failures. I wasn't keeping tally to be mean, but the way anybody who witnesses an accident or a crime expects justice to be served.

Time was not only ticking on my mother's 'deed' to the Chevy, but our house *was* indeed for sale, "Just to see if we get any nibbles," my father had said. And since our place was on the market, my father thought it was a good idea to drive around to check out the competition, eyeball other houses that were more or less looking to get bitten.

Aside from the fact that we didn't want to be with our parents when they were trying too hard to be nice to each other, any trip in the car could make Johnny-Boy puke. Occasions of throwing up are part of every family's history and passed down punch bowls. Our legend began with the story of the ziti classic. As I recall it, a storm hit the backseat on Easter, 1967, while we were traveling south on I-95. Our mother yelled for our father to pull over. Like a stunt car driver, he muscled our vehicle to the breakdown lane in a matter of seconds. Our mother did her best to steady the kid against a Jersey barrier, to console him, give him room, and the right amount of air. He retched again as soon as our father merged back into traffic. Chunks of pure pandemonium spewed everywhere except out of that open window.

It seemed to me that the Caddy was asking for trouble. It was alive, a complex organ. Its red leather interior was fleshy and plump—all of us swallowed up together—minor rumblings inside of a huge upset stomach.

My father held on to my mother's hand.

"Look," my father said as our car inched along the curb. "A lot like ours but that house doesn't have shutters."

"Our shutters really do make a difference," my mother said.

"And look at this place over here," my father pointed. "I appreciate antique blue clapboard and dental molding. But look how the house is situated—out in the open, on Hughes

Avenue. No sense of privacy—no security."

"Nice house," my mother said. "Unfortunate lot."

Johnny-Boy belched.

"I think I did right by us with that picket fence," my father said.

"No doubt about it," my mother said. "Our fence defines the property, serves as the frame, sort of sets our place in the world. You kids ought to know your father made our house what it is. The second bathroom, the finished basement, the kitchen he remodeled from ceiling to floor, even the white brick walls, do you remember who did all that?"

As citizens of the backseat, we had nothing to say about property, about lots or houses, about remembering or remodeling. In fact, we recalled more about things our father broke than anything he built. I hated it when my mother extolled the virtues of our father. It made it harder not to think about what I was looking at when I saw his calloused knees and swollen fingers. Our father: builder of shutters and fences and additions and so many things we couldn't bear to owe him for.

My mother pulled down the visor to check her lipstick. "It's just that there are so many houses up for sale right now."

The Krasners, the Scarpettis, the Flanagans—everybody in our neighborhood had moved or were trying to get away from the problem called urban blight. The Sheehan's house was broken into. There was a popular exodus from Bridgeport, to towns like Fairfield, Trumbull, and Stratford. Later I would learn that the migration was called white flight.

Wherever our father thought about moving us to, he never told us. We continued to prowl in the Caddy, gawk and squawk at the sudden availability of places almost as nice or nicer than ours.

"You know, before we got married, cruising was the thing to do," my mother said. "We'd get in the car and just drive around...."

"And it was innocent," my father said. "Not the way they gallivant around today."

"Sometimes I'd see a sky so beautiful," my mother said, "and I'd think, this is as good as it gets—this is the best day anyone can have."

Johnny-Boy rubbed his belly. Joe-Bins flipped the lids of the ashtrays open and shut, over and over, while Big-A napped.

"I never knew I'd have so many happy days like today, like the day each of you were born. Sometimes the best days of your life come as little surprises—you have to take care not to miss them. How does it go? *The afternoon knows what the morning never suspected.* Something like that. I'm not sure who said it." My mother lit a cigarette. "Point is—God has been good to us, better than we'll ever know." My mother leaned over towards my father and snuggled his arm. She asked, "Why don't we drive through Seaside Park, take in the ocean air?"

"For what—a whiff of the dump?" my father said. "Hey Johnny, how's your tummy? Still have agita?"

"I feel fine," Johnny replied.

"I don't mind driving, but I hate mob scenes," my father said. "Being gridlocked with idiots. The fourth of July was sheer hell. People too high to know they're trapped and too stupid to get out of the way."

Before we knew it, we were rolling through the big cement arches of Seaside Park. It was a glorious and grand entrance—a road that followed the shore. Of course, my father was right about the garbage dump, but it wasn't much different than the smell of low tide.

It was late March; the air was still raw, so people weren't cramming the place with cars or gallivanting half-naked around on the beach. The sky was a true blue instead of the usual gray smudge that most often hovered over Connecticut. The salty air hinted of spring—a thawing smell—like a body just beginning to sweat. The moisture of spring seeped into everything. Bare branches were buttoned with pearls so green they looked fake. Statues along the esplanade had glistening cheekbones. A freshly painted bench beckoned us to stop the car and sit down. It amazed me how alive the Park City could be.

The University of Bridgeport dorms towered at the far end of the park—mountainous high-rises with sheets hanging out of the windows—sheets that were spray-painted with colorful daisies, big-grinning happy faces, and peace signs. Young people walked around in patched jeans and army jackets, holding hands; they kissed on the hoods of cars, on blankets, and huddled against statues.

The university students used their bedding to make public statements, personal billboards. The idea hit me, ironic and embarrassing even, the reality that they were sleeping together, on bare mattresses. Messages hung out of almost every window and hung far enough to drape the apartments beneath them. One sheet said **MAKE LOVE NOT WAR**. The word **LOVE** rippled in rainbow-colors, and the word **WAR** flared in red letters that dripped like blood. I sat perfectly still. I didn't even turn my head.

"Over my dead body," my father said.

"What?" my mother said.

My father glared at me in the rearview mirror. "It'll be a cold day in Hell before you ever step foot in one of those commie factories."

I asked, "How come you never say garbage like this to my brothers?"

"Patricia!" my mother said.

"I didn't do anything."

"I won't have sassing your father and ruining this day," my mother said.

"We knew this was an ambush," I said.

"John," my mother said, "let's spin around to that place on Grand Street where they sell the real Italian Ices."

We pulled up to Angelo's Pear Tree Shop: A Variety Store. A Coke-a-Cola bottletop the size of a hubcap floated above the storefront—a real seal of authenticity. It was old-fashioned, a place that seemed to have been there for generations, started out as a hardware store, and except for some freezers, hadn't changed all that much and didn't want to.

My father left the car running. He stood outside in a blue-green plaid shirt and beige corduroys and he leaned in through his open window. He asked, "What'll it be?"

I chose watermelon. Johnny-Boy asked for lemon, and the boys stuck with cherry.

"I'm fine," my mother said.

"Come on," my father said.

"No, really." My mother patted my father's arm before he headed into Angelo's.

We watched my father pass a couple of guys who were playing checkers by the door. Other men sat around a table as parched as driftwood. The men weren't old, but they looked wise and weathered, tans, thick cable cardigans and caps I assigned to mariners. They nodded to my father and then looked at us and waved, as if we were all okay.

My mother turned toward us. "Never disrespect your family. It's like spitting into the wind. And I want you all to remember this—no matter what happens, no matter what we say when we fight, your father is a good man. The man you just saw walk into that store, that's one of the finest men you'll ever know."

"Is he letting us have ice cream in the car or do we need to get out?" I asked.

"Don't forget what I say to you here today," my mother said.

"Where does this come from? The Bible? Shakespeare? Gettysburg Address?"

"Did you hear me?" she shouted. "Nod yes."

I nodded.

"John, Anthony, Joseph," my mother said. "You're good boys. You are the very definition of happiness and you are sweet as the day is long. Patricia, look at me. You are strength."

"Great. Can you please stop? We're not in a movie. You can't talk to us this way."

"No matter what our mistakes, we will love each other

until the end of time."

"Are we eating inside or out?"

"Let's stay right where we are," my mother said. "Just be still." Her eyes were glassy but bright. "These are the days, my children. These are the days."

"We know, Mommy," Big-A said.

I would know by the wad of napkins what my father wanted us to do.

Mom and the Caddy. Mom was classy and stylish, even in a kerchief....

On Good Authority

I spent hours mesmerized by the way my Nonnie washed dishes, the way she circled the bottom of each one with a pink sponge dripping with suds. She rinsed each plate under the spigot with a rolling motion—like a 49er sifting out a nugget. My Nonnie filled the drain board with a row of gold-rimmed plates that gleamed like halos. It was simply natural for me to gaze into the pool of suds and to get lost. I'd heard the term, dishpan hands, on TV but my Nonnie never wore gloves. She enlisted a sponge on a handle that looked like a magic wand, so the notion that washing dishes was a monotonous chore never settled in my mind. I was drawn to the busy smell of pink detergent and graceful gestures.

"Before your stories come on, why don't we move the furniture so that the couch faces the TV—the way Grandpa's chair does?"

"Oh no. Your grandfather would kill me."

"What do you mean—he'd kill you? He can't kill you. I think it's even against the law for him to hit you."

"He'd hit the roof," she said. "He doesn't like surprises."

"But this would be a nice surprise."

"There's no such thing to your Grandfather."

"Nonnie, you have to stick up for yourself," I said. "You live here too."

"But it's your grandfather's house, Patty-cake. And I owe him."

"What do you owe him?"

My Nonnie headed toward the back door. I followed her out into the yard and we pinched wooden clothespins and slipped towels off the line.

"Can you keep a secret?"

"Of course."

"I was a young girl when I met your grandfather. I was gonna have a baby and I needed help and so Grandpa married me."

"Okay, so he married you. You cook and clean for him, so it's as fair as war."

"Some things just won't be fair."

"But Nonnie, you have just as much right to move the furniture as he does. Since you don't drive or mow the lawn, he should let you have run of the house. You've got to stand up for yourself or he won't respect you."

"That baby I was supposed to have, it died."

"What?"

"My baby died. But your grandfather stayed married to me. He didn't have to do that. A few years later I had your uncle Joe and then your father."

"You got married for nothing? Oh Nonnie," I followed her back to the kitchen with fresh, clean dishtowels. I leaned into her as she stood before the sink. Silky skin and the scent of Sweetheart Soap, she was the right size for my hugs.

I understood how babies came to be, but my Nonnie had a paperback titled *The Virgin Birth*. I knew I had to read it because if anybody besides the Blessed Mother could become blessed with child by words alone, my Nonnie was that woman. And I was certain the Blessed Mother stayed with St. Joseph after Jesus was gone. God tested women more than he ever tested men. I knew she was a saint but I never knew the details. I thought somebody ought to write a book about my Nonnie.

I asked, "Why did God put you through all this?"

"God's been good to me. Listen, I could wring your grandfather's neck sometimes but I'll never betray him."

"Can't you sit down and reason with him?"

"No," she said. "That's why I have you. This is a secret."

"You're an honorable woman, Nonnie. Even your secret is honorable."

❈ ❈ ❈

I barreled into the kitchen only to forget what I came for in the first place. It seemed to me my mother was always reaching into a cloud of bubbles and coming up with something better than new: a clean jelly jar that would serve as a drinking glass, a handful of silverware that she held like a bouquet. When she skimmed the bottom of the aluminum sink for what looked like the last time, I wanted a miracle. Jesus fed thousands on a few loaves and fishes. I wanted her to come up with one more thing. She dipped down and resurrected —a turkey baster—when we hadn't had turkey. A simple but magical act.

"Mom, I think Nonnie's afraid of Grandpa."

"What makes you think that?"

"She can't rearrange the furniture because she's worried that Grandpa will lose his temper."

"What does she want to move furniture for?"

"For fun," I said.

"George is mostly hot air," my mother said. "He'd like to have the world think he rules with an iron fist."

"He should be nicer to Nonnie. She's had a hard life."

"What do you mean—hard life? What did he do?"

"Nothing," I said.

"Well, living with George is no picnic."

"I just don't know how much more she can take."

My mother looked puzzled. "What in the name of God are you talking about?"

"I'm supposed to keep it to myself. It's girl-talk."

"Do I look like The Marlboro Man to you?"

"You can't let Nonnie know that I told you," I said. "You absolutely can't tell dad."

My mother rested her sudsy hand on my shoulder. "Don't you know you can tell me anything?"

"When Dad calls his mother a saint, he's right," I said. "But he doesn't know how right he is." I proceeded to tell my mother the story of how my Nonnie married Grandpa, and about the baby that died.

"Rose told you this? When?"

"I don't know. Last time I slept over. She's an honorable woman, Mom. She has decorating ideas. It's the least Grandpa can do. Maybe we can get him let her move the couch and buy some new curtains to boot."

My mother raised her hand for me to stop talking. "Not another word, Patricia. For now, let's keep a secret a secret."

But that very night my parents came up to my room.

"Tell your father everything you told me," my mother said. "Word for word."

Of course I complied.

"Your grandmother is a very good woman," my mother said. "But she takes medicine for epilepsy and so she gets confused."

"We have to protect Nonnie," my father said. "She repeats what she hears on television sometimes. She doesn't know any better." My father drew closer, hand on my chin. "You hear? Look me in the eye. It's TV rubbish."

"That story," my mother said. "Don't believe it, best to forget it, and you certainly can't repeat it."

"Or you can button your lip and take it to your grave," my father said.

I listened and gave all the promises they asked for but I never, not even for one minute, believed a word they said about my Nonnie.

A few weeks later, we went to my Nonnie and Grandpa's for our usual Sunday dinner but the spread was more than the table could hold: Homemade ravioli with Ragu Marinara sauce, meatball and sausage grinders on Portuguese rolls from Lisbon Bakery, Sicilian chicken and potatoes. They tossed a salad inside of the punch bowl: iceberg lettuce, plum tomatoes and basil from Grandpa's garden with a heavy dose of Wishbone Italian dressing.

Nonnie wore a simple black dress and a brooch like a satellite with pink and green gemstones. She smiled but looked glassy-eyed and far away. Before grace, Grandpa stood up, a jolly man in a lime shirt and brown tie with white polka dots. "I toast to family and to Ross and I. We solda the house and we gonna move to Hollywood."

"What?" I asked. "When did you become movie stars?"

"Hollywood in Florida, Petty-girl," Grandpa said. "The cold is too cold for Ross."

I looked at my mother but she looked down at Joe-Bins' plate as she cut his food.

I turned to my father. "You told!"

"They're my parents," my father said. "Aren't you going to congratulate them, give them hugs?"

"How can you let them leave?"

I ran from the table and locked myself in my Nonnie's pink bathroom. I blew my nose with rose-colored tissue and I lifted my head as soon as I heard her sweet, unbelievably faint knock on the other side of the hollow bathroom door.

"Oh, Nonnie, I'm sorry for what I've done. Please forgive me for betraying you. Don't go. Tell me how to make it right."

I opened the door and my mother stood in the hallway holding the framed picture of the Virgin Mary. She said, "Nonnie said you could have this."

"I'm not talking, especially not to you." I took the frame out of my mother's hands and marveled at the detail, the gold filligre, the pastel gown, the peach face of Mary, her Immaculate Heart and her eyes that never left me alone.

"I have it on good authority that they both wanted to go," my mother said. "That's what people do. They get old and they need to move to a kinder climate. It's nobody's fault."

I bent forward, dizzy with tears, hugging the picture, wondering if it was all a dream. "Oh, Nonnie."

I accidently said it out loud.

❊ ❊ ❊

"You're blocking the television," my father said.

"Can I take your glass into the kitchen? I'm about to wash the dishes," I said.

"Another day, another plane crash," my father said. "The idiots are still willing to pay for a seat on the Titanic."

"I'd fly on a plane if I got the chance," I said.

"Are you out of your mind?"

"A plane is as close as I'll get to space. Flying is a gift from God."

"God gifted the birds," my father said. "Aren't you afraid?"

"No."

"Well, you ought to be. A whole football team burnt to a crisp! Planes are dropping out of the sky every day. What kind of stupid ass are you?"

"I'm not stupid. Stands to reason—planes fly every day—thousands of takeoffs and landings, thousands of cities. A crash makes the news so that's what sticks in your mind."

"It sticks in my mind because I'm not brainwashed."

"I heard you have a greater chance of getting killed on the road than if you're flying."

"Let me tell you something, genius. I can have an accident every day of my life for an entire year, and there's a good chance that I'll live to see another day. Broken bones, fractured skull, loss of limbs, punctured lungs or kidneys—all possible and possibly fatal injuries. But there is no such thing as an accident on a plane. It's always a catastrophe and everybody dies."

"You can't think past your own fear. But you don't see everything."

"You think you're smart, don't you? You're actually trying to impress me with this half-assed, lame-brain attempt to present an intelligent opinion. Well, you picked the wrong side of the wrong issue. Only a jackass would get on an airplane."

"Normal people, interesting people, intelligent people with places to go travel by plane."

"You've been brainwashed by those ads with the go-go girl stewardesses handing out trays of steak while passengers lean toward the window for their pie-in-the-sky sunset."

"That's a pretty nice image."

"That's a cattle car, you fool."

"I'm tired of you calling me names. This is the United States of America and I'm entitled to my opinion."

"Not in my house you're not."

"I'm just not going to talk."

"So this is it—I guess we've lost you. Oh—*Flying is wonderful, safe, modern...close as I'll ever get to God.* You're a moron and a huge disappointment."

My father stormed out of the room, darted up the stairs and before I could guess what he was up to, he came down carrying my globe. He held it out by the pedestal. He asked, "What do you see?"

"Water, continents, countries? What am I supposed to say?"

"Name this?" He placed his finger on the tip. I said, "That's India."

"Oh, India, you say! You must be smart. Barely had to look. Have you ever been to India?"

"You know darn well I haven't."

"Have you ever met someone who told you they came from India?"

"No."

"Do you have a friend, or friend of a friend who can claim to have seen India?"

"No, I don't believe I do."

"So you're convinced India exists because Rand McNally says so."

"What?"

"You look stymied. Don't feel too bad. Millions of people

believe French fries are good for them because of Ronald McDonald. It's called being duped."

"What does India have to do with airplanes or French fries?"

"You don't know the truth!"

I looked at my father in his crushed velvet recliner. He reached for the end table, the lamp adorned with cherubs and decorated with tear shaped crystals; he grabbed a handful of peanuts out of a small bowl. "Prove that you haven't been brainwashed." He shook the nuts in his hand like they were dice before he popped a few into his mouth. "Say it. Say that you've come to see that flying is not now, nor has it ever been safe."

He popped more nuts into his mouth, chewed and sucked his teeth like my father but he was an imposter. I wanted to grab the receiver, dial zero and plead for help, but who could help me? The Pope? A psychiatrist? The FBI? Who were the proper authorities? I stifled the urge to run out into the street and yell, "—in our living room—there's a man who doesn't believe in India!"

Just Like on Television

My mother often said she'd take me downtown to shop for clothes as a way to pay me back for babysitting and once in a while she made good on the promise. Downtown Bridgeport buzzed with people, all kinds of people who had somewhere to go but liked to look good getting there. Main Street pulsed with the pop tunes that boomed out of cars, and the sidewalks became runways of bold clothes and righteous sunglasses. I especially felt happy being around black people, their tumbleweeds of hair with fancy combs sticking out, their wide lapels, tight pants and platform shoes. The world was wearing cool clothes. Black people wore them better.

    I made a habit of keeping behind my mother a bit so I could practice my walk, a strut somewhere between a sashay I thought fit for the *Soul Train* line, and the hobble associated with the new sheriff in town. I didn't know if I was smiling at every black person, but it seemed they were always smiling at me. Of course walking behind my mother put me front and center for the display of how men shamelessly stared at her, her hair teased for the effect of windblown curls, frosted lips, smoky eyes, silver hoop earrings. My mother's walk called for one foot pointed ahead of the other, hips arriving before her head, a deliberate gesture that was meant to look carefree, similar to the way it took my mother hours to apply makeup to achieve that natural look.

Lafayette Mall boasted a see-through elevator and a splashy fountain pool shiny with pennies. We entered the world of Lerner's of New York. My mother tried on entire outfits and an outfit often meant a matching scarf and color-coordinated shoes.

The fitting room opened like a big empty barn with hot lights and pop music; it lacked cubicles, doors or curtains, a room buzzing with chatty, half-naked strangers. It smelled like antiperspirant spray and sweaty feet. I felt like a peeping tom as I watched my mother. She undressed in public as if nobody else was there. She gazed at herself, front, back, side and head angled for effect, tossed clothes off and moved on to the next set, hit-and-run fashion, and I was always tailing her.

Just when I was convinced the trip was not about me, my mother grabbed a blouse with bell sleeves, and a denim skirt off end racks—all this as we dashed to the checkout. Flowing paisley teamed with classic khaki and denim, and the clothes would fit perfectly. She was that good. Sometimes we stopped at Beechmont Dairy, sat at the lunch counter just for fries and a hot fudge sundae and so more people could look at us.

As soon as we got home we retreated to our rooms, unpinned the price tags, put garments in the drawer or closet so that if asked where they came from, the appropriate answer would be, "I had it." It was a silent understanding.

Like any starlet, my mother never walked into a place—she made an entrance—an entrance with attitude; sometimes her clothes happened to match it. I was thirteen. I was into attitude and special effects. I sprung from the couch and to the bottom of the stairs to watch her slow descent—a vision in suede, leather, and nylon—she moved like a smooth song that didn't need a name. Her body followed her boots to the

U.S. and Them

landing. And I watched her touch down. I couldn't take my eyes off her legs.

Blouse, jumper, vest—the whole outfit was thigh-high. Brushed-silver studs ran the length of the suede vest. Her wide-collared blouse spilled over with ruffles. She continued to glide over the moss-colored carpet, past my father in his recliner.

"In the name of God, where do you think you're going?" my father asked. He kicked the footrest back into upright.

My mother said her lines, "Undercover operation. With the police. Tonight."

"What are you going under cover as, a prostitute?"

"What's the matter with you?" my mother said. She headed to the spring water dispenser with my father in pursuit. She tapped a splash of water in a paper cup and sipped it carefully.

My father crept up behind her. "What's the matter with me? Look at this!" He slid his hand under her skirt. She flinched. "You can't bend. You can't stretch. You're not fit for public, Jane! One sneeze and it's a free show."

My mother pushed his hand away. "You've got a coarse mind and a foul mouth. There's nothing showing—and I'm wearing leotards."

"Leo-tards? That's what you call this sausage skin you're busting out of?"

"Enough," my mother said.

"Enough what?" he asked.

My mother jerked her head in the direction of the room. "The boys are in earshot," she said. "We've talked about this already."

"I don't remember a discussion about you dressing like you're twenty and going out for trick-or-treat," my father said. "What did we talk about?"

"—You know darn well. The sting operation."

"But, Ma," I said. "What is a sting operation? And what do the cops want with you?"

"Yeah," my father said. "Just who's stinging who? Explain

it to your daughter."

My mother shot me a stony look. "It just means that I'm working undercover—infiltrating a meeting of the Black Panthers—with detectives from the PD."

So she was. There was nothing strange about my mother's call to civic duty. She stood as a patriot, a member of Support your Local Police, a Bircher. She *had* told us something about working with the Bridgeport Police Department. She'd mentioned it before, but it never sounded like anything that would account for the way she looked. Anyone could see that celestial forces were about to pull her out the door. That night, she belonged to the world, not us. If I could have stepped out of the daughter role for a moment, I would have explained this to my father. When you see a star about to take its rightful place, the only thing you can do is stare. I wanted to pull him aside and say, Let her go—*she'll be back*.

Of course, I didn't say any such thing. My mind was occupied. The plan to go unnoticed didn't make sense. Her hair was done up in a flip, teased higher than I'd ever seen it before. I guessed that the Black Panthers liked it that way. Being beautiful gets you places. But if sneaking in under the radar was the plan, why was she dressed like a flare?

The plot was bad—but the casting was worse. The first thing someone needed to tell my mother was that she wasn't black. The Panthers were bound to notice. Why would they discuss the location of their unregistered weapons or share the place and time of their next riot—with her? I had a better chance of finding out. I was more likely to blend in with the deep olive complexion and what my cousin called an ethnic butt. If this episode of *Mission Impossible* had been handed to me in a top-secret manila envelope, I would have curled and teased my hair, glazed it with some Afro Sheen, and kicked my strut into gear. If the cops were interested in real skills, I was their girl. My mother's look was trouble, the kind where the innocent bystanders are the ones to get hurt.

The room filled with the smell of Charlie perfume and White Rain hairspray. My mother walked back into the foyer, turned on the light, and stood under the luminous glow of our small brass chandelier. She paused in front of the hallway mirror and pinched the tip of the curl that grazed her jawbone. She dug into her purse, pulled out a frosted lipstick, and patted her lower lip with the wand. She pressed her lips together and said, "It's time to go."

"You're not going out like that," my father said. He paced the hallway in his sloppy paint pants, dingy white tee shirt, and his socks. When he came to a halt, he positioned himself at the front door, hands on his hips, and he trained his eyes on her. "As of right now, your covert activities are confined to this house."

My mother went to the hall closet. She reached for her trench coat; a metal hangar tipped, fell to the floor with a chime but she made no attempt to pick it up. "I'm due at the PD for a briefing in 15 minutes."

"The PD. You've got no business at the PD. Get with the real world! You're not a cop, and this ain't television!"

But it *was* like television. She glowed. My mother slipped into her raincoat. She tied the belt loosely at the waist. She was Agent 99 on *Get Smart!* A brunette Angie Dickenson on *Police Woman.*

"We're going over the plan at headquarters before we stake out the Snake Pit," my mother said.

"The Snake Pit? You're a mother for cryin' out loud."

My mother gave a pat to her hairdo. "It goes like this— the Panthers are plotting. I'm just posing as a new recruit. All I have to do is sit there, look pale and interesting—they'll talk."

"This is outrageous and flat-out dangerous." My father looked at me as if I should say something, but I knew I'd said enough. He lowered his gaze, combed his hair back with fingers, and his voice softened. "Come on, Jane. Let's be serious. You're no detective. You're supposed to stay *away* from those animals. I'll call the detective bureau and tell them to get somebody else."

"No dice," my mother said. She fished around in her

quilted handbag and came up with the car keys. "Don't worry about me. I'll be safe. Detectives carry guns too, and they're going to wire me."

"They're gonna tape a *microphone* to your body?" The question darted out of my mouth.

"I told you," my mother said. "Now is not the time."

My brothers pulled away from the TV and planted themselves in the foyer. Joe-Bins stood by my mother, petting the fake leather of her go-go boots.

"Kids, mommy has to go to a meeting," my mother said. "John, please get away from the door."

My father didn't budge. "Patty," he said without moving anything but his lips, "take the boys outside."

"But it's dark," I said.

"Put the light on in the garage."

I marched into the kitchen, grabbed a package of Oreo cookies, and my brothers followed me.

We were used to being cast out to the garage. That's what garages were for. We took our place among a host of gadgets and were consoled by the fact that most of them were broken before we got there: tire jacks, hedge-clippers, fondue sets, push mowers, everything slimy with grease or cranky with rust. We sat on five-gallon buckets—listening and not. We swiped at mosquitoes and moths. We had Oreos—real ones, not the bargain brand.

Johnny unscrewed his Oreos and ate the filling first—just like the commercials tell you to do. Big-A liked to nibble on his Oreo, make it last. Joe-Bins crammed the entire cookie into his mouth and smiled so that the black stuff looked like missing teeth. I didn't eat Oreo Cookies because I'd read the bag and they were nutritionally void.

Joe-Bins could hardly take his eyes off his feet; he sported new Converse All-Stars and he was looking to put on some miles. He stuffed his mouth with more cookie and twisted into a pose so he could get a view of his sneakers from the side. When he got tired of that, he collected pieces of wood from the scrap heap in the corner that used to be the trim in our pantry. He laid down wooden strips and stomped them the way Godzilla traipses over Tokyo. The wood tinkered, sounded like the harmless tumble of Lincoln Logs.

"I bet you think you can fly in them shoes, don't you, kid," I said.

Joe-Bins raised his fists. "I can run fast as a car," he said. "See my tire marks?"

"Yeah." I said. "Sure-sure."

"I can speed over rocks and pricker-bushes. I'm indestructible."

I flinched when I heard the sound of wood snapping. It wasn't from Joe-Bins woodpile. It came from inside the house. I imagined it was a spindle knocked out of the staircase like a tooth. We told each other to shhh and we heard swearing and glass breaking.

I kept my transistor radio in a secluded area in our garage. I thought about taking it out, coming clean with the boys. Music would've blurred the noise. There were radio stations that were always happy. I could have saved the day. But tomorrow or the next the little finks would rat me out,

Daddy, we listened to music out in the garage.

Whose garage? my father would demand. *What music? Where's the radio?* The my father would begin his own detective work until he wound up beating the transistors out of the culprit. I decided I needed music more than my brothers did.

The boys took turns coming to me for Oreos. "I'm not gonna ration anymore," I said. "I give up." I handed the bag to my brother Johnny. "Now you're in charge. Eat the whole bag if you want to."

His face lit up.

We heard the squeal of rubber when the Chevy took the corner out front. Obviously, our mother had made a getaway. I stepped up on the porch with the boys pushing me to go in. We heard the shatter of more glass coming from inside.

 We scurried back to the garage.

Johnny dug deeper into the bag of cookies. Big-A built a

stack of lids, balanced the cookie-tops on a shelf like a stack of black poker chips. Joe-Bins threw more wood into his pile; it kerplunked when he added scraps of trim and 2 x 4s.

"What are you building over there, Bins? A bonfire? C'mere, kid." I frisked him.

"What are you looking for?" he asked.

"I better not find any matches." I checked his back pockets. "He's clean," I announced.

Joe-Bins held his foot in the air and leaned on me to keep his balance. "See the bottom of these sneakers? Same treads as Firestone tires—just like on TV."

"They're not Firestones," Big-A protested.

Johnny chimed in, "This kid thinks his sneakers are steel-belted radials!"

"They are!" Bins insisted.

"Knock it off already," I said. Johnny left the bag of cookies on a bucket of Spackle, and he studied the shelves. "What are you looking for?"

"I wanna count my lures," Johnny said.

I stood between him and the shelf, placed my hand square on his chest. "The last thing I need right now is a handful of kids playing with dangerous fish hooks, capisce? Mellow out! Go throw some darts."

Joe-Bins stood on an upturned bucket and leaped. He landed on his little pile of wood scraps, shrieked and flapped his arms like a crazy bird.

"Hey! Cut that out before you bring Dad out here," I said.

Joe-Bins yelped, "ow-ow-ow!"

"You're not a bird. Now stop it." I turned to see him hobble toward me on short stilts, stilts made of blocks. I asked, "What the heck? How'd you get 2x4s to stick to the bottom of your sneakers? Crazy Glue?"

Joe-Bins sat down right where he stood—on an oil stain the size of a bath mat. He held both feet up in the air and I saw nail heads. The blocks weren't glued—they were nailed—flush into the bottom of each sneaker.

"Oh my God! Both feet? You little moron—you'll get us

all killed!"

Bins didn't cry. He panted. I grabbed one of the blocks and pulled but I couldn't get it to budge and my effort made him shriek. The nails seemed deep. I thought of an oil change, pictured the kid's blood spouting out of the hole in his shoe.

I asked, "What can we use for a tourniquet?"

Big-A said, "We need an ambulance, on the double!"

Johnny said, "We need Dad." He grabbed Joe-Bins under both arms and lifted him off the ground. Big-A held one foot with its block of wood and I held the other.

I told myself it wasn't happening. It was another simple disaster dream. But Joe-Bins was really hurt. I was in over my head.

We carried him, bumbled our way into the house. Big-A and Johnny began to cry.

My father faced the stove, seemed to be staring at his reflection in the upper oven. We held our littlest brother like a spider or a crab—appendages extended. When my father turned and saw us he appeared stunned. For a moment he looked afraid of us.

"Right here," my father said. He slapped the Formica and slid napkins and a stack of bills to the floor. Let's get him up on the counter." He tore out the laces, pulled back the tongue and Joe-Bins yelled as our father gave a swift pull to each block. When the sneakers came off fluids didn't pour. I looked inside the sneakers and found a penny size spot of blood, same with his socks. I studied the kid's feet but I was darned if I could see the entrance wound.

My father sighed. He said, "We're gonna need to get you a tetanus shot."

Big-A said, "Make that two tetanus shots!"

Joe-Bins sniffled. He held both arms out in a pleading gesture. He seemed to be begging to be delivered from his misery or maybe he needed someone to hold him.

My father kissed him on both cheeks. "You're gonna be okay, son." He descended on the kid with bear hug gestures; he rocked my brother back and forth, as if getting to the emergency room was not so imperative.

But Bins kept squirming. He managed to slip his arms out of my father's hold. His hands said gimme, gimme, gimme...

"Daddy's right here," my father said. "Everything's all right, son."

Big-A yelled, "Say something. Does it hurt?"

"Nod if you're in too much agony to speak," I said. "No? Try!"

Big-A said, "Maybe he wants Mom."

Johnny didn't say anything but he picked up one of the Converse All-Stars my father had just pried off and handed it to Joe-Bins.

The kid sniffled and sighed. Whatever tormented him was instantly gone. I waited for Joe-Bins to say something profound and true because he'd been chastened—nails driven deep into both feet. You can't get much closer to God than that.

Joe-Bins took great care, inspected the treads, traced the design with his fingers, bent the soles, and smelled the rubber. He held his sneaker to his cheek the way a baby poses with a teddy bear and he kissed the rubber toe.

"See, Anthony! I told you! These are the tires that never go flat."

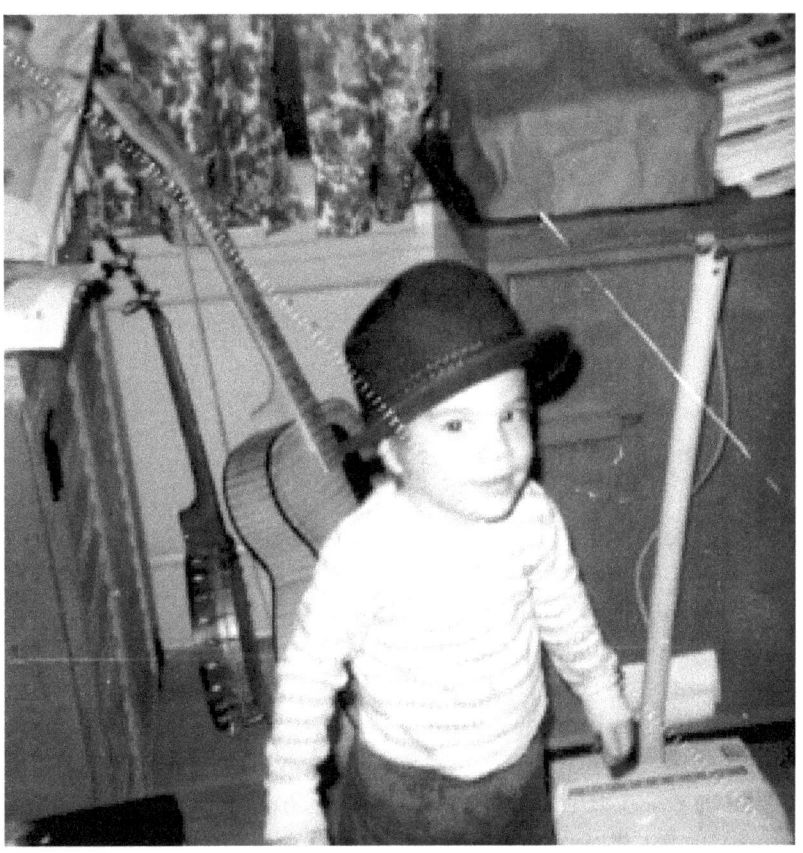

Joe-Bins in Dad's hat....

My Two Favorite Subjects

I didn't know how to read music. I knew how to remember it—sometimes I couldn't forget. If civilization collapsed and if the crumbs of culture were indeed left in my hands, I'd offer the world a museum of musical remnants. I had music on my tape recorder; though my father smashed the first one, I managed to get another. I had Al Green, Marvin Gaye, The Spinners, Stevie Wonder, and more. The words and the pulse to every tune that mattered was in my head, a Rolodex of music for when we lost power and more.

When people suffered and there was no medicine left, I could give them beautiful music to ease their souls and lift them back to life or back to God. If I had just a small chunk of happiness, I would be able to figure out the pieces that fit around it. Any structure could be rebuilt when the right music plays. And because music was the sound of hope, whether set to paper or tape or memory, part of my job was to keep hope in a place my parents wouldn't find it. As soon as we became forced to take refuge, everything we owned would have the greatest value. My father wouldn't break anything. Everyone would thank God that I'd been a little sneaky.

I was a Motown girl, but as the custodian of culture, I kept other genres in mind. I taped a section of *I Love Lucy*, specifically the episode where Harpo Marx plays a harp because most people didn't know the instrument existed in the first place. I taped classical music: Beethoven's 4th Symphony, the Strauss that played in *2001: A Space Odyssey*. I taped the first episode of *Lost in Space,* the score from *West Side Story*, my parents' Henry Mancini—"Moon River" and some Mitch Miller for the boys. I taped the opening to the *Twilight Zone*, the howl from *Chiller Theater*, the 'Control Voice' opening to *The Outer Limits* reruns, shows that truly haunted our TV set and I'd taped the National Anthem, the tune that shut the TV down.

For weeks I chased a song that had already caught me. I heard the end of it a couple of times but then it was gone, out of my head and off the airwaves before I could capture or master it. It wasn't a hit, and since I'd made a life of embracing what the average American failed to see, I grew afraid I'd never hear it again. *Sail on, sail on, sailor, something, something*...It seemed to hit high, sad notes. Could have been the Beach Boys but I hoped it wasn't. I was allergic to soulless music, especially the kind pedaled by white guys whose trademark was a surfboard and the promise to never grow up.

I stretched out in the grass one day and gazed up at an anyday sky and the everyday tree, the big airy maple that shaded the lot behind Hellwig's, just me and my transistor radio. I ran my finger along the dial and I bumped into the sleepy sailor song. As I lay there with it, I thought I could feel the separate cells of myself spreading out on the high seas, *sail on, sail on*...I imagined myself beaming like a newly created bronze, mirroring gold heavens, beloved. Priceless. But the next time I heard the same refrain: *sail on, sail on*...a slashed painting came to mind, a canvas raft, cast out and reeled in by tides and gray skies with no moon, no stars, no shores.

I wanted to understand, figure out the why it had such power, how I could be lifted and crushed by the same line of a simple song. I was certain there had to be a secret. And there was nothing more powerful than a secret—and secrets and power were my two favorite subjects.

I wrote a letter to WICC:

> Can you please send the words to the sailor song? I think the Beach Boys sing it and I'm unsure of the title.

I asked Maria Vasquez if I could use her name and return address; I floated an eight-cent postage stamp in with my request and dropped the small white envelope into the mailbox on Wood Avenue. Every day I loved longing for a sound I could hardly remember. I loved waiting for a message to decode, lyrics as words that would reveal something more than words, something like a treasure map with dotted lines that led to an X that marked the spot where the magic happened.

Someone answered. Someone from the radio station sent a typed sheet of white paper with lyrics.

It was the Beach Boys, my first disappointment—silly music for the endless summer crowd, music from men who called themselves boys. Blondie Chaplin's name sat at the top of the page as lead vocals. Maybe he was less sappy than the Wilson Brothers. I read down the page quickly. *Seldom stumble, never crumble, try to tumble, life's a rumble*...My second disappointment—Joe-Bins could have come up with better lyrics for such a rudimentary rhyme scheme. My skin itched and my ears burned. I crumbled the paper.

"You know what that means, Maria?" I said. "You have to get your parents to let you buy the record. I'll pay."

"I do?"

"We have to listen to it on your record player. I have to do some interpreting. You'll get a record out of the deal," I said. "You gonna help me?"

"I'll do it!" she said.

I uncrumpled the lyrics, took them home, and hid them in the shoebox under my bed.

❈ ❈ ❈

I was nervous before Maria put the needle to the record. First, crackles of vinyl, then the piano. It came back to me, the snippets of joy I heard on the radio. Every possible emotion strung together seemed to pull through me like a knotted rope.

I followed the words as I listened. *I sailed an ocean, unsettled ocean, through restful waters and deep commotion, often frightened, unenlightened*...the lyrics eased me along until the Wilson brothers beamed in with background vocals—the refrain: *Sail on, sail on sailor*...That was it. That was the buried treasure, the wave of power, a choir of voices. I played it over and again.

"Do you hear this, Maria? My God, what a sound."

"They're famous por la armonia," Maria said.

"What? Can you speak American, please?"

"It is nice, pero no muy bueno."

"I've got to hear it again."

"Too loud!" Maria said.

"Well, shut your soundproof doors," I said.

"What?"

"Well, they look like fancy bank vaults," I said. "They close like a vacuum seal, don't you hear it?"

"What?" Maria asked. Then said something in Spanish.

"What did you just say?"

"I said you get on my nerve."

When I got home and back up to my room, I took the lyrics out of my pocket and read them again. *I sailed an ocean, unsettled ocean, through restful waters and deep commotion, often frightened, unenlightened...I rest the waters, fight Neptune's waters, sail through the sorrows, of life's marauders...unrepenting, often empty....*

The song was simply about a broken heart.

Maybe I was the sailor. But if God had given me a choice, I'd have chosen to be a soldier. A soldier takes up arms, touches ground, completes a mission, and comes home to someplace. Sailors are tragic. They see what looks like home, get close, and they crash into rocks beneath the surface of the cruel sea. The sailor is the most heroic figure and appears unassailable until you set your eyes on him a moment too long—and you are crushed with the knowledge of his loneliness. I heard myself singing a lament, the song of a person pleading his case to God, and getting answered with a beautiful chorus. *Sail on, sail on...sailor.*

It meant: make friends with pain.

Stop the crying, and the sighing, and the lying, and my dying...Sail on, sail on sailor...

I sang my song. Blondie Chaplin, Brian Wilson, Carl Wilson.

I signed my name next to theirs.

The Lion Sleeps

Pipe, gun, candlestick, rope, the boys and I sat around the Clue board on the floor in my room on a dark rainy Saturday. We all knew who done it—we just kept guessing wrong so the game could go on.

My father popped his head in the doorway, and then he came around with the rest of his body, a half eaten banana in his hand. "Come fall, you'll be attending Zion Lutheran," he said. He tugged at the peel and took another bite.

"Who?" The boys hooted.

"*She* will," he said.

I noticed my mother was standing sheepishly behind my father in the doorway. My parents had been discussing some form of what I considered unnatural schooling since I started kindergarten, and I could have considered myself lucky that it had taken them about eight years to actually go through with it, but I didn't.

"*Zi*-on Lutheran," I said. I stood up and set my hands on my hips. "Sounds like a church on a hostile planet."

"Oh, Patricia," my mother said. "Don't start with your warped sense of humor already."

"Okay. What do I know about this monument to education? It draws an assortment of kids from various states to pursue reading, writing, and arithmetic—underground—

in yet another church basement. I've lived my whole life in basements and cellars, waiting for a trip to the bomb shelter."

My brothers repeatedly whispered the word Zion, pointed their finger guns at each other and made pulsing ray gun sounds.

"Knock it off, boys," my father said.

"The Zion basement is supposedly modeled after the one-room schoolhouse," I said. "In the twentieth century we call that a nut house."

My mother edged her way into the room. "Or you could choose to say it's a one-room school that models itself like a close-knit family."

"Family? What about the other school kids in this room? Where will they be and why is it you didn't prowl up here and leave details of their future on my doorstep like a dead bird?"

"For now, your brothers are going to stay at their public school," my father said.

"What kind of family does that?" I asked.

"Your brothers aren't affected by school," my father said, "Because, one—nothing much happens in the lower grades. And two—they're boys." My father dropped the banana peel in my wastebasket. "So let's go," he said. He dusted his hands off. "We're heading over to the Sheehan's right now. We've got brochures you and Carly can look at."

Big-A and Joe-Bins sprung right up. Johnny-Boy moved slowly as he balanced and then lifted his stocky frame up from the floor.

I leapt over the sprawling game and bounced down on my bed. Then I ceremoniously propped my pillows, cracked open *A Tale of Two Cities*, and blocked my face.

"Look, Jane. We've got a young scholar over here," my father said. "She's serious about reading. Let her read!"

My mother took a step toward my bed. "I understand why you want to be alone right now." She gazed at the floor and shook her head. "Sheesh. Look how they left this game. We should've had them help you. You always get stuck with the mess, don't you?" She started to gather the Clue cards. "Come on. You and me, let's straighten your room and go to the Sheehan's."

"Suit yourself, kiddo," my father said. "But we're going to be working out the logistics. Books, carpools, things you'll need to know." He grabbed my big toe and wiggled it. "It may interest you to know that the school runs from 8am to 4pm, Monday through Thursday. Your Fridays will be free."

"There are no free days for a slave!" I said.

"Watch your mouth," my father said.

From the window in my room, I watched my parents pop open umbrellas and hustle across the street with my brothers. As they disappeared into the Sheehan's yard, I bounced down the stairs and out to the garage for my radio.

I ran back up the porch and saw Carly from the corner of my eye. She ran toward me, inside her clear dome umbrella. We stepped out of our shoes, shook the rain off, and sat at the dining room table in my quiet house.

"Don't you want to hear the details?" Carly asked.

"We've got forever for the details," I said. "What's that on your hand?"

"A mood-ring. My mother got it for me."

"For no reason? Let me see. Looks like a round tinted window in the center." I slipped it on my middle finger. "It was green on you," I said. "Now it's going gray. Is that supposed to mean I'm getting older by the day?"

"Each shade is supposed to show strong emotion," Carly said.

"At least the Magic 8 Ball tells you something specific," I said. I gave Carly back her ring.

"At least neither of us is alone, Patty. Don't you think about that? When the conspiracy isn't a conspiracy anymore, we get to take shelter together."

"Yeah. That's what they say."

"And we'll have Fridays…."

" —To do what? It's still living like Anne Frank." I turned on the radio and thumbed through the static. "Don't let them lie to you, Carly. Zion Lutheran's more of a concentration camp than a school."

"But nothing's really changed," Carly said. "No matter where we are, it's still us versus them. A happy ending."

I turned the transistor off. "Listen, if the bomb drops or a revolution starts today—I'll be more than happy to hunker down, you and me and this radio here—and we'll start up our auxiliary-power life."

"The new school is just temporary," Carly said. "A deeper level of preparation."

"What's wrong with you? Life is temporary! Preparation for what? Aren't you tired of this already?"

"I don't know, Patty."

"I don't hear a bomb. Do you hear a bomb? I don't see total anarchy. Do you see total anarchy?"

"No, and we should be grateful."

"And we should be in regular schools until there are none left! I want to be above ground and among the living—every day and until God says we can't."

"Patty, you're making it sound so bleak."

"It is! Don't you see? That school is the catacombs, oddballs who don't care about suede clogs, shags, or mood rings. Rosary beads around their necks and oversized clothes, they zombie around like they've already got radiation sickness. We're still alive, in the prime of our lives and we're being signed up for early death by our own parents!"

"You're crazy. What exactly are you accusing our parents of?"

"I don't know. Hurting us! People get divorced all the time for intolerable cruelty."

"Patty, I can't take this. I can't be happy if you're not happy." Carly looked at the ends of her hair as if she was looking for split ends. She never had any. Her hair was long, blunt cut, and beautiful. She wore it pulled back from her face with a wide barrette; her hairline came to a point that dipped low on her forehead and gave her face the shape of a genuine heart, a sad, pale heart. "My head hurts bad. Can't we make believe we're happy? Please? Just be on my side. I'll do anything if we can turn this into a good day."

"I *am* on your side. And you're right. It *is* a good day! We're cool."

I turned the radio back on. "Maybe we can find our new favorite song on here."

"What would that be?" Carly asked.

"The Zion Lutheran school song," I said. "Guess what it is."

"I don't know, Patty." Carly rolled her eyes and put her head on the table. "Just tell me."

"Don't get nervous. I'm trying to make you laugh. Our new favorite song is 'The Zion Sleeps Tonight.'"

Carly laughed and snorted a little. "Taken from 'The Lion Sleeps Tonight'?"

"Yup! Get ready to sing it with me. I feel there's a Zion out there somewhere…."

"What is a Zion?" Carly asked.

"Damned if I know."

We listened to radio advertisements, our own local *Twilight Zone* of insane places and products: a chipmunk-voice calling us to Raceway Park, and a woman's shrill euphoria over a jumbo freezer from Mudrick's. I doodled on the back of a Southern New England Telephone bill, scribbled out big crazy eyeballs, and stick houses with smoke coming out of the chimneys, and drew my name in 3-D block letters.

"We're the only ones that make any sense," Carly said.

She hugged me. I hugged her back. Her hair smelled the way it looked, like sweet maple syrup. Her dress was a hand-me-down from her sister, long and a little loose under the arms but she seemed to rest in a clean bed of daisies, her face over the open field of wildflowers.

Elton John began to sing "Rocket Man." I took the radio out of my shirt pocket, turned the volume up, and stood it on the table between us. *And I think it's gonna be a long, long time….*We both knew the words and we started to sing.

I heard a quick knock and before I could hide the radio,

Mrs. Sheehan had let herself in. "Still raining," she said as if we'd asked for such a report. She untied her plastic kerchief and glanced at the radio. She said, "It's okay with me."

I shut the radio off and put an *American Opinion* over it just the same.

"Listen, girls, I was thinking maybe I could talk to you like the brilliant young women you are."

"Would you like a Coke or something?" I asked.

"Good idea," Mrs. Sheehan said. "You relax. I'll get us all Cokes." I looked at Carly to see if she knew what her mom was up to, but she shrugged her shoulders.

"I need your help," Mrs. Sheehan said from the kitchen. "How can I find ways to be positive about change?" She put cans of cola on the table. "What can we do? We're in this together. Ladies, how can we make this new school work for us?"

"Work for us?" I looked at Mrs. Sheehan and, for a moment, at Carly. She was expressionless, and it occurred to me maybe my best friend was in on this—her mother's plan to cozy us up to the idea. I said, "Maybe I'm only speaking for myself, but the only way Zion Lutheran can work for me is if they close it down."

"I'm trying to speak to you as young adults because you do have a say," Mrs. Sheehan said.

"We're not being treated like adults and we don't have a say, at least my parents are not listening to me. For the record, the very idea of enrolling in a one-room schoolhouse is Cro-Magnon. We should only be stuck with such a setup if there's no modern version of school available. Nobody's going to convince me otherwise."

"Maybe you're looking at this all wrong," Mrs. Sheehan said.

"We've already got the end of the world to contend with," I said. "Why make us suffer so much now?"

"No, you don't understand," Mrs. Sheehan said. "A small, private school can give you an educational advantage."

"An advantage where—at the Apocalypse?"

"Patty, you're smart," Mrs. Sheehan said. She got up, stood behind my chair and pulled my long hair over one of my shoulders. "I don't think you know how smart and pretty you are—that's true for both of you." She came back around and knelt down in front of me. "I see you're wearing earrings," she said. She held the dangling turquoise teardrop and when she let go of the earring, I felt the gravity and sway of the tear.

"These are just clip-ons," I said. "My mother's thinking about letting me have pierced ears."

"They're nice. But smaller earrings would be even more attractive on you—a simple pearl or a gemstone on the lobe of your ear and your face wouldn't seem so long."

"In other words, I don't wear the right earrings," I said.

"Patty, what I'm saying is that I see potential. A haircut and shorter earrings and a smile would reveal your unique beauty. Small pick-me-ups can make all the difference! But you can't see that—and I can."

I looked down at the carpet, embarrassed by the implications of my potential beauty.

"I'm trying to say you don't see the bigger picture, either of you. It's not your fault. It's natural. But I'm here to say you can be happy if you set your mind to it."

"Trust me, we're happy." I said. "We were laughing our heads off before you got here."

"Do you really mean that?" Mrs. Sheehan said. "Come on, Patty." She looked at me with what seemed to be impossible patience. "I'm trying to talk to you about life. Attitude is everything. Your health and happiness is what's at stake." Mrs. Sheehan pulled her chair closer. "Did Carly tell you she's been taking special vitamins?"

"No." I looked at my friend. "What, are you sick? Is that why your head hurts?"

"I'm not exactly sick, Patty," Carly said. She rummaged through her quilted purse.

"She's taking a nutritional supplement," Mrs. Sheehan said.

"For what?" I asked.

"We're giving her a supplement because she's tired and she hasn't been eating...."

"—Wait just a minute," I said. "I know for a fact that Carly eats."

"She hasn't been eating enough. And it's hard for her to keep food in her stomach."

"What's wrong with her stomach?"

"Nothing. She's had a case of nerves. And a couple of times she's done some silly but dangerous things."

I was afraid to hear what Mrs. Sheehan would say next. I knew she was about to feed me the type of lie only a parent could tell.

"She runs out in the street—in front of cars."

"No! How can you say such a thing about your own daughter?"

"It's the truth, Patty," Mrs. Sheehan said.

"It's a lie," I said.

"I wish it weren't true but it is. And we are stuck with it—the truth."

"We've never been stuck with the truth before!" I said.

"I won't argue with you," Mrs. Sheehan said. "I want both you girls to know that no good can come from being self-destructive."

I looked at Carly and she finally produced something from her purse, a dark medicinal bottle with a dropper.

"This is the supplement. It's made from sea kelp and it thickens hair naturally," Carly said. The three of us sat around the dining room table, looking and not looking at each other over a bowl of plastic fruit.

"I'm getting ready to serve hot apple pie," Mrs. Sheehan said. "Let's have fun together. We'll be waiting."

When Mrs. Sheehan had gone, I examined the medicine bottle. Carly laid her arm across the table and rested her head on it. The mood-ring on her finger turned brown and milkish, like the eyeball of a dog with a cataract.

I picked at my thumbnail. I knew she'd been doing me a favor. I didn't want to hear. I didn't want to look. I didn't want to see what sadness looked like on her pale, heart-shaped face, or even on her ring.

I saw her run out into the road. She did it now and again, for no particular reason. But I kept an eye on her. She never got hurt—and some kids just do things like that—don't they? I looked at the daisies that roamed her dress. I wanted to ask Carly why she acted like she didn't want to live. Where exactly was all her hair that was falling out? Did she flush it or save it? Was the seaweed for swallowing or to put on her scalp? I didn't speak because maybe I'd start crying and never be able to stop, or maybe I wouldn't be able to get out of my bed anymore. I once heard about a woman who was sent to the nuthouse for being too sad.

I turned the radio back on. I settled on the only tune I could find, some whiney song about the distant future: *In the year 2525, if man is still alive, if woman can survive, they may find....*

I asked, "You like this?"

"No," she said.

"Me neither."

Sail On, Sailor

On my way home from Star Market, the raw wind ripped through the bruised sky and wrenched my umbrella inside out. The angry rain fell so hard it seemed to take the air with it. Mrs. Flanagan pulled up. Her station wagon blocked my driveway, and she rolled down her window to a tidy blue interior. She sat tall in a clear plastic scarf that protected her hair, hair that looked like all she did was take the rollers out. Her lips were brake-light red and her eyebrows were painted into paisley shapes. "I'm on my way to market," she said. "I'd have given you a ride but I see I'm too late!"

"Thanks anyway," I hollered into the wind.

"Holy Moses. This rain. How many days can it go on?"

"I ask myself the same question."

"But everything happens for a reason," Mrs. Flanagan said. "Such is life in the land of four seasons."

No one really talked about the chronically ill weather in Connecticut—the damp disappointment that darkened the days and blighted the seasons.

"Yup, such is life," I said.

"Well, my goodness, I hear you folks will be moving to the country!"

I hadn't heard. Moving to the country? What country? I was discombobulated and didn't want her to see. I fidgeted with the umbrella and hoisted the damp grocery bag higher on my hip. Cans of corn tore through the bag and fell on to the sidewalk. I chased the cans a step and cradled what was left of the bag.

"Well, I'm happy for you people!"

I didn't know which part I believed less—that we were moving, or the *happy for you people* part. I couldn't be moving north *and* go to school in Bridgeport. Nothing made sense. I didn't buy it.

It didn't take long for me to realize what was really going on. Something big had happened. Somewhere there was a mushroom cloud sucking up the sky, or a metropolitan city lit up by a mob and Molotov cocktails—and word must have started to get out—to jettison out of Bridgeport and hunker down quietly. The stuff about moving was just a cover story—a ruse designed to fool people like Mrs. Flanagan, people who might try to follow us. My ears felt hot and I could hear my pulse.

"I'm sorry," Mrs. Flanagan said. "I'm keeping you out in the rain, aren't I?"

"Don't worry about it."

"Smile! You know what we say—if you don't like the weather in the Nutmeg State, just wait a minute."

My father's paint truck was in the driveway, much too early. The truck's appearance lent credence to all this madness with Mrs. Flanagan.

I left the skeleton of the umbrella splayed out on the back porch and flung the storm door open. I reached for the knob and felt it pull out of my hand. My father opened the door, took the grocery bag from my arms, and offered me a towel. The rain, my father's truck, Mrs. Flanagan's propaganda—it all stirred me into a damp, agitated state. I hung my slicker, stepped out of my shoes, and wiped a trickle of water out of my ear.

Weary eyes and chapped lips, my father's face verified disaster. I figured we needed to get the boys out of school, wait for my mother to get home, and head out to wherever the secret destination was. My father was silent. He was nervous, swallowed as if something just wouldn't go down. He didn't know how to break the news to me.

Action was my best reaction. "I'm going upstairs and get ready," I said. He'd see I was focused and unafraid. He followed me upstairs. I bent down next to my bed, slid out my old shoebox and shopping bag from Reads with flannel pajamas and winter-wear, everything still with price tags. My father stood in the doorway to my room. I stopped to give him my full attention. "Well?" I asked after long spell of silence. I folded my arms. I yelled at him. "Just say it!"

"Did you go to school today?" he asked.

"*What*?"

My father's hands jiggled in his pockets, sounding off keys and change.

"Just answer the question. Did you go to school today? Yes or no?"

"Did I go to school today? No."

"Where are the boys?" he asked.

"School."

"Where'd she go?"

"I don't know."

"The hell you don't."

"She said she had errands to run."

My father pulled his key ring out of his pocket and threw the silver wad at me. I ducked and the keys darted into the wall and took out a chunk of sheetrock on the old Nina, the Pinta, and the Santa Maria wallpaper.

"You know she's been seeing him, don't you? You know damn well she's been sneaking around with that cop."

But she was on the SYLP committee, working for the John Birch Society. She'd been making sausage and peppers first thing in the morning, taking Tupperware lunches somewhere. She'd been asking me to stay home in case she was late. I felt as if someone poured ice water over my head. I could have known if I wanted to.

"You've been in on this," my father said. "The pinnacle of

her godforsaken covert activities."

"That's not true."

"She can take-up with that Lieutenant, but she's not getting one thin dime from me—and she's not getting my boys."

My father poked me in the shoulder. "As for you—you're old enough to choose—though your life may well be ruined already, you get to decide who you want to live with. I'm going to save your brothers if it's the last thing I do. And I'll tell you something else—I've taken 15 years of shit from her, and I'm not going take another 15 minutes of it from you. If you stay—you make meals, you babysit, you do everything I tell you to do—and not a sonofabitching peep out of you. Get it?"

I didn't know I had not answered until my father picked up his keys, stormed downstairs. I scrambled after him. He stopped at the back door and turned toward me suddenly. "You know what? Know what kind of an ass I am? She told me she wasn't going to see him anymore. I was going to take her on a cruise."

His eyes crinkled and his lips bent into a cartoon shape, a look on my father I was sure I was never meant to see. He lowered his head and uttered sounds that I was never supposed to hear. Maybe I had known about my mother and the cop but I didn't want my father to die. I thought of a song: Roberta Flack and Donny Hathaway—"Where is the Love?"

"I know a beautiful song," I said. "A duet of broken hearts. It's your song."

He bolted through the kitchen door. He kicked my umbrella off the porch, hopped into his truck, and slammed the door. I chased him. Barefooted and hair-soaked, I followed as he inched down the driveway. He stopped before the rear of his truck hit the street. Then cranked his window down.

"And since we're stuffing ten pounds of shit into a five-pound bag," my father said, "you may as well know the Sheehans are moving."

"What?"

"Out to Long Island." Of all the cruelties, this seemed the worst. The raindrops hit the open window ledge and splashed my father's face. He left the window open and pulled away.

I called Carly to find it was true. Harvey Hubbell had reassigned her dad and just like that—they were being relocated—sent off to Levittown, Long Island. Carly's dad once said he'd rather serve hard-time on Riker's or pitch a tent on a New Jersey landfill before he'd live on Long Island. He said it was the worst place to be when anything catastrophic happened. I thought we had time, the time it would take to sell their house, but Carly told me they'd only rented it. In a few short weeks, everything they owned would be packed up and shipped out and they would be off to an island.

I believed we'd always be together, suffer school, suffer parents, take shelter, and survive whether we wanted to or not. As soon as I heard she was moving I blamed her. If she didn't fight, she betrayed me. I always wanted a sister but I didn't have one and making believe was just no good. Carly turned into one of those people who came and went when you least expected it. People disappeared. Life was a Bermuda Triangle. I spoke to Carly a couple of times on the phone even though she still lived across the street. If we stopped trying to hold on we would get over each other quicker. If anyone knew how useless it is to say goodbye, it should have been us.

I made Hamburger Helper. It wasn't healthy, but my father said it was okay since the boys liked it. We sat at the dining room table slurping noodles and meat, and my father told us we were indeed moving to Monroe in a few months, and I didn't have to go to Zion Lutheran. And we were still slurping the same slop when he said our mother probably wasn't coming back but she would be calling. We didn't ask a single question.

My mother called right before it was time for the boys to go to bed. Their little behinds fit together on a footstool in the kitchen. One at a time they listened on a rotary wall phone. When Joe-Bins was done listening, he said goodbye and handed the receiver to me.

I promised my mother everything was going to be okay. I didn't say how. I didn't ask specific questions or stay on the phone very long. I was afraid to know more than I already knew—for instance, I had already decided to stay with my father and the boys and not with her. I didn't know when—or even if—I made the choice, or maybe it was I who was chosen. I just knew she was stronger and he was broken.

I came home from school the next day and saw my mother had come while we were gone. She left drawers open so I could see she left me her coral frosted lipstick and a gemstone American flag pin. She took curlers and makeup and some clothes. She took my pillow and left me hers. I never told anyone.

Keep on Truckin'

I stood at our kitchen counter and made all our lunches in the morning. I laid out ten slices of wheat bread, two-by-two. I was spreading peanut butter when my father walked in buttoning his flannel shirt.

"How old are you?" he asked.

"What?"

"When the hell were you born?"

"1959," I said.

"You must be older than you look. You seem to specialize in Depression-era sandwiches. We're not on rations here! Double the amount of peanut butter you slap on there, don't spare the jelly—maybe slice some bananas. Throw more than just an apple and two Oreos in my lunch pail. What do you want me to do, lose weight?"

"Of course not."

"Well, you need to start fixing man-sized meals. I'm not some kid. And these messages here."

"Huh?"

"What's this? 'Undie Joe called about a wedgie?' You think your pranks are funny? I have customers calling me for jobs and estimates. That's how we survive and don't you forget it."

"No! That must've been Johnny. I don't make jokes of

your messages." He took the note pad, dropped it on the counter next to me, and headed out to work. I looked. It was my handwriting, alright. It said *Uncle Joe called*. My c and my l ran too close together, and I tried to abbreviate wedgewood, a shade of blue paint. It wasn't easy to hold the receiver between my ear and my shoulder and write. I thought about pointing it out to my father when he came home. Maybe he'd laugh, but I just plain forgot.

❃ ❃ ❃

Our house hadn't sold yet but we packed a box or so every day, an enterprise that made small boxy cities of each room: brown sky lines, pulpy-smelling alleyways, the sense of needing directions or a map, the dread of curbside type places where unboxed items just got dumped.

Fall was not far and it was clear that parochial and private schools were out.

"I'd keep you home permanently if they wouldn't throw me in jail for it," my father said. "You'll be serving time at Maplewood Junior High School. The school that the City of Bridgeport has assigned you. All I can say is welcome to the jungle and I promise it'll be a short stay."

I still found ways to steal time and run up to Maria's house so I could listen to my song. When I closed my eyes and listened, the world could be the same as it was last time I heard it. I sat on the white carpet in her pink room and swayed and rocked—almost free and almost lost.

"This is a powerful song. I've been studying it, keeping track of what music does to me. I write my ideas down. I'm trying to see how power works."

Maria rifled through her box of 45s. "I want this." She held up a Donny Osmond record.

"He has no talent," I said. "You know how you can tell really good music? It messes with your mind."

"Your mind, Patricia, no es mio."

"Don't you want a real friend, Maria?"

"I have you for friend, yes."

"Yeah but I'm trying to tell you things no one else knows. See, this silly little Beach Boys song, it holds up for the entire three minutes and nineteen seconds that it plays—floats in the air like a cloud and a prayer, not even one extra note, not a single wasted second."

Maria looked at her watch. "My turn to choose."

"Try this," I said. "Get in front of the mirror and look at your face as you sing the words...*Sail on Sailor*. You'll see that your mouth stays open almost the entire time. You'll look as if you're wailing, or gasping for a breath, or praying more deeply than you ever have before."

"I won't do any of those things."

"Why not?"

"It's stupid."

"Come on, just give it a chance! Let's do it together. Let's sing."

Maria shut off the record player. She said, "I have to do homework."

I sat on the bed next to her. "Maria, do you want to know a secret?"

"Sure."

"You know Carly was my only best friend—right?"

Maria nodded.

"And you know she's gone—right? Her whole family moved."

"Of course," Maria said.

"And did I tell you about my Nonnie who left me?"

"You told me."

"And now my *family* is moving to Monroe, to a house I haven't seen yet?"

"I know this too."

"What you don't know—is about my parents. They split. My mother—she's not coming with us."

"Oh? Maybe they fix and get back together."

"She's at her mother's place now, but I can tell you it's over. She's got an apartment over a flooring store in

Bridgeport. She had wall-to-wall gold shag carpet put down already."

"Well, don't expect sympathy from me!" Maria said. "Siempre dices…You always say you hate your mother."

"That's not true. What a terrible thing to say! You make me sick, Maria."

She said, "Stop singing to the mirror, Patricia, and look at yourself!"

"I'm leaving, and taking my record with me."

"I thought you were gifting it to me," Maria said. "Not to be generous, because you can't bring it with you. You are afraid de tu padre!"

Maplewood Junior High was a rough mile away, way down Wood Avenue, a tough part of Bridgeport. The sprawl of concrete at Assumption seemed luxurious and modern by comparison. Maplewood was brick but like a tenement, not a town hall. In fact, the school reminded me of Father Panik Village, the ghetto on the east-side that we could see from the highway, a place where groups of tough, street people circled cars with open trunks and blaring speakers during the day and huddled around trashcan fires at night.

The morning routine was very different from Assumption's. No one lined up in the morning. Of course we didn't pray, but we didn't even say the pledge. When the bell rang, kids poured in from around the building where they'd congregated all over the streets. They took their binders off the hoods of other peoples' parked cars and strutted into the building as if there was time to spare.

I was amused by artifacts that hinted of Maplewood's noble days. Roman numeral clocks and antique wooden doors in the classrooms—I stared at these details. The faceted knobs looked like real crystal, and I wondered why no one had stolen them. The floors throughout the school were like straw—parched, unvarnished wood planks close to the color of a manila envelope. The principal's office reminded me of the detective bureau on *Dragnet*, dropped balls for light fixtures, wire bins full of papers, army-green filing cabinets, and old courtroom chairs. Everyone in the principal's office seemed old enough to be in an old folks' home.

In my classroom, the desks were connected in vertical rows, with wrought iron filigreed legs that were bolted to the floor. The desktops were etched with graffiti—crosses and knives, and names like Tikie and Delgado. The surface of every desk was intensely pitted and scarred so deeply that we were given clipboards to write on. The desks didn't open. They were designed so students could slide books inside. No one was assigned a particular seat, and no one needed to tell me that anything left in the desk would disappear. At the top right corner there was a hole that seemed sized to hold a can of Coke.

Mrs. Texiera, my homeroom teacher, was a rotund elderly woman who sported a poncho and brassy red hair that she always wore up with clips. Pale patches of her scalp and flecks of dandruff were part of her everyday hairstyle. On my third day I got up the nerve to ask her what the cutouts in our desks were for.

"They're inkwells," she said. "Just ignore them. Make sure you bring two ballpoint pens, two three-subject notebooks, and spit your gum out before you come into this room."

My elderly history teacher made an impression as she got up to go out for a puff, mid-lesson. Mrs. Crawford was the voice of the lifetime smoker. She barked a wonderful lecture at us, gruff and urgent, rapid-fire pace. Coughing. Current events sounded like a secret that leaked.

"You are witnesses to a major historical moment," Mrs. Crawford said. She had long painted nails, heavy gold baubles and dark red lipstick. A face of authority with a German physique. "Go home and tell your loved ones that the significance of this moment will never be erased. The President of the United States is facing impeachment. What are your people at home talking about?"

We hadn't had a JBS meeting or any other reason to talk much. We tackled the day to day and packed in between. I finished the dishes. I asked my father, "What do think will happen to Tricky Dick?"

"Don't let me hear you say that again," he said. "I don't care if they hang him, but young ladies choose better words."

I wore simple blouses and khaki or denim skirts that just touched my knee. Except for the outfit I got from my mother, my clothes weren't cool, but I wasn't guilty of trying too hard which was worse. Understated fashion was a good strategy in a school full of kids with afros and hair-picks. Lots of people wore polyester shirts that featured skylines of cities like New York and Las Vegas.

When I wanted to be cool I'd pull on my hip hugger jeans, tight and low, bellbottoms with pink triangles sewn in. When I wanted to be cool, I'd wear the jeans underneath a maxi-skirt so my father couldn't see. When I wanted to be cool, I'd drop the skirt and come out of the bathroom at school like Wonder Woman.

I was really struck by the maxi-skirts and the wide-legged pants that dragged on the floor. For the most part, the fashion at Maplewood meant that you couldn't see anyone's feet. My father wouldn't have allowed skirts or pants that dragged—and I would not have such attire, not just because the look was so ratty but because the coolest part of my look was my shoes. I got them from Lerner's. My mother bought them for me before she left. I earned them by babysitting: suede slip-ons with lavender, grape, and maroon-colored patches sewn together with wide, zigzagged stitches. My shoes reminded me of a Keep on Truckin' poster I'd seen—the kind of awesome footwear you'd see on a *Soul Train* dancer. My shoes didn't have high heels or platforms, so my father didn't see them as a threat; he didn't throw them into the garbage can during one of his clothing inspections. He said they were Bozo the Clown shoes.

White, Black, and Latino, Maplewood was racially mixed at a time when so much of the world was demanding attention or outright power: black power, woman power, flower power. In some ways, our inner-city school seemed incredibly free and advanced in the early 70s: white girls went out with black and Hispanic boys; black girls went out with black and Hispanic boys; Jewish kids went out with Catholics. But two or three times a week, it seemed everyone hated each other for it. The halls erupted in fights that drew blood and brought cops and metal detectors. The fights came out of nowhere and became routine, and as pointless as they were, they generated wild energy and more participation than any pep rally. Kids at Maplewood talked about seeing our school on TV or in the paper at night; they spray-painted the words **KENT STATE** on the buildings as if it meant something, but nobody knew what it was.

All this agitation led to rules which dictated which bathroom we wound up using—but we made the choices on our own. The white girls gravitated toward the lavatory closest to the office; the lav at the opposite end of the hall was used by Latino girls, and the one downstairs was where the black girls were. All the bathrooms were full of smoke, just like the teachers' lounge. Everybody was puffin' and everybody knew it. It was as if they let the school calm down by smoking.

From day-one, I used the black girl's bathroom. No one ever said a cross word or gave me an evil eye. I went when I had to use the toilet, and I stopped in for no particular reason, sometimes to stand in front of the mirror and put on lip gloss. Girls sat on the sinks and painted their names on the wall with nail polish. Several cigarettes burned at once, and when somebody asked me if I wanted a hit, I said sure.

One day I was hanging out in the black lav, listening to a girl named Shirley, who wore yellow better than a queen bee. Poised on the edge of the sink, she graced a gold halter-top, sported a righteous glittering afro, and told us what was going down between "some jive fool who was messin with some honky chick." I was posing against the wall with my hands in my pockets, as interested as everybody else. Out of the corner of my eye, I saw a thumb-sized bug scamper right by my shoulder— creepy, dark against the beige tiles. I jumped and screamed. The bug scampered off somewhere but I couldn't shake the idea of it—the idea that the bug was in my hair. I bent forward and swatted at my own head. "Oh my God, get it off me!"

Everybody laughed.

"It's not on you," Shirley said. "It's in the sink."

I stood up without smoothing my hair. I looked in the sink, screamed again, and backed into the paper towel dispenser.

"Girl! Ain't you never seen a cockroach before?"

"I've never seen a bug like that in my life!" I said.

Another black girl spoke up. "I bet you ain't! Look at you, all scared and shit! What you got your candy-ass in our bathroom for anyway?"

"Yeah," Shirley said. "Why you here, skinny little tan girl?"

Several of the girls who had been tolerating my existence and liking me for weeks suddenly acted like they'd never seen me before.

Shirley pursed her lips and slid them side-to-side making faces and sucking her tongue as if she was smacking on sour apple candy. "You best take move on down the road to the honky bathroom," she said. "What's your name anyway?"

"Patty."

"Oh, yeah—Peppermint Patty, you need to get your candy-ass outta here." Her afro and her boobs shook a little when she said it.

"I ain't no candy-ass," I said.

"I *said* you best be headed down the white way." Shirley moved up close, blew smoke in my face, and flung her Marlboro into one of the stalls.

"Get her, Shirl," somebody shouted.

Then the other girls stopped talking and surrounded us.

"You 'bout to get messed up," somebody said.

"I'm not going," I said. I locked eyes with this girl. I was convinced she was waiting for some cue to hit me. I balled my fists and waited. I knew how to throw a damn punch.

Shirley pointed down at my feet and started to laugh. "Where'd you get them pimp shoes? That's why you don't like the cracker bathroom. They won't let your shoes in there!"

Everybody laughed.

"My mother got these for me and—and what are you talking about?" I asked. "Everybody loves these shoes! You wish you had them. They're the coolest shoes in this whole damn school."

Shirley set her hands on her hips, ran her fingers along the top of those denim hip huggers and she circled me, went into a strut and checked me out head-to-toe. She pulled out another cigarette, put it between her lips, and waited.

I pulled out my lighter and lit it.

Shirley said, "She's cool."

I was.

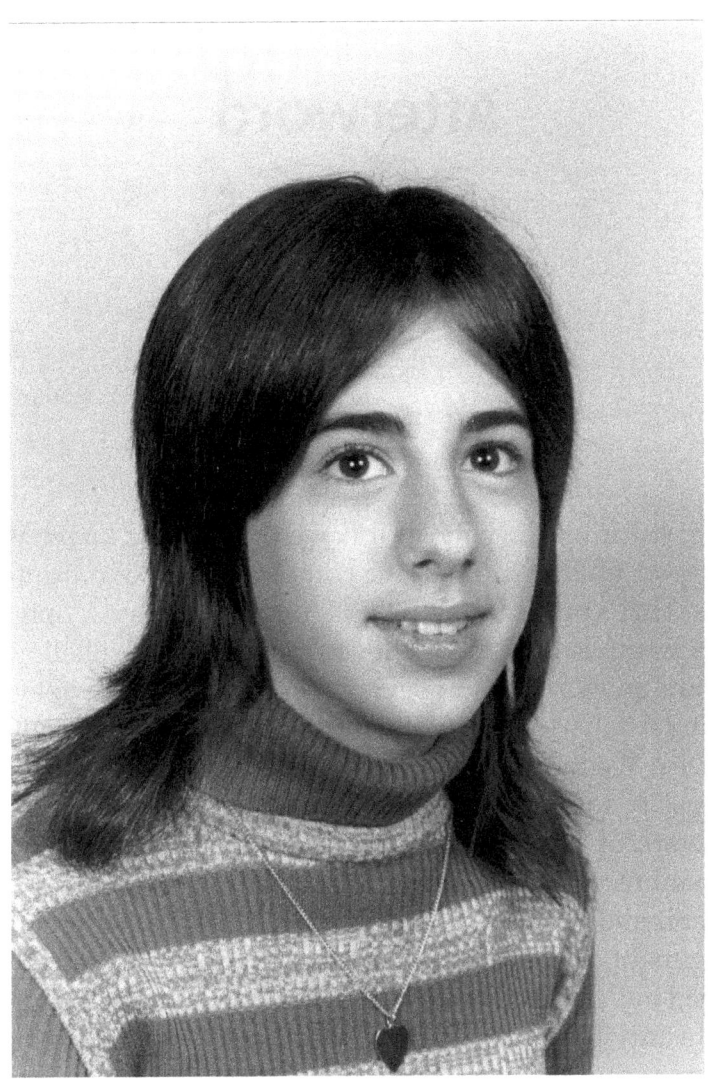

Age thirteen. The shag and me.

Afterword

We're stuck with whatever it is we thought we knew, with whatever filtered through the complex screen of our limitations. That's our legacy, that's all there is…and now only the work which is love and the love which is work will allow us to come anywhere near obeying the dictum laid down by the great Ray Charles, and—to tell the truth—James Baldwin.

Dear reader, I believe each of us holds within ourselves a capacity to understand the human condition, and for me the work of understanding human nature begins at home. The embrace of complexity—this is central to the ethos of my memoir and is the driving force of my work. I am grateful for the gifts of memory and imagination and for those who've helped me, especially my own children, to look back at where my history began and reckon with the love I was unable to embrace and the tears I refused to allow. My view of family and growing up is neither over-sentimentalized nor vilified. I believe this view constitutes a healthy legacy.

This memoir is written with a loving heart. It reflects the work of many years, the maximum understanding of which I'm capable. I chose to use the names of family members only, and all the characterizations and events are honest and based on the people, places, and things I knew. I see this work as a re-enchantment, a troublesome joyride, the place where *Soul*

Train meets bomb shelter!

Part of me is a reflection of the times in which I lived and the environment in which I was raised. For a long time, I thought the brand of cold war fear and depression I grew up with was unique but now I tend to think we all deal with some measure of a cold war—an us versus them—way of seeing the world. I would like to believe that those people from my childhood who were measuring the time until doomsday by their watches no longer live in absolute terror, that they believe in the future, and they've grown to see how important a belief in fundamental goodness is—to all of us—especially the children. I'm saddened to see the bulk of a generation who should be enjoying their golden years tethered to screencrawling tickertapes of bad news and paranoia on blaring 24-hour TV channels and radio shows, feeding on fear, waiting on death. Like all kids, I wanted my parents to look at me and be happy. I still do. I still believe no matter how old we are we need the faith of those who came before us—faith that problems will be solved and life is worth living.

I look at my own children, who are now adults, and I sometimes wonder what have I brought forward from the impressionable days of my childhood. What have I left behind? What can I do now to make up for my fears, which must have manifested somehow?

Or better yet—how can I say yes to life today?

Acknowledgments

Sincere appreciation to all the remarkable people whose friendship and support were essential to the writing of this book. Thank you to my mentors, friends, and colleagues from the Creative Writing Department at the University of North Carolina at Wilmington, notably: Wendy Brenner, Philip Gerard, David Gessner, Virginia Holman, Haven Kimmel, and my deepest appreciation to Clyde Edgerton. Many thanks to generous MFA peers: Katherine Sweeney, Douglass Bourne, Miriam Parker, Joel Moore, Xhenet Aliu, and Sally Smits. I am indebted to the community at Southern Connecticut State University, including Nicole Henderson and Brian Johnson, and especially to Tim Parrish for his wisdom and generosity. Profound thanks to my gracious family and others who've inspired and sustained me, including Charlotte Meehan, Edward Bjorklund, T. D'ho, Kate Newcomer, and Ernest Wilder; thank heavens for copy editors Andrea Barilla, Ella Jo Sellers, and Andrea Bates. Deepest appreciation goes to my kind and heroic editor, Lowell Mick White. I am thankful for the support of the folks at Alamo Bay Press.

Thanks to my students at UNC Wilmington, Southern Connecticut State University, and Southeastern Community College for their energizing encouragement, and to the members of the Downtown Writer's Workshop in Wilmington, especially Amy Ott Young, Risa Kell, and Anthony Lees.

This project stalled—or, actually, I struggled for lack of courage—but it finally sailed ahead on the sage advice and encouragement of my son, Richard Bjorklund.

And it would not be complete without the love and support of my husband, David Wilson Roberts. Back at ya.

❀ ❀ ❀

Much gratitude also to my fellow *Folio* and *Aries* editors and to the following literary magazines and presses for having provided a home to several chapters of this book:

Missouri Review: "U.S. and Them"
Sou-wester: "Just Like on Television"
Palooka: "Countdown for Leaving"
Press 53: "Almost Happy"
Wilma: "A World Still Flat" and "Good Catholic Motorists"
American Writing: "Soul Train"
Cedars: "A Taste of the Cold War"
Folio: "Soul Train"

About the Photographs

- Page 3: *Cascone Family, 1963....*
  This photo was taken at Nana and Grandpa Nastasia's, their stucco house on Thorme Street in Bridgeport, Connecticut—screened porch, weeping willow, and bunny in backyard. My mother's brother, Mike, worked for a local newspaper so he had a high-resolution camera. I stuck out my foot and struck a pose, and while I remember being chastised (and the multiple 'takes'), this is the shot he gave to my parents.

- Page 13: *The fence Dad built, post to pickets, and me in my Assumption uniform....*
  The picture was taken in front of our house at 327 Wade Street, with Pacific Street and the backyards of Laurel Avenue behind me. The tall pine in our front yard gave us a childhood of sappy pinecones—grenades and table settings. Seven or eight years old, I was wearing my crisp Our Lady of the Assumption uniform—but the picture says so much about my parents—that picket fence that my father built around our corner lot, and the time my mother spent on my hair.

- Page 31: *Mom and us: Johnny-boy, Big-A, and myself, about nine months before Joe-Bins was born....*

    My mother had a photographer come to the house for this portrait, a surprise birthday present for my father—the bigger surprise would be my mother's announcement that she was expecting again. Portrait was taken right in our living room, the triangle of our moss colored sectional sofa. My favorite fake plant stands behind us, the elephant ears my mother kept fresh by dusting and shining with Pledge.

- Page 63: *Nonnie and Grandpa, their forever smiles....*

    My father's parents, George and Rose Cascone, lived on Lennox Avenue in Milford, Connecticut. In the backyard—a picnic bench stood on a small cement patio below a short tin awning. Half of the humble yard was vegetable garden. I'm not sure why I believed Grandpa smuggled special seeds from Sicily for 'imported' basil and tomatoes, whereas the cucumbers, I was certain, were boring-domestics. We saw Nonnie and Grandpa most every Sunday until they moved to Hollywood, Florida.

- Page 102: *Stylish Mom and Dad entertain at our home, circa 1970....*

    My parents generally didn't have parties. There is definitely some tension here, but I know my mother already cleaned the whole house and prepared a perfect spread, and my father probably worked at least a half-day before coming home to mow the lawn and trim the hedges. The wonder is in the detail. My father stands with his hand on his hip—just like his father—and of course the likeness didn't register with me at the time. No matter what they said, my parents did change with the times, and they had a classy, elevated sense of 70s style. I get hung up on the crystal teardrop lamp, the shine of the end table, and size of the ashtray. The sectional has slipcovers! They wanted me to get them in the picture head to toe. This shot is good, but I missed the mark and I still wish I could see the shoes they were wearing.

- Page 138: *Johnny and myself—holiday time at Nana and Grandpa Nastasia's home....*

    Another wonderful shot taken by Uncle Mike. My brother was adorable, something lost on me until I grew up enough to look at pictures of us and see more than just myself. It seems to me most of our friendly poses required coaxing, and tended to render images that suggest we'd just been fighting. But this time I think we both came down with a fever and wound up in bed early on Easter Sunday.

- Page 204: *Mom and the Caddy. Mom was classy and stylish, even in a kerchief....*

    My mother put a shine on everything. She's the *long cool woman in the black dress*, even when she was sporting a kerchief and cut-off shorts. She could have sold Rally Wax in her curlers. I imagine my father taking this picture and feeling happy.

- Page 223: *Joe-Bins in Dad's hat....*

    I have an image in my mind from way back, Dad in a hat—at the end of an era—and so this picture belongs in the family museum. Joe-Bins, in the prime of his Healthtex life, notoriously cute, the only kid with nerve enough to put Dad's hat on—and simply have his picture taken for it. The sunroom was Dad's office. My mother saved up to have curtains custom made. The bigger deal was Dad's binoculars and the shuttered blinds he installed on the top half of each window. Each section of blinds was angled a bit differently, which allowed him so see what was going on 180 degrees around our house from right where he sat. He also had his spies out, agents who followed my every move as soon as I walked out the door—and I believed it all. Behind Joe-Bins and atop the cabinet, Dad's adding machine and protective sheath. Guitar and banjo! How? Why? When? I was uneasy when he played and sang, "Oh, Maybelene—why can't you be true...?" But now, of course, I wish he'd fiddled around with these instruments more often. This photo would have made it to a frame and claimed a spot on top of our TV set or mantle, if it were not for the Sears Roebuck vacuum cleaner head and neck, which, my mother pointed out, was not a member of the family.

- Page 253: *Age thirteen. The shag and me.*
  What can I say? The secret is to sleep on your back and to not wash your hair for three days.

About Patricia Bjorklund

Patricia Bjorklund's writing has been published in many journals, including *The Missouri Review*, *Connecticut Review*, *Post Road*, and *Wilma! Wilmington's Magazine for Women*. Director of the Downtown Writer's Workshop in historic Wilmington, North Carolina, she earned an MFA in Creative Writing from UNC-Wilmington and a BA and an MS from Southern Connecticut State University.

She can be contacted at www.coldwarchildhood.com